WOLFPACK WARRIORS

WOLFPACK WARRIORS

The Story of World War II's Most
Successful Fighter Outfit

Roger A. Freeman

GRUB STREET · LONDON

Published by
Grub Street
4 Rainham Close
London
SW11 6SS

Copyright © 2004 Grub Street, London
Text copyright © 2004 Roger A. Freeman

British Library Cataloguing in Publication Data
Freeman, Roger Anthony
  Wolfpack warriors: the story of World War II's
  most successful fighter outfit
  1. Zemke, Hubert, 1914- 2. United States. Army Air Forces.
  Fighter Group, 56th 3. World War, 1939-1945 – Aerial
  operations, American 4. World War, 1939-1945 – Personnel
  narratives,American 5. World War, 1939-1945 – Campaigns –
  Western Front 6. Fighter pilots – United States – Biography
  I. Title
  940.5′44973

ISBN 1 904010 93 8

Typeset by Pearl Graphics, Hemel Hempstead

Printed and bound in Great Britain by Biddles Ltd, King's Lynn

Contents

Author's Note

Some 150 veterans were consulted during the research for the following narrative, many of whom are quoted. In the cause of presenting a true picture of their youthful experiences, statements have not been sanitised.

The research programme for this book took place over fourteen years and space herein precludes the individual acknowledgement of all who contributed. This in no way indicates any lessening of the author's appreciation, and to all who helped he offers his sincere thanks.

NB: Most of the material I have quoted in the book has been attributed, but where it is not it has been taken from private conversations, official papers and published works.

Introduction

Progress wrought by the passage of time changes the character of a nation. If honest endeavour backed by a charitable religious faith is the best mould of mankind, then for the citizens of the United States of America that period approaching the mid-twentieth century was the zenith. The good and bad, the strong and weak, are with all nations; but in general, by the yardstick of moral human assessment, the generation of young Americans raised in the nineteen-twenties and thirties were of the best. Decent people with an ingrained sense of duty to what in their sub-conscious was God's own country. Thus were they with an ethos that would serve them well but test them severely.

The conflict of arms during the years 1939-1945 was the true world war of the twentieth century, albeit that it became known as the Second World War or World War II. It was distinguished by the scale of mechanisation employed; not only by armies and navies but air forces, which for the first time came to be a crucial element in the successful outcome of many campaigns, not least the defeat of Nazi Germany in western Europe. In both the tactical support of land forces and the strategic bombing campaign post-war analysts deemed air power to have played a decisive part in securing victory. The belief that enemy capitulation could be achieved by strategic bombardment was an unproved ambition of the bomber commands of both the Royal Air Force (RAF) and the United States Army Air Forces (USAAF). The onslaught was too slow in gathering pace and the resilience of the enemy underestimated. Yet, in the final months of the campaign strategic bombing denied the enemy much of the materiel needed to sustain his forces in the field, most importantly petroleum products. For the bombers, whether strategic or tactical, to go about their work, domination of the enemy air force was essential. Moreover, it was vital to the success of land campaigns, allowing Allied armies to advance without the continual harassment from the sky that was their opponents' lot.

Air superiority was predominantly dependent on fighters, aircraft designed to destroy enemy aircraft and equipping units committed to this objective. The effort of the USAAF to afford its strategic bombers protection from hostile fighter interceptions during daylight operations eventually resulted in a state of air superiority, even over the enemy homeland. Although desirable, this was an objective not thought possible in the early years of the war because it was believed a fighter having long-range ability for escort duties could not compete with a short-range interceptor. While technical advances played a major part in this achievement there were other factors, not least the tenacity and skill of the airmen. While RAF and other USAAF formations played a part in the establishment of air superiority, it was the fighter units of the US Eighth Air Force, based in south-east England, that were primarily responsible. Of these several had outstanding records, but the most successful, in terms of enemy aircraft shot from the sky, was also to some extent the catalyst that imbued men of other units to succeed. This is the story of that unit and its ethos, an ethos that was to some extent the general hallmark of the fighter command of which it was part. Much of what follows has its parallel in other fighter units, but I have chosen to write about the most famous as I was an observer of this unit's progress for much of its operational commitment. In later years I came to know many of its men and their personal accounts provide the quintessence of this story.

1 Born and Weaned

The US Army and US Navy had both established their own formations for the use of aircraft prior to the 1914-1918 war. Although the air element of the army strove to emulate the British and become a separate service during the inter-war years, this was resisted by the traditionalists who considered the use of aircraft no more than a useful innovation and the operatives only worthy of corps status. The massive re-armament programme begun by the United States in 1940 included considerable investment in many types of aircraft predominately for the army. In view of this a large degree of autonomy was accorded the airmen with the creation of the Army Air Forces in June 1941 at which date the United States was not yet involved in hostilities, although its government was becoming increasingly hostile toward the Axis powers. Orders placed for military aircraft totalled some 30,000 by the summer of 1941 and the USAAF was in the process of creating new units to operate these machines when they were built.

In common with the British, who had been influential when the United States entered the First World War in 1917, the basic flying unit of the US Army was the squadron composed of about a dozen aircraft and a staff of pilots and servicing personnel to operate them. To create a stronger force and more economy in support, squadrons with the same mission were organised into groups, mainly bomber, fighter and observation. The group equated to an army regiment. By the nineteen forties the standard strength of a bomber group was four squadrons and for a fighter group three, numbered squadrons generally becoming a permanent assignment to a numbered group. From a dozen groups in the late 1930s, by 1941 the US Army Air Corps, predecessor of the Army Air Forces, had begun to constitute and activate a number of new groups to meet the vast expansion programme planned following the government's fear that the nation would eventually be drawn into hostilities.

In compliance with an order from the commanding general, on 20 November 1940 the Army Air Corps constituted 35 new combat groups, which simply entailed a Washington headquarters clerk entering selected numeral designations in the paperwork. One of the 15 for fighters was the 56th Pursuit Group, composed of a Headquarters Squadron and three Pursuit Squadrons, the 61st, 62nd and 63rd. Activation was the word for giving a new unit a physical entity; for the 56th Pursuit Group this entailed orders posted on the morning of 14 January 1941 for three officers and 150 enlisted men, selected from the 27th Bombardment Group and its 15th and 17th Bombardment Squadrons, to move from Hunter Field, Georgia, to the National Guard armoury in nearby Savannah, to become the nucleus of the new unit. It mattered not that these were men from a bomber organisation for in giving the 56th Pursuit Group substance they were to build the domestic and administrative facilities. For the next few weeks personnel were assigned and transferred out again as the Army Air Corps struggled to honour its commitments, creating new units by taking part of the personnel from existing units. Even so, there were a few individuals from the original cadre who remained with the group throughout its wartime existence. It would be the pilots who earned fame but the ground men would provide the continuity of the organisation. Not until late May was the 56th more than a neophyte unit far removed from its mission. In that month orders were received to move 200 miles north to Charlotte airport in North Carolina where Major Davis Graves assumed command. On its arrival the lack of equipment and living conditions were considered abysmal in comparison with permanent Air Corps establishments.

Just prior to the move to Charlotte the designation 'Pursuit', a legacy of the First World War, was replaced by the more fitting term 'Fighter', and at the same time the three squadrons were also redesignated with the new term. However, the P designation for an aircraft's role remained unchanged. (In June the Army Air Corps gave way to the Army Air Forces to distinguish a semi-autonomous status in the United States' military organisation.) At the new location the 56th received its first fighters, ten Curtiss P-36s, and later in June three Bell YP-39 Airacobras, all worn hand-me-downs. The aircraft strength was rarely more than a dozen during summer of 1941 and often half that number because of accident or withdrawal. Personnel strength continued to fluctuate as men were assigned for service elsewhere. In the autumn the US Army planned large scale manoeuvres in the Carolinas during October, which included a test of Army Air Forces fighter defences against bombers. To make the 56th Fighter Group's involvement more effective ten new Bell P-39s were received. The fighters were adjudged to have acquitted themselves well.

While the US government planned for possible hostilities, its abrupt entry in to the war occasioned by the Japanese attack on Pearl Harbor was not anticipated. On the afternoon of 7 December 1941 the 56th's personnel were brought together for an address by Major Graves who cautioned that they should be prepared to move at short notice. Rumour soon held that they were destined for overseas immediately, but the excitement was dispelled when the men learned they were to go no further than the seaboard of South and North Carolina. On 10 December the group headquarters and the 61st Fighter Squadron moved to Charleston, the 63rd to Myrtle Beach and the 62nd to Wilmington, The squadrons were separated to give cover along the 100 miles of Atlantic coastline of an air defence section. Although defence was an unlikely requirement for the area, the group received reinforcements in both men and equipment. In the final weeks of that month 24 newly commissioned 2nd lieutenants arrived at Charleston. Captains Richard Games and Loren McCollom of the 61st Fighter Squadron, who had been given the task of assessing the capabilities of the newcomers, set up a checkout school in a tent on the Municipal Airport. Their task was difficult in that the extra fighter aircraft received were of five different models: Seversky P-35s, Curtiss P-36s, Republic P-43s, in addition to more worn P-39s and P-40s. After being checked out in a particular type each pilot was ordered to take the aircraft to his assigned squadron. Accommodation at all three locations was either requisitioned buildings and huts or army tents. At Wilmington Municipal Airport most personnel lived four to a tent in woodland beside the airfield. The headquarters staff of the 62nd Squadron occupied a former filling station and their bunks were little better owing to the unwanted ventilation occasioned by the neglected state of the building. At Myrtle Beach a similar situation existed although there were some barrack huts. In all three squadrons there were now more pilots than aircraft. To quote the Engineering Officer of the 62nd, John M. Schneider, the aircraft were "an assortment of junk – flying junk with point 30 calibre machine guns firing through the propeller arc. The timing was never perfected, resulting in many forced landings with shot up propellers." Such was the shortage of aircraft in the rapidly expanding Army Air Forces that units with a low priority were given a variety of obsolescent types.

If there were difficulties in obtaining new aircraft there was no shortage of personnel, only in training and equipping them. In the depression years of the nineteen thirties the army or navy had been an attractive alternative to the dole for many young men, albeit that the intake was restricted. Political and budget limitations resulted in the United States having meagre armed forces and the total Air Corps personnel hovered around 15,000 for several years. With the late 'thirties expansion, brought about by the significant use of aircraft in the European and Asian conflicts, more volunteers were accepted. With the attack on Pearl Harbor there was a veritable deluge of men wanting to enlist. John Sipek gives an insight on the patriotic mood of the nation:

"In early 1941 I was seriously thinking of enlisting in the service to get my one year of compulsory military duty over with so I could get on with my life without interruptions. I mentioned it to my parents and my father, who was a veteran of World War I, talked me out of it and said he would not sign since I was a minor. On December 7th, 1941 I was returning from a football game and as I approached my home, neighbours were going back and forth discussing a Japanese attack on Pearl Harbor. As I came in the house my parents were talking about the bombing and my father asked me what I was going to do. I told them I was going to the recruiting office in downtown Chicago the following morning to enlist. His reply was 'Good, son.' I found out this was much easier said than done.

"When I arrived near the recruiting office the area was flooded with men wanting to enlist. This situation was so unexpected the office was not equipped to handle the thousands of volunteers. Most of us never got near the building. It was cold but with so many bodies and the adrenaline stimulation we were warm. At lunchtime we were given tickets to nearby restaurants for a sandwich and coffee. We returned and waited until late afternoon when the recruiting officer told us to return home and come back in the morning. This situation went on for weeks. I would say goodbye to my parents in the morning and come home in the evening. I had been working at Western Electric, and hadn't told them of my intentions, so on December 19th I went to the plant before going to the recruiting office. They sent me to the employment department and gave me an exit interview and physical. The personnel department told me when I walked out the door I was severing all relations with the company because I was not drafted but enlisted of my own accord. I didn't care as I only had three months' service with the company and our country was at war. The doctor wished me luck and said you will be accepted because your physical showed you A1. About six months later I received a letter from the company stating that they had changed their policy since war was declared. Upon my return from the service I would be reinstated at the job I left or the equivalent and given credit for my time in the military plus all the rises and promotions I would have received had I kept working. They also included a $50 cheque to show their appreciation. Finally, on December 27th, I made it into the recruiting office."

For aspiring pilots among the influx of volunteers following the United States entry into hostilities, it would be some time before those accepted would reach the squadrons. The pilots of the 56th Fighter Group who eventually went to war were mostly young men who had an ambition to make flying a career in the immediate pre-Pearl Harbor years. The determination to achieve that goal is well illustrated by the efforts of Harold Comstock:

"When I was 16 I did part time work for the Boy Scouts, cleaning and polishing their premises in Fresno. With my very first pay cheque I cycled out to the airport and spent it all on airplane rides. My father was most unhappy that I'd spent my money on flying. From the Boy Scouts I got a job with my uncle running a propane station at night. I kept that job for two years working at night until I went to college when working at night became something of a chore. I then went to a regular service station at 20 cents an hour, again working until midnight. Then for a car dealer delivering, servicing and collecting cars. All this time I was sinking some of my money into aviation. One had to have sixty units of college education to be accepted by the army and as soon as I had them I applied, which was just after my twentieth birthday in 1940. I wanted to be an airline pilot because that was good money but I was having trouble getting in the required 200 hours flying and one of my instructors suggested I join the Army Air Corps first. Although I'd soloed in 1936 I didn't get my pilots' licence until I was 19. I cheated. The government put up a scheme called Civilian Pilot Training. One of the stipulations was that no one who had already soloed privately could enter it. But I got my instructor to sign off as if I hadn't. The people running the CPT were local and knew who I was but they turned a blind eye, probably because here was a young fellow they would not have any trouble teaching how to solo! I got my 35-plus hours which I had to have and got my licence. Then I took the secondary course flying a Waco for acrobatics which I thought was great. To celebrate I took my future wife for a flight and hung her upside down, and, as she was sunburned, the straps didn't do her blisters any good. Although my application for the Army hadn't been rejected the months went by and I got tired of waiting so went down to try and join the Navy. Then in October 1941 the Army finally did call me up for cadet training down at San Antonio, Texas. There the first mail I got was from the US Navy telling me to report in!"

The US Navy held more appeal for many would-be aviators than the Army Air Forces, apparently having a superior status in many young minds. Leslie Smith was one:

"In July 1941 I tried to get into the Navy. I took my physical and passed that. Was sitting down answering questions from the interviewer who asked have I had chicken pox, have I had syphilis, and so on, and I could answer 'No' to everything. I considered myself a perfect physical specimen. He was almost through when he asked if I had ever had hay fever. I was happy to say 'Oh yes, I had hay fever.' He closed his notebook and said, 'We don't take anyone who has hay fever.' So I was rejected on the spot. At the time I was living in Colorado and working in a bank: I'd gotten out of school about a year. I was really downcast because I had been rejected by the Navy for physical reasons. After a week or so I decided to try the Army Air Corps who had a recruiting station at Moffat Field. I applied for Cadet training and passed all their tests until I got near the end and was asked about various illnesses I'd had including had I had hay fever. Well, I'd never had that! I was brought up very strictly and to tell a lie was very serious crime. So I worried about saying 'No'. The old Master Sergeant who conducted the interview took me in for the Snyder test which related to blood pressure and other things. I failed, although I'd passed when trying to get into the Navy. It made me think I'd failed it because I'd told a lie. The sergeant did this test two or three times but it was still too high. He suggested I go out, have lunch, relax. He asked me if I smoked. I told him I didn't. He then handed me a big cigar and said after lunch smoke this thing and then come back and take the test. So I did as he said, had lunch and then went outside and lit up the cigar. I got definitely ill and lost my entire lunch and felt awful. So I went back and found him and he looked at me and

said: 'Fine. Let's go get the test.' I guess he knew I'd get sick, but this
time the test was too low. So he told me to wait in the waiting room for
a half hour and to come back again. This time I passed perfectly."

The boosting of the 56th's strength in December 1941 was preparatory to
a new assignment. On the anniversary day of its activation in Savannah
the group was moving to the New York area where it was to provide air
defence for the city. Having tried to get through the Hudson river toll
tunnel without money and New York traffic without escort, the ground
echelon's movement in a convoy of old trucks and private cars was
hilarious or frustrating, depending on one's responsibility. Headquarters
and the 62nd Fighter Squadron went to Bendix Airport at Hasbrouck
Heights to the south of Hackensack, New Jersey, the 63rd to a new
airfield adjoining the Republic aircraft factory at Farmingdale on Long
Island and the 61st moved to Bridgeport Municipal Airport, Connecticut,
right on the coast some 40 miles north-east of New York city. The group's
squadrons had the task of intercepting unidentified aircraft approaching
the New York area. A plotting centre had been set up along British lines
and fighters were given three minutes from receipt of an instruction to
intercept to becoming airborne. The RAF's term 'scramble' was adopted
for this procedure. Located on the 11th floor of the American Telephone
and Telegram building in New York city, the plotting centre was a crucial
part of the air defence sector for which Major Graves assumed command
responsibility, in addition to being boss of the 56th. The group's pilots
took turns in manning the intercept board for two-week spells, a popular
move as accommodation was in a city hotel.

While there was some thought of the Luftwaffe staging a one-way
attack on the city from secret bases in the Arctic, the likelihood was
remote. Nevertheless, for the air defence for New York some upgrading
equipment was deemed advisable and selected pilots were sent to Bradley
Field, Windsor Locks, to learn to fly the Lockheed P-38 Lightning, an
unconventional twin-engine fighter that was the great hope of the Army
Air Forces. A few P-38E models were then delivered to each squadron
and it was assumed that the 56th would eventually standardise on the
Lightning – so much so that the 63rd Fighter Squadron embodied a
stylised P-38 in its unofficial insignia.

To facilitate P-38 re-equipment, entailing a far more complex change
for maintenance crews, a few Lockheed trained or approved specialists
were brought in to help. Co-ordination of air force and civilian mechanics
with maintenance tasks was not easily achieved as the latter,
understandably, were not happy about taking instructions from military
personnel. Sergeant Sylvester Walker, one of the few men still with the
group who had been part of the original complement at Savannah, was
involved in an incident that brought matters to a head:

"One afternoon at Bridgeport, Sgt 'Orbie' Owens and I were pulling a

25-hour inspection on a P-38's Allison engines. We were checking the valve gap, me on the left side and Orbie on the right. We would turn the prop' by hand to get the valves top dead centre. The engine cowlings we had taken off had been put on top of the crew chief work stands. Suddenly the props whirled round, cutting one of the cowlings into two pieces. What we didn't know was that a civilian engineer was in the cockpit doing some instrument work and he had accidentally hit the start button. Could have killed us. Shook us up so bad we went to the Orderly Room. Captain McCollom came out of his office and seeing us two sitting drinking Coca Cola, wanted to know what was going on. We told him what happened. He was so mad he had a directive issued that no GIs and civilians work on the same planes simultaneously. We never told him that we did not disconnect the battery cables, which was the first item we were supposed to do before conducting any engineering work on the engines!"

Of the three locations, Farmingdale had the best facilities being recently enlarged and having hard surface runways and taxiing areas. Accommodation was mostly in newly erected huts. Bendix, a small civil airport contracted to the Army Air Forces, had a thousand yard sod runway, a wooden control tower and two small hangars. Somewhat basic – peach baskets were used as runway markers – the sod surface became muddied with the winter thaw and often hazardous for aircraft operations. The 62nd's headquarters was in the regular airport building but most personnel were billeted a few miles away at Teaneck where the National Guard Armory served the group headquarters. Some of the pilots became friendly with the Peppys family living nearby who bred English bulldogs. One aged dog, named Buddy and given to the 62nd, became something of a mascot, not least through amusement caused by its regular flatulence. Bridgeport was another small local airport but it did have a hard runway. Located on a peninsula jutting out into Long Island Sound between Bridgeport and Stratford it was bordered by beach houses and sand dunes. Personnel of the 61st were billeted locally in appropriated civilian property. Until new huts were built the sleeping accommodation for the squadron's 22 officers were cots in the upper room of a building belonging to Stratford Baptist Church.

The expected build-up to authorised strength did not materialise in the early months of 1942. The aircraft complement was still mainly a mixture of P-38s and P-40s and personnel were often taken to form the cadres of new units. Among newcomers the new group Materiel Officer, 1st Lieutenant Hubert Zemke, drew attention as he had been in Russia teaching Soviet pilots how to handle the P-40. This unusual assignment came about through the British deciding to pass on Lend-Lease P-40s, which they named Tomahawks, to the Russians as a gesture of support shortly after Hitler's forces had struck east in June 1941. Zemke, who had been sent to Britain to advise the RAF on P-40 operation, found himself on a ship with RAF technicians bound for the USSR. When the United States entered hostilities he actually received notice of assignment to the 56th Fighter Group at Charlotte while still in Russia. As a pilot he was not pleased with the post he was given on arrival at Teaneck and made representations to Graves; eventually he was made Operations Officer at the Air Defense Center and promoted captain, before being reassigned to oversee advanced training to a contingent of Chinese pilots.

Another pilot joining the 56th around the same time was 1st Lieutenant David C. Schilling who had been delivering Bell P-39s and Curtiss P-40s from the manufacturers' airfields. He had actually been assigned to the 56th several months earlier but had continued on detachment at Buffalo. With orders to join the 63rd Fighter Squadron at Farmingdale he was made a flight leader. Schilling was not only a self-assured and able pilot, he was possessed of a disposition that quickly won him friends. From a relatively well-to-do family he had joined the Army Air Corps in 1939 for the fun of flying; that he was intent on having fun is illustrated by an anecdote from David Hubler:

"I was with a bunch of mechanics at Bradley Field, Connecticut going into transition on P-38s, when one Saturday afternoon I was working on the flight line and I see this 1st Lieutenant come across the ramp with a parachute on his shoulder. He said: 'Sergeant, is that airplane ready to go?' and I said 'Yes'. I didn't know who he was. He wanted to take the airplane, so I assumed he had permission. Strapped him in and off he went. About an hour later he comes back. I'm helping him out and he says 'God. That was a lot of fun'. I asked him what he had been doing. Apparently he had heard on the radio that a friend, who was a delivery pilot at the Curtiss field when Schilling had been there doing similar work, was going to be heading this way in a P-40. Schilling thought it would be fun to take off and intercept this man and show him what a P-38 could do."

As production of the favoured Lockheed P-38 Lightning could not meet demand, the squadrons of the 56th began to re-equip with late model Curtiss P-40s. Although the P-38s were taken away the group continued to receive new pilots with the twin-engine training until higher command caught up with the situation. In April 1942 some P-40s with 'pink' camouflage finish were received, diverted from assignment to the North African deserts. A number of pilots and P-40s were detached to join a large formation drawn from several fighter groups on the east coast to fly west to San Francisco, to meet concern about a Japanese attack on that city. The emergency over, the detachment returned, although two pilots of the 62nd Fighter Squadron were lost in a collision over the Pacific coastline. New P-40F models with Packard-built Merlin engines, were received and it seemed that the group was to standardise on this version. But command had other plans.

2 First with Thunderbolts

Across the airfield from the 63rd Fighter Squadron site at Farmingdale the Republic Aircraft Corporation plant was commencing production of a new fighter, the P-47 Thunderbolt. The prototype had first taken to the air in May 1941, soon the subject of 'fastest and best' hyperbole by the news media. Compared with the P-39 and P-40 fighters the 63rd had been flying, the new type was a giant. In the late 1930s the Army Air Corps had developed turbo-supercharging to enable bomber aircraft to operate at what was then the great height of 25,000 to 30,000 feet, and with the expectation that an enemy might also come to operate at such altitudes an interceptor fighter with this capability was desirable. An engine turbo-supercharger was a bulky piece of equipment and to reduce frontal area Alexander Kartveli, Republic's chief designer, placed the turbine in the rear fuselage. Other designs of the period for land-based fighters mostly favoured liquid-cooled engines effecting better streamlining than air-cooled radials with their exposed cylinders. In the P-47B Kartveli made use of the new Pratt & Whitney R-2800 radial, rated at some 2,000 horse power and supercharged, promising a top speed of more than 400 mph at 30,000 feet. For armament the P-47 had eight wing mounted guns; not the rifle calibre weapons that armed RAF Spitfires and Hurricanes during the Battle of Britain but the larger .50-inch calibre Browning with more destructive capability. To incorporate the power plant, sufficient fuel storage and armament, the aircraft had to be substantially larger than its single-engine contemporaries, both US and foreign.

The first production aircraft appeared in March 1942 and by the summer some 50 a month were coming out of the Farmingdale factory. First deliveries to the Army Air Forces were expected mid-May and high command concluded that as technical problems were bound to arise with the new product the first units equipped should be those in the vicinity of Republic's plant. An obvious choice was the 56th Fighter Group, with one squadron on the doorstep and others close by. On 26 May the AAF officially received its first Thunderbolt, the tenth P-47B off the production line, and shortly thereafter the 63rd became the first fighter squadron to fly Thunderbolts.

A few days later the 62nd was moved to Newark Municipal Airport, 12 miles south-west of Bendix. There the landing ground was considered in better condition than that at the vacated base. Squadron headquarters operated out of an airport administrative building along Pulaski Highway but most personnel had to be found accommodation off the station. Training and coastal patrols continued with P-40s and the exuberance of young pilots was occasionally evidenced by such unapproved actions as flying under the George Washington bridge on the Hudson river or very low passes over some objective – 'buzzing'. Mostly the perpetrators got away with their aerial escapades; sometimes there was 'big trouble'.

James C. Stewart, who, understandably, was tired of linked references to James Stewart the great Hollywood star, was a senior 1st Lieutenant in the 62nd. While patrolling over Long Island with 2nd Lieutenant John McClure, Stewart decided to buzz his girl friend's house at Montauk Point at the extreme eastern end. In the swoop down over the coastal inlet Stewart's and the following P-40 flown by McClure hit electricity support cables and local residents lost their power. The duo were positively identified before getting back to Newark where examination of the undersides of the P-40 fuselages revealed scrapes and a missing breather stack. Both pilots were driven in separate staff cars to Colonel Graves' New York office where each was interviewed separately and given a severe reprimand. Stewart was taken off flying status and banished to a ground job at group headquarters for three months. McClure, who was simply following his leader, returned to his squadron and had to fly the dawn patrol – take-off at 6 am – for several weeks.

Major David Terry, the 62nd's CO of a year, was hospitalised for appendix surgery with additional medical treatment in June 1942 and remained there for some weeks. George Reeves, the squadron Operations Officer and second in command, had recently been killed in an air collision while with the California detachment. With no one of sufficient service seniority in the 62nd to succeed these men, Colonel Graves transferred David C. Schilling from the 63rd to take command and Schilling made Horace Craig Operations Officer. Self-confident and eager to succeed, Schilling also had an effervescent personality, which quickly made him popular, particularly with the enlisted men. His coming was recalled by Line Chief Sergeant David Hubler:

"One morning at Newark this Captain rolls up with a black eye and one arm in a sling and says, 'I'm your new commanding officer'. Comes out with several things you couldn't say in front of ladies. Then he asks, 'You wonder why I look like this?' He was in a New York night club and they told him to leave. Said he wasn't going so they threw him out via a plate glass window. Seemed the sort of man we could relate to. Full of energy. He was Mister Personality; all things to all people. Always on the go. Soon called everybody by their first name."

Intelligent, Schilling was also a natural exhibitionist, which aided his standing with the men. One day he walked into the mess hall with Buddy the bulldog who was wearing a pair of pilot's goggles. Buddy later inspired the squadron's 'patch' insignia which featured a cartoon boxing bulldog with thunderbolt decorated gloves.

John McClure, who was considered one of the most able and experienced pilots in the 62nd, went by staff car to Farmingdale to collect the squadron's first Thunderbolt. After an intensive cockpit check and briefing by a Republic test pilot, McClure took off and flew the 'monster' back to Newark. As he made his landing approach only one wing flap would lower and then when he abandoned the landing this flap would not retract. Orbiting the airfield, McClure sought advice through radio contact but all his efforts to retract the flap were in vain. Further advice included abandoning the aircraft over Long Island sound and baling out. Parachuting into the sea seemed more hazardous than attempting to land the ailing Thunderbolt so McClure decided on the latter. By keeping a high speed and cross-controlling with ailerons a safe wheels-down landing was made. The errant flap was found to be jammed in the fully down position, caused by a slight misalignment of the actuating mounts. This was the first of many malfunctions the 62nd and the other squadrons were to experience during the next few months. The 56th Fighter Group was to be the service troubleshooter for the P-47.

Pilots who had flown P-38s, P-39s and P-40s found the P-47 easy to handle but acceleration was slow and take-offs required a long runway. Take-off was simple if the rudder trim tab was set properly as the tail wheel automatically locked straight ahead. In the air the climb rate was slow and turning radius more than desirable. Above 25,000 feet when the turbo was giving full power the P-47 was far faster than the other types and could out-dive all. With hands off the stick the aircraft would recover without assistance, but there were instances of flat spins from which there was no recovery. Occasional accidents through pilot error or mechanical failure occurred in every fighter group. In the 56th, which had to train with a new make and act as a test unit for the type at the same time, accidents were to be expected, particularly as the pilots, mostly fresh from training grounds, lacked experience. Even so, accidents came with frightening regularity in the early weeks of the new type going into service. Two were badly damaged in a landing collision of 17 June and another next day in a landing over-shoot. The first fatality came three days later when Lieutenant Robert Knowle, the Operations Officer, did a full power run across the airfield and went straight into the ground in a cloud of dust. There was little left of either pilot or aircraft that GIs with shovels could find in the crater estimated to be 30 feet wide by 15 deep. The impact was next to a chicken yard, and many of the birds had been killed and others defeathered. Ballooning of the fabric-covered control surfaces, which would have made the aircraft uncontrollable during the high speed dive, was the suspected cause of the crash. Metal-covered elevators and rudder were an early modification on P-47 production.

Four days later Lt Colonel Graves had to bale out from a Thunderbolt when it caught fire after the turbo-supercharger disintegrated. This also proved to be his exit from command of the group. At the beginning of July 1942 some major changes took place. The so-called Headquarters Squadron was disbanded, and a new group headquarters established at

Bridgeport alongside the 61st Fighter Squadron. Lt Colonel Graves departed to take command of the New York Air Defense Wing, and his position with the 56th was filled by Lt Colonel John Crosthwaite. Many men of both group and squadrons were transferred to other units, mostly to a new embryo fighter group that had taken the 56th's place at Farmingdale. Several P-40 pilots joined a group despatched to North Africa in July. Incoming were contingents of freshly commissioned 2nd lieutenants from advanced flight schools whose first introduction to flying fighters would be with the Thunderbolt. Most of the new pilots were checked out in the type at Bradley Field, a recently upgraded AAF airfield with concrete runways at Windsor Locks, Connecticut, 45 miles from the coast north of Hartford. In keeping with military tradition it was named Bradley Field in honour of the first pilot killed while stationed there. In flying the sole P-47B received at Newark it was immediately clear that this airfield was not suitable for safe operation of the type which required at least a 700 yard take-off run. In late July the 62nd Fighter Squadron moved to the more suitable Bradley Field where its inventory was soon increased to a dozen Thunderbolts.

Bridgeport also left much to be desired when it came to operating Thunderbolts. Gerald W. Johnson was one of the spring influx of 2nd lieutenants:

"There were sand dunes and beach houses. Our runway went right up against these houses and it was only 3,800 feet long. It wasn't much of a place to check out the P-47. I must have spent hours around that P-47 when the first arrived. It was the biggest aeroplane I'd ever seen with one engine. We had to have a little ground school on the airplane before we first flew it. The nose was so big you had to S to taxi. On take-off you could only see a little bit of the runway going by. When airborne it took forever to get a decent climb speed. The first P-47s had a prop' that wasn't matched with the engines at all. I finally got it high enough to do some rolls and turns but it appeared that with most everything you did it lost altitude. It seemed under-powered to me. It was not easy to get that airplane down with the approach we had coming over these houses.

"After that we started taking new pilots up to Bradley Field because it had a longer and wider runway. As one of the first to check out in a P-47, I went up there on several occasions just to teach new pilots how to fly the thing. One pilot, Albert Biales, whom I was checking out, dropped that airplane in from so high on the right wheel when landing that it hit the runway so hard it drove the entire landing gear right through the top of the wing. The canopy was open and the strut of that landing gear was lying right across the cockpit in front of the pilot."

One of the pilots who made his first flight in a Thunderbolt from Bradley was Leslie Smith:

"I went straight from AT-6s (advanced trainers) to P-47s. At first I was intimidated by this thing. I was scared to death on my first flight. But I knew where everything was; I could find them blindfolded. Whoever checked me out told me what the aircraft was going to do: that it would try to run off the runway to the left and you had to fight the torque. Initially I had to look out to the side because you can't see over the nose. Watch the edge of the runway and hold direction. Build up speed to 120 then gently pull it off and let it climb. Most of us forgot to pull up the gear and were reluctant to pull back on the throttle. Every new pilot's first flight was watched by other pilots and ground crew who were around. Well, I got off, raised the gear, edged the throttle back and was sitting there in amazement that I'd got the thing airborne. Continued to fly in a straight line. I'd never flown over Massachusetts before and didn't know any landmarks. Knew the field was not many miles north of Hartford and that the Connecticut river ran right along beside the field. I finally decided to turn and take a look back at the base but I couldn't see it. I was lost. I kept flying up and down the river trying to recognise the field which I knew was on the left above Hartford. It had been camouflaged, the runways painted to look like fields. I finally recognised the hangars which weren't camouflaged. Didn't have any trouble landing, it was so heavy and stable."

For the first eighteen months of its existence the 56th Fighter Group had been just another air force unit to those who manned it. Such was the turnover in personnel that there was little scope for the development of esprit de corps. With the coming of the Thunderbolt, however, the men had a reason to feel special, as the group was the first in the Army Air Forces to be equipped with 'the super fighter' as the press hailed it. The feeling of being somewhat elite was particularly strong with the 2nd lieutenant newcomers who had little or no experience in other fighter types. Moreover, arriving in batches on completion of the various training classes they had already established friendships with one another and these usually endured in their new assignment. As personnel numbers expanded towards the Technical Order (TO) requirements for a fighter squadron, the remaining pilots that had arrived from Classes 41-H and 41-I shortly after the attack on Pearl Harbor were elevated to flight leaders there being three flights in each squadron. While some flight leaders and senior squadron officers tolerated the excesses of the young pilots and often turned a blind eye or gave but a mild reprimand, there were others who stuck fairly rigidly to the code of military conduct. This resulted in some uneasy relationships.

Harold Comstock was typical of his generation whose aspirations to fly had only been achieved through determination and effort. Self-confident and already an able pilot, he had not taken easily, as he saw it, to being talked to like a novice when first checked out in a P-47. His instructor was 1st Lieutenant Lucian Dade, always known as Pete in the 56th, a Class 41-I man who believed in correct procedure. Comstock made the mistake of being, as he put it, 'snippy' with Dade during this check-out which led to an enduring resentment between the two. Comstock, recently married, was permitted to live with his wife 'off base'. The couple had found rented accommodation by the coast some distance from Farmingdale. As Comstock did not have a car he was forced to catch the 3 am bus, which took three hours to reach the airfield where his duty commenced at 6 am for the first flights of the day. Often the bus was five minutes late, and though Comstock ran across the field to reach the 63rd office, on arrival he was usually confronted by Dade who fined him a dollar. A dollar a day was then a considerable amount to part with for a pilot on $200 a month. But Dade – who did not think fighter pilots should be married – could see no reason for allowing this breach of duty.

Pete Dade was not alone in his views about fighter pilots being married. The question was raised in many commanders' minds as to whether or not when her husband was committed to combat operations a wife at home might undermine a pilot's will to fight. However, it was obvious in many cases that the young wife took second place in a fighter pilot's life. For the single men, being a dashing fighter pilot was a draw to the girls, which many were happy to take advantage of and play the field. The majority of these young men were probably more confident in the cockpit of a Thunderbolt than in the company of women. This was a time when nice girls were for marriage and nice boys didn't go with bad girls. Away from home influence, however, these attitudes would change – just as it did to alcohol. Drinking with the rest of the boys was part of service life and 'off base' one sought out a good establishment to indulge the habit. Gerald Johnson:

"I became friends with Justus Foster who, like me, was from Kentucky. He bought a Chevrolet for $28 and it provided transportation for us to get from our Stratford billet into Bridgeport. The radiator had a few holes but if it was filled right up before we went to town it would get us there, although the last few miles it would start steaming. We liked to go to a bar in the hotel at Bridgeport, listening to the stories of the bartender, who was such a colourful guy. He wore a different tie every night we were there. They were hand painted and he said they cost him ten dollars apiece. None of us really knew how to drink. We were just learning how to drink. Cocktails were the thing. Usually four of us would go in, park the car. The bartender would be talking all the time and we would order Manhattans. We didn't drink Martinis at the time, we didn't think they were very good, we wanted something a little sweeter. Manhattans were the favourite drink. The bartender would keep talking, he'd have the shaker, he'd line up four or however many glasses were required on the bar, then he'd fill the first glass right up to the rim. When he got to the last glass he was still able to fill that right up to the rim. I saw him do that many times but he never measured anything. We were learning some things about the real world. When we got ready to go overseas, Foster left the car with the keys in it parked just outside the base. A free gift for somebody."

The real buzz in life for these 2nd lieutenants, however, was the cockpit of a Thunderbolt high in the sky. Despite the loss of life in accidents, caution often gave way to the exhilaration of being in command of a 400 mph machine. The 'it always happens to the other guy' belief held true, if sometimes there were sobering reminders that it didn't. Harold Comstock:

"Once I followed my flight leader, Walker Mahurin, up to Windsor Locks and we took on some people from the 62nd Fighter Squadron and did quite well with them. They landed and he decided we ought to rub their nose in it a little with a buzz job. So he said, 'Okay you take the taxi track and I'll take the runway.' Fine with me, the taxi track was as long as the runway. There were trees between the taxi track and the runway and in among the trees were revetments where the airplanes were kept. So I come down as low as I dare and am going as fast as I can go. Mahurin is over the other side going down the runway. And I'm watching where I'm going when a little truck slips right out in front of me. I barely had time to lift the right wing; it was almost an automatic reaction. I lifted the wing no more than a foot or two. It proceeded to peel the front off the top of the cab, just like a can opener. If he had been going a little faster I would have got him with the propeller. Had I been a foot lower I'd have taken his head off. It was an Italian fellow and he spent several days in hospital with shock. My right wing was pretty well banged up so I thought I better put it on the ground before I compounded my problems, rather than fly back to Bridgeport. So I landed at Windsor Locks and I'm in deep trouble. Mahurin goes home. He didn't even tell Tukey [the 63rd CO] what happened. Bob Stover, a guy who didn't quite make it through the war, flew me back to Bridgeport. When I landed Tukey said I was grounded and restricted to the base to serve in the Operations Room for ten days. So I stayed in the Ops Room for ten days, ate with the GIs in the squadron mess and slept on the parachutes."

Another 'near thing' occasioned by exhilaration blinding caution befell Ralph Johnson on one of his first flights in a Thunderbolt:

"Jimmy Jones and I were brand new second lieutenants and our bars shined like new pennies. I liked Jimmy from day one. He was another Southerner and grinned from ear to ear. I can truthful say that he could make the most difficult conditions seem pleasant. After standing in line half the day, he and I finally got Craig at 62nd Operations to let us fly. The squadron only had around a dozen P-47s at the time so we had to take turns. Off we went into the not so wild blue yonder. It was a pleasant day for New England with broken clouds and light drizzles at about a thousand feet. We found a hole in the clouds and climbed on top. After twenty or thirty minutes of 'Hey! Watch me' or 'Can you do this?', we found ourselves still on top with that nice round hole nowhere in sight. After a short discussion we finally convinced ourselves that we were over the base and would soon see the girls lined up in their cars at the main gate. Down through the clouds we went and everything was fine until the clouds had trees in them. We had let down into a small valley in the hills west of the base. Just enough room for two P-47s and no more. Fifty feet in either direction we would have been short two Thunderbolts. Back up with full throttle, and, oh, how wonderful it looked on top. After much more radio discussion we decided to fly down to the coast and let down over the ocean. This we did and when we returned and landed at beautiful Bradley Field we caught holy heck from Craig because he had scheduled us for one hour and we had been gone for almost two. Messed up his schedule but we never told him how stupid we had been. Jimmy and I agreed that a good chewing-out was little punishment for endangering military property and, oh yes, two second lieutenants' government issue. Needless to say, I never let down again unless I knew what to expect. After many more 'I'll never do that again' we completed training; but the hills at Bradley taught me a lesson that I never forgot."

Jimmy Jones became known to the ground crews as 'Full Throttle Jones'. Sergeant David Hubler: "Jones was a better. He'd bet you two birds sitting on a fence which one would fly first. He'd bet you on anything. He'd come down and pitch pennies."

There were other escapades, some elation always to be had in cheating authority. In this respect 2nd Lieutenant Anthony Carcione was unfortunate. As a pilot of one of two P-47s despatched on a 20-minute training flight, Carcione failed to return when expected. The other pilot said Carcione's P-47 had just disappeared. As time for his fuel supply to be exhausted was approaching, the squadron was about to signal a crash alert when the missing P-47 appeared and landed. Carcione's excuse was getting lost. His ground crew chief was somewhat suspicious on discovering that not much fuel was required to replenish the tank in the aircraft that had been gone so long. Nothing more was said about the mystery until a few days later when somebody on the squadron came by a copy of Carcione's home town newspaper, for which he had worked in civilian life. The newspaper carried a photograph of its smiling ex-employee standing up on the wing of a P-47. Carcione had landed at the home town local airfield and spent some minutes enjoying celebrity status. The punishment from his CO for this unscheduled visit was 30 days as Duty Officer of the Day, a task looked upon by hot-rod 2nd lieutenants as confinement.

Tony Carcione was later in more serious trouble. Short, stocky with good Latin looks, during his off-duty time he had made the acquaintance of some girls at the University of Connecticut campus. Again on a training flight, Carcione decided to enhance his status with the university girls by making several low passes over their dormitory building. He was so absorbed in this buzzing he failed to watch the lowering fuel supply and switch to the second tank. On his third pass the engine suddenly faltered and Carcione was committed to belly-landing the Thunderbolt on a small lake. The aircraft overshot and finished up in a grove knocking down several small trees before coming to a halt. Carcione immediately opened the cockpit hood and stood up to make a hasty exit, only to be struck on the head by a falling tree branch and rendered unconscious. Fortunately the aircraft did not catch fire and Tony ended up in the university hospital where he had a fine time entertaining the staff and a number of students. This was the only P-47 lost by the 62nd Fighter Squadron while at Bradley.

3 Hub takes Command

At the beginning of September 1942 a decision was taken in high command to prepare the 56th Fighter Group for overseas. The 63rd Fighter Squadron was moved to Bridgeport to join Headquarters and the 61st. Although this put two of the squadrons on the same station for the first time since Charlotte, training operations still continued on a squadron basis and there was little contact between the two units. To provide a younger group commanding officer with experience of a war zone, Lt Colonel Crosthwaite was moved to command a fighter wing on the west coast and his place taken by the 28-year-old Major Hubert Zemke. Zemke had been raising a neophyte fighter squadron elsewhere as well as teaching the class of Chinese pilots to fly fighters since his original assignment to the 56th. Because of his service in Britain and Russia he was the object of some curiosity among the 2nd lieutenant hot-rods. For them, the group headquarters was an area of administration outside their squadron world, and the group commander was rarely seen. Zemke, however, took a more active part in flying from the outset, leading squadron training missions, often in non-regulation flying gear. Gerald Johnson:

"The first time he briefed us I noticed that his flying suit was tucked into some ten inch high boots. Later I asked him where he got them and he told me Macey's in New York. So the first opportunity I had to get down to New York I bought two pairs of the same boots. They were a hunting boot, soft leather with some kind of synthetic sole. They were just wonderfully comfortable boots and if my commander was going to wear them that's what I wanted."

Zemke, 5ft 9in, trim and handsome featured, sometimes wore a black flying suit which he had acquired in London the previous year and had used during his work for the Soviets. If his flying garb was non-regulation, his conduct was definitely military, however, as any officer or enlisted man who erred soon found out. Zemke's flying was another matter. His air leadership from a piloting viewpoint could be erratic and soon led to 'The Big Wheel' being considered a poor pilot, despite his experience. Harold Comstock:

"One time Hub Zemke came over to fly with the 63rd and was going to go down to Harrisburg which was the Army camouflage school. I was to fly his wing. They had done an outstanding job of camouflaging the base. Hub and I found the runway all right but Johnny Vogt landed over in the golf course and Ed Whitley landed across the runway and there were 63rd planes in various parts of that airport. We went to that base for the people there to take a look at the P-47 and be able to identify the aeroplane in flight. So we are gathered and back we come, and we get close to Bridgeport, and the Old Man wiggles his wings to close it up and then pumps the stick up and down which means go into string. So I'm intent on making a good impression and get up close behind. We come around and suddenly there's fire coming out of his turbo and wheels coming down. I pitch off to the left so I don't run into him, and Roger Dyar who was No 3 goes to the right, blowing the formation all to hell. We landed and Zemke had his critique and we were told what we did wrong. I very meekly asked: 'Sir, I didn't see your landing signal.' He just looked at me and said, 'I didn't give any.' It ended the conversation right there."

The leader's lack of indication referred to a system of visual signals used by pilots. A fist pushed forward repeatedly was a warning to the wingman that the throttle was about to be opened and speed increased. If power was to be reduced, the signal was an open hand with the fingers pointed up and moved rearwards in a beckoning movement. When running low on fuel, each finger stood for ten gallons. A crooked finger was five gallons. To move the element to one side or another the leader would sharply dip the wing on the desired side. To close up the flight the leader would rock his wings slightly. To put your formation into string, the leader would pump the elevators. In preparation for levelling off, the leader used his hand with fingers straight ahead and the palm down. To open out the formation the leader pumped his rudder. Most of these signals were passed from the two people on the leader's wing to other aircraft.

A facet of Zemke's character was a doggedness of purpose, although his detractors may have seen this as obstinacy. If he believed he was right or that those of his command were right, he would not easily be persuaded otherwise. An early example of his loyalty in this respect was an incident that occurred at Bradley where the 62nd Fighter Squadron remained, though sharing the airfield with other units training on Thunderbolts. John McClure and his flight returned from a training exercise low on fuel to find P-47s from another unit using the runway. A request to the tower for a priority to land because of the fuel position only brought radioed response to keep out of the traffic pattern until called. Further requests for a priority landing were also disregarded. Angry that the seriousness of his flight's situation was ignored, McClure threatened that unless he was allowed to land he would fly through the tower. Then with his wingman following he proceeded to conduct an extremely low pass over the building, entered the traffic pattern and landed.

Unfortunately, the other P-47s that were using the runway were those of the 326th Fighter Group, a recently activated unit under the command of Major Gilbert Meyers, who prior to his promotion earlier in the year had been CO of the 63rd Fighter Squadron. It was Meyers who was in the tower directing his pilots when McClure buzzed it. Meyers was livid and threatened McClure with a court martial even when the depleted fuel supplies of McClure's P-47 flight were confirmed. Schilling was sent for and in his defence of McClure decided to contact Zemke by telephone. Zemke wanted to speak to McClure and asked him to give him the truth 'with no bullshit'. Convinced of the seriousness of the situation in which McClure had found himself when not being allowed into the traffic pattern on return to Bradley, Zemke – recently promoted Lt Colonel – then spoke with Meyers and told him to bring Schilling with him and drive down to Bridgeport to settle the matter. McClure was ordered to stay in Bradley Operations where he remained for seven hours until Schilling and Meyers returned. Meyers was not a happy man, as while not endorsing McClure's angry swoop on the Bradley tower, Zemke had rebuked Meyers for not responding to an emergency situation which could have resulted in aircraft crashing and loss of lives. McClure never heard any more of the incident.

Since first receiving P-47s the 56th's squadrons had written up well over a hundred unsatisfactory reports on technical matters involving the aircraft. The electrical pitch control of the Curtiss propellers and the supercharger to carburettor linkage setting for the engine were particularly troublesome. A new model, the P-47C incorporating improvements, was in production by September and a few were received by the squadrons. Accidents continued but less frequently. Second Lieutenant Milton Anderson had an engine detonation immediately after take-off from Bridgeport and ended up in Long Island Sound. Despite the disintegration of the aircraft he was able to get out and wade ashore. But uncautioned flying by cocky young pilots still brought fatalities. One day Glen Schiltz and Richard Craghill of the 63rd were 'rat-racing' around when Craghill's Thunderbolt hit somebody's propwash (turbulence) which turned the aircraft on its back. This wasn't unusual but instead of rolling the P-47 back up Craghill proceeded to do a half loop, known as a Split-S, which would have reversed his direction of flight. It was a misjudgement that cost him his life for with only 3,000 feet of altitude he was unable to complete the manoeuvre. The aircraft crashed on a house in Darien, Connecticut. Fortunately, the occupants of the house had just gone outside the front door to say farewell to visitors when the P-47 impacted in the back.

On 13 November Lieutenants Roger Dyar and Harold Comstock of the 63rd were sent out to test a new type of radio antenna on P-47Cs because the original type kept breaking off. They made their first runs at 35,000 feet at over 400 mph then still at high speed entered dives to conduct runs at lower levels. Almost immediately both aircraft encountered compressibility, and the forces on control surfaces made it impossible to move the normal flight controls in the rarefied air. Only at lower altitudes could recovery be effected, first by winding out the elevator trim tabs until the denser atmosphere dissipated compressibility and enabled the normal flight controls to function. Similar experiences had led to speed restrictions in August but on this occasion the cockpit indicators had shown maximum figures of 725 mph, beyond the speed of sound! Republic took advantage of this for some laudatory publicity while the press went still further and pronounced that Thunderbolts had exceeded the speed of sound. In reality the speed indicators were wrong and the true speed in the dive was probably in the vicinity of 500 mph. In any case, the terminal velocity of a Thunderbolt would have been no more than 600 mph. The speed of sound varies with altitude being 760 mph in the rarified conditions at 30,000 feet and lower in denser air. Approaching the speed of sound, the behaviour of air against an aircraft wing suddenly changes. Instead of flowing over the airfoils in common use at that time it piles up in front. The aircraft is buffeted, its tail surfaces are blanked out in the unstable air. Long before sonic speed is reached, local compressibility conditions develop over rivet heads and other projections.

Modifications and grounding of the P-47s restricted flying time even when the aircraft complements of the squadrons were increased. Many pilots had no gunnery practice and little experience of bad weather flying. In early November word was passed around that the group would most likely be going overseas to Europe. Gerald Johnson:

"Our squadron commander came in one morning saying he'd learnt where we were going: England. There's lots of bad weather in England so if any of you don't feel you can fly instruments as well as you should you'd better start practicing flying instruments. I had been through the clouds a few times but all of my training, except primary, had been in Texas and they don't have that many clouds in Texas. I didn't know much about flying instruments apart from using the Link ground trainer. At that time we were shooting gunnery most every day down on the south side of Long Island. I told my flight that on coming back I'm going to climb up into clouds if we've got any clouds. You don't have to come with me, you know how to get back to Bridgeport. So we shot our gunnery – rationed to the use of one gun – and on the way back I said, okay I'm going up in the clouds. So I'm now up in the clouds at maybe 4,000 feet and I'm thinking to myself there's nothing in flying instruments. I'm just knocking along here and the instruments were reading okay. Thought to myself that if I'm going to combat you may have to do some fighting in clouds as well. So I decided I'd roll it. When I rolled it the gyros spun all over the place and before completing the roll I suddenly realised the airplane was getting out of control. Fortunately the cloud base was not too far below but I came out in a semi-spin. I got straightened up and flew back to the base at Bridgeport. Thought I ought to talk to someone about this experience as there's a whole lot I don't know. I'm either dumb or not very qualified. So I decided to talk to our Operations Officer, Wetherbee. He was an old man it seemed to me. Believe he had graduated with class 41-H: I was in class 42-D. So I approached him and

said I need to talk with you about something. And I told him what I'd
done. He was very nice about it. He said you don't normally do that. The
clouds you're gonna find in England you're going to be trying to fly
through them and get on top of them. You don't normally do aerobatics
in the clouds."

In Johnson's mocking of his own inexperience there is a glimpse of the
limited and hurried training of these young pilots who on average had
about 150 flying hours each in fighters by mid November when the
personnel requirements of the Technical Order had finally been reached.
Each squadron was authorised 27 pilots, of which three were the
commanding officer, his deputy the Operations Officer and an Assistant
Operations Officer. A squadron was divided into flights designated A, B
and C with eight or nine pilots and aircraft assigned to each. The aircraft
complement was 25 and it was usual for junior pilots to share a fighter
while the senior men had one assigned for their use only. In practice,
owing to unserviceability and other factors, a pilot often had to fly other
machines than his own. Promotions, as wartime temporary, had been rapid
with the approved rank of a squadron CO being major and flight leaders
captain. In addition to the 27 flying officers there were ten ground officers,
usually older men or those not medically acceptable for flying. These were
an Adjutant, Intelligence, Assistant Intelligence, Engineering, Supply,
Communications, Ordnance, and Statistical Officers, and a Flight
Surgeon. Enlisted personnel totalled between 240 and 250 per squadron of
which some 115 were sergeants, 70 corporals and 60 privates at this time.

The aircraft maintenance force was also divided among the three
flights under a flight chief. Each aircraft usually had a ground crew
complement of three, Crew Chief, Assistant Crew Chief and Armament
Engineer, although this depended on the availability of trained men.
There was an influx of new ground specialists in November although
there were several unfilled vacancies, particularly with regard to engine
mechanics. Without word to his superiors, Dave Schilling went over to
Pratt & Whitney's factory at East Hartford, not far from Bradley Field,
and endeavoured to recruit some of their engineers. Understandably, the
firm's management were not happy when they got word of an
effervescent Air Force major trying to proselyte their workforce. This
brought a strong reprimand for Zemke from General Cannon, chief of I
Fighter Command, and Zemke was equally vexed with his enterprising
squadron commander. This and other uncautioned actions by Schilling
made Zemke a little wary of what the 62nd's CO might do next.

When the group was activated several of the enlisted men sent to form
the initial cadre were long service soldiers with no particular expertise.
With the prospect of overseas movement many of these older men were
replaced by younger blood, better trained and more suited to the task
ahead. Some older men though relatively uneducated had become able
mechanics without any formal instruction. Dave Hubler:

"I worked for a sergeant in the 62nd called 'Jeep' Thurman at Bradley Field. He was an old cavalry trooper with some 15 years service. Somehow he got into aviation maintenance. After a while I noticed that when there was some problem with an airplane we were working on he'd say 'Go get the technical order (instruction manual). I'd bring it over and then he would say, 'Read it loud so we'll all know.' On the maintenance forms he'd put red dashes and crosses in the right places but then he'd tell me to fill in the rest of the form because I printed better than he did. He would sit in the barracks at night and look at a magazine or newspaper and we'd hear him chuckling and sometimes he'd make an occasional remark about pictures in there. I got to thinking about this and when Jeep wasn't around I said to a friend 'Do you think Jeep really knows how to read and write or is he just pretending he does?' My friend grins and all he says is, 'So you finally figured it out!'"

Despite the numerous transfers several of the enlisted men from the original cadre were still with the squadrons at this juncture and did go overseas. In fact, it was the ground echelon rather than the pilots that made the 56th Fighter Group an enduring entity.

On Thanksgiving Day 1942 the 56th Fighter Group was finally alerted for overseas. In the next few days the P-47s were withdrawn and word was that they were being made ready for shipment. In fact all were transferred to other units in training. For a month while the ground personnel packed maintenance and other essential equipment the pilots attended instructional classes, frustrated that they could not fly. Gerald Johnson:

"We had a great spirit in the 61st. We were competitive, great guys. We all had so much energy. We were young, physically fit. When the airplanes were taken away we had literally nothing to do. We managed to get some jeeps by talking our way into this by saying that every flight commander should have a jeep. We had jeep races. It was snowing by that time and it was kinda rough around there. By the time we had to leave we had just about destroyed those jeeps. We had run into sand dunes, each other and banged them up in every way."

With less re-assignment of personnel more stability was evident in the squadrons and a growing camaraderie, particularly among the young pilots. Personal friendships developed and inevitably this was marked by bestowing nicknames that became the normal terms of reference. Harold Comstock's wife Barbara called her husband 'Bunny' at home and when his squadron mates got wind of this Comstock was thereafter Bunny. Horace Craig, 62nd Operations Officer, took a lot of ribbing about an incident when a girl referred to him as 'Grandpappy'. With time this became abbreviated to 'Pappy' and the moniker stuck. There was also the status accorded fighter pilots by society, which understandably boosted egos, untried and untested as they may have been. It carried a lot of kudos with the girls who were generally eager to 'walk out' with a fighter pilot. And with self-importance came some recognition of belonging to a gathering which was something more than just a numerical designation. The 56th Fighter Group and its squadrons had become an objective reality.

4 The Move Overseas

While the 56th Fighter Group awaited movement orders, another organisation was being prepared for commitment overseas on the same vessel. This was the 33rd Service Group. Army Air Forces organisation of aircraft maintenance was based on what were identified as four defined areas, known as first, second, third and fourth echelon maintenance. First echelon was the work by squadron ground crews in servicing their charges and making minor repairs. Second echelon maintenance covered work that required specialist knowledge and equipment but could be carried out on the home airfield. Third and fourth echelon maintenance was performed at special locations and involved major repair and overhaul. It was realised that in committing a unit to a theatre of combat operations it was essential that second echelon maintenance be readily to hand. This led to one of the two squadrons of a service group being attached to a combat group to provide the desired maintenance support. Although answerable to the local service command the service squadron would in practice become merged and part of the combat group.

Its associations yet unknown, the 33rd Service Group at Grenier Field, near Manchester in New Hampshire, received notification to prepare for assignment to a combat zone. John Sipek:

"Getting prepared for overseas movement was an enormous task. It was much more complex than a move in the USA. All our tools had to be covered with cosmoline to prevent rust. The most difficult items we had to treat were a couple of heavy duty chain hoists. The next step was to construct crates to pack all our equipment in. A shopping number, 8569 P, was assigned to our squadron and had to be stencilled on all the crates with black paint. Those of us who held out during the shake-down inspections and didn't turn in all their excess clothing now had an opportunity to stuff it into the crates with our equipment. I saved extra pairs of stockings, coveralls and a mattress cover which I packed. We were told that the mattress covers we turned in would be used as body bags for the dead.

"A notice on the orderly room bulletin board informed us to get tags and wire from the quartermaster supply room to attach to our barrack bags. Examples of the information to print on the tags were illustrated. We also had to stencil a white 'A' on one bag and 'B' on the other one plus our shipping number 85669P. These instructions were to be carried out immediately and the bags were to be tied to the end of our bunks ready for inspection the following morning. Our daily routine was to read the orderly room bulletin board on the way to the mess hall for lunch, and next day there was a long list of names of men who were to report to our CO's office after lunch with their A and B bags. After lunch I grabbed my bags and lined up with the rest of the bad boys outside the CO's office. When my turn came I walked in and stood to attention in front of his desk. He was sitting at his desk, looking down at some papers ignoring my presence. I waited to be recognised and when he finally looked up I saluted him holding it until he returned the salute. I said, 'Private First Class Sipek reporting as ordered, sir'. In a very calm manner he asked, 'Why are you here, private?' (As if he didn't know after needlessly chewing out a couple of dozen of my buddies.) I replied it must concern my barrack bags as I was ordered to bring them, and report to you. He had a copy of the instructions and illustration of the tags to be attached to our bags. He told me to compare my tags and tell him of any dissimilarity. The only difference I found was that the instruction specified wire to attach the tags and I used cord. He preceded to chew me out and then asked me how I expected to help win the war if I couldn't follow the simple instructions. He ordered me to make the necessary changes and have the bags tied to the end of my bunk ready for his inspection the following morning. He could make a mountain out of a molehill and was a major drawback in our squadron.

"When we finished packing all our equipment and stencilling all the crates with our shipping number everything was delivered to the port of embarkation, including our vehicles. It would all be shipped overseas on a cargo ship and we were told that we may never see it again. Our officers told us not to worry about losing our equipment because we would be supplied with replacements when we arrived at our destination. I didn't want any of our crates to get lost because I had packed extra tools in addition to the extra clothing in them that would not be replaced."

The 56th Fighter Group and its squadrons finally received orders to move by train to Camp Kilmer, New Brunswick, New Jersey, two days after Christmas to be ready for embarkation. For seven days a cycle of showdown inspections, inoculations, orientation lectures and so on, kept the men occupied, plus speculation as to where they were going. Those not in the know were now sure it was England until a rumour that some items of warm weather clothing were being issued reasserted Africa as the likely destination. Other units were also arriving at the same location, including the 33rd Service Group. John Sipek:

"In late December we moved to Camp Kilmer, New Jersey, our last stop before going overseas. We were informed that our stay would be short. It had a much different appearance than any of our previous bases. The exteriors of all the barracks were painted a different colour and took on a weird guise. Since the camp was located near the east coast there was a blackout in effect. The GIs that occupied the camp before us left their signatures in all the latrines. They drew little faces staring at you with the caption 'Kilroy was here'. We added more Kilroy graffiti during our stay. Camp Kilmer was a staging area near the New York port of embarkation. We were checked for physical condition, inoculations, pay, personal records, insurance and equipment. We had some practice drills carrying all our personal equipment walking up a makeshift gang plank. In the evenings we were free to go to the recreation hall, base movies, or relax in the barracks. New Brunswick was near the camp and the city bus stopped at the main gate. An evening pass was available but fellows who went said it was dull walking around in the blackout. An all-day pass was offered to anyone who lived or had relatives living within a 25-mile radius of the camp. Sam Fil told me his uncle lived in Brooklyn and I could come along as his guest to visit him. We were issued passes with instructions with few dos and many do nots. The most important thing they stressed was for us to zip our lips and not discuss military matters or where we were stationed. Sam gave me a well guided quick tour of Brooklyn. When we arrived at his uncle's apartment and salutations were completed, the next words out of his uncle's mouth were, 'You boys stationed at Camp Kilmer? That's the jumping off place.' We stood looking at each other wondering what to reply. His uncle broke the silence by saying, 'Don't worry, the civilians know more of what's going on round here than the military'. We had a few drinks and talked for a while, being careful not to discuss military affairs.

"Our bus ride back to camp was uneventful until we arrived at the main gate. There we witnessed a very smooth smuggling job. Liquor was prohibited at the camp, which only presented a challenge to the resourceful fellows of the squadron. Two MPs were waiting at the front of the bus as it opened to check our passes and confiscate any liquor found. We noticed a couple of the first fellows off the bus walk round to the rear. One of our fellows inside the bus at an open rear window started passing out bottles to the fellows outside that had already been checked by the MPs.

"When the time finally came for us to leave Camp Kilmer, we travelled by rail to the New York port of embarkation. The dock area was loaded with GIs all eager to go overseas into the unknown. Everything seemed to be in a state of confusion. Our officers were running around trying to find out what ship our squadron was assigned to, so we had to stand and wait for instructions. While we were waiting, some women came through our ranks carrying arm loads of sleeveless sweaters and gave one to each of us. The sweaters had been knitted by a group of women in Needham, Massachusetts. They had each sewed little tags in the back of the collar with their chapter identity. It was a great feeling to get this gift from a complete stranger who would never see us again. They were real Americans with a heart. There was no crowd of people or band playing at the dock to cheer us on as is usually portrayed in the movies when troops are going overseas. We finally got our ship assignment and had to walk a long distance on the dock to reach it. The weather was cold so we were wearing our overcoats, rubber overshoes, cap, helmet, field pack and gas mask carrier. In addition we were carrying our rifle and two loaded barracks bags which made the walk very tiring. Fortunately we had lined up, as was our custom, by height so I was at the front of the column right on the heels of our officers. Watching them struggle with their bags helped to get our adrenaline flowing and made our march easier. Finally, up the real gangplank we climbed, giving our name and serial number to the officer in charge so he could check each one of us against his list. Our B bags were taken from us and stored in the swimming pool. We were then assigned our state rooms. The last sentence really sounds grandiose. I had to share a stateroom with 26 other buddies plus our A bags and rifles. According to the information on the wall, this stateroom accommodated two so I think we were a little overcrowded. The bunks were three high with wood slats attached across the width, covered by a thin pad which served as a mattress. We had to use our own blankets to keep warm. Sleeping on a hard surface on land is uncomfortable enough but on a moving rolling troop transport it was miserable. The three bunks were so close together that in order to climb in or out we had to do it sideways. There were many bumped heads caused by fellows awaking and attempting to sit up in bed. There was also the danger of the heavier fellows breaking through the slats and injuring the bunk-mate underneath. It was very late at night when we settled in our bunks. A short time later we were awakened by strange noises and felt the ship moving away from the dock. It was the 6th of January 1943 and we were on our way to the UK as passengers in the fastest ship afloat."

Some, expecting a long sea journey, sought to lighten the passing of time with a little liquid refreshment, although it did not lighten the load in the unexpectedly lengthy troop along the New York docks. Gerald Johnson:

"One of my best friends at the time, Dick Ellis, suggested that we dispense with some of the clothing packed in our bags and take a little liquor. We bought a case of bourbon and took six bottles each, only we never reckoned on having to walk so far. I have no idea how far we walked as it was so dark, but it must have been miles. To ease my aching arms I had that bag in every position I could think of, moved around on top of my head, shoulders and back; first held by one arm, then the other. All the time the bag got heavier and heavier. Having got so far I simply wasn't going to throw that bourbon away. But was I mighty relieved when we finally got aboard."

The personnel of the 56th Fighter Group and 33rd Service Group amounted to about a sixth of the near 12,000 souls on board the Cunard liner *Queen Elizabeth*, impressed as a troop transport. Among the units was a hospital complete with nurses. For the vast majority this was their first time outside the United States and in the 56th Fighter Group only two men are known to have previously been to Europe. Before enlisting many had never travelled outside their own state. A great adventure for some, but apprehension generated by the reports of sinkings in the Atlantic frequently seen in newspapers was in many minds. And it was disquieting to find that the vessel relied on speed rather than an escort to survive U-boat interception. The once luxury liner had been stripped of its furnishing to accommodate the maximum number of persons and discomfort was added to unease. Most bunks had to be shared, eight hours each for three people. The B bags, which were stored at various points throughout the ship held gas-proof clothing impregnated with a chemical the smell of which pervaded the whole ship below deck. All that could be said in its favour was that it hid the stench of vomit: there were many poor sailors. Feeding the multitude was another matter. Max Victor, a 63rd Fighter Squadron crew chief:

"Getting into the mess hall twice a day with 12,000 troops on board was no easy task. We would wait in line for at least two hours before we could get to food. Abrupt changes of course didn't help digestion. During the voyage the ship would zigzag by turning every seven minutes. We were told it would take that much time for an enemy submarine to prepare to fire its torpedoes. We were out on the ocean alone with no escort. There wasn't a navy warship built that could keep up with the speedy *Queen*. During the trip it was rumoured that an enemy sub did in fact fire two torpedoes at us and missed. We did hear big guns on the deck go off numerous times but we were told the gunners were just firing them for practice."

In the early hours of 12 January 1943, after six days sailing, the *Queen Elizabeth* dropped anchors off Gourock, Scotland, and several thousand young Americans got their first look at a foreign land. A damp, dull grey day with a skyline of hills and cranes was the unexciting panorama that greeted those who went out on deck to look. The 33rd Service Group had been the last to board and now it was the first to be disembarked by tender and ferried to the docks where trains were waiting. Men of the 56th had occupied an area in the forward part of the vessel and were some of the last to leave, late in the afternoon. There were more delays while awaiting train transport, locomotives and carriages that were diminutive in comparison with those in the US. Women came amongst the waiting troops dispensing hot tea. They seemed friendly but conversation was limited by failure to understand what was said with strong Glaswegian accents. The first contingents travelled in daylight but there were many stops. The weather was damp and despite the packed humanity the journey was cold. While the train was held in a Newcastle siding for several minutes, Mike Sidisin, a 62nd Fighter Squadron radio man, got into conversation with a British soldier and traded his GI overcoat for the more substantial if less well tailored British Army greatcoat. The last 56th contingent departed Gourock shortly after 5 pm but made better progress through the night.

That afternoon the staff at the small country railway station at King's Cliffe, Northamptonshire, had been amazed when an American truck unloaded a military band in the yard – and even more amazed when another vehicle with doughnut making equipment arrived and its crew proceeded to provide for the bandsmen. The US authorities had arranged a welcome for the expected troops; it was to be a long wait as the first train did not arrive at the little station until deep in the night, at 3 am. One officer asked the local policeman, who was on hand, how close they were to the sea. Evidently the place name and the noise of a stiff wind made the American think they had arrived at a coastal location, when they were actually near the middle of England. In the dark the arrivees were taken by trucks and buses and shown into huts on a nearby airfield. Some pilots were put in hotels at Peterborough and others in reasonable barracks at an RAF station nearby owing to lack of accommodation at King's Cliffe. One of the first impressions of Britain was the dominance of darkness at night. There had been a blackout of sorts in New York; in Britain it seemed total. A GI who switched on a flashlight was immediately warned to 'Put that light out' by an unseen Briton and by his officer to 'Remember you're in a war zone.'

5 Introduction to England

Dawn brought a bleak morning, soon found to be the norm at King's Cliffe in winter. The day was taken up with sorting out barrack sites for the various units. HQ 56th Fighter Group and 33rd Service Group, 61st and 62nd Fighter Squadron and 41st Service Squadron were present, but insufficient accommodation put the 63rd Fighter Squadron at RAF Wittering a few miles to the north. A pre-war RAF station, the barracks were substantial with hot running water in sharp contrast to the damp and chill of King's Cliffe. Men of the 63rd were reasonably happy with their situation. Ed Lanham, a crew chief:

> "Wittering was an active Mosquito airfield so on our first day in the European Theatre of Operations (ETO) we were close to those fighting the war. As this was a permanent base the facilities were very nice. The barracks were brick and situated around a square. The marching on the square woke us up the first morning; young lady soldiers! WAAFs and boy could they drill, the shoes all hitting the asphalt in unison. You had to admire them."

Initial contact with RAF suggested a harder and more disciplined regime than that of the Army Air Forces. Conversely, the British would view the newcomers as lax and undisciplined, even if they politely kept these opinions to themselves.

With their own equipment still to arrive, the 56th command kept the small liaison staff provided by the RAF at King's Cliffe busy seeking temporary replacements. Colonel Zemke, who had set up his office in the airfield control tower, made arrangements to replace the RAF cookhouse staff with men from his own quartermaster attachment as an early move. Many GIs were not happy with the bland British fare that had been served on the *Queen Elizabeth*; and while the RAF had thoughtfully provided a beef stew for the weary travellers when they arrived in the dark hours US rations were missed. Hopefully something more favourable to an American palate would soon be provided.

Motor transport was an urgent requirement and on 14 January it was arranged for Sergeant William Billings and Corporal John 'Red Dog' Woods to be taken to an RAF depot to collect vehicles. Billings:

> "We received one Humber staff car and one English 3 ton Dodge truck

(which we later called Old Lend Lease). Red drove the staff car and I the truck. At this time and date I was the only one in the outfit with experience of driving on the left side of the road as pre-war I had driven on the left in Trinidad. Back at the base I was despatched to pick up a detail, and drive back to the railhead in the village of King's Cliffe to recover our B-Bags and TAT Equipment. As the truck was being loaded someone spotted a pallet of Scotch whisky on the loading dock. The bill of lading (delivery note) was handwritten, to me unusual as on our railroads they were typewritten. I saved the bill of lading with the idea of sending it to my dad but never did. My dad spent all his life railroading. The bill of lading was addressed to the RAF Wittering Officers' Mess. The temptation was too great. Three of the men in the detail grabbed two boxes apiece. The Scotch was packed four bottles to a box, then stuffed with straw. In our haste one bottle fell and smashed, it was kicked under the truck before it was seen. In all 23 bottles made the trip to the 62nd Squadron living site."

Evidently the theft was noticed by the railway station staff and the local constabulary notified. Next day the British law arrived at the airfield and, identifying the vehicle and crew involved, it was directed to the 62nd living site. Major Schilling, who was aware of the crime, ordered a barracks inspection. Before Captain Virgil Durrance, the squadron Adjutant, First Sergeant Raymond Hancock and two English police officers entered the barracks, Schilling took Billings and went ahead collecting both full and empty bottles. The wood boxes had already been burnt in the hut stoves for heat. The bottles were secreted in the trunk (boot) of the Humber staff car until the police had left empty-handed. Understandably this episode increased Schilling's popularity with the enlisted men of his squadron. Morally a reprehensible act, Schilling only saw his men depriving the Wittering Officers' Mess of its precious whisky as a huge joke, whereas the other squadron commanders and Zemke would never have done such a thing, let alone approve. When word eventually leaked out Schilling would plead no knowledge of the event with a big smile and a chuckle. The chuckle was Dave Schilling's audible hallmark, frequently heard in the lodgings of the 56th, particularly if he was involved in some piece of social devilment. Even so, the flamboyant persona hid a more serious side and probably a degree of insecurity.

The English roads and traffic system were an early puzzlement, being narrow, winding and metalled where one kept to the left side, if the lane was wide enough. Hazardous for driving and also walking. John Sipek:

"A public road separated our barrack site from the technical and mess sites. A group of us were on the way to the mess site with Edward Deveau leading the pack. Ed started to cross the road after looking to the left for traffic and carelessly stepped into the roadway where he was struck by an English fellow riding a bicycle. The fellow was travelling down a little grade in the road so he was moving fast. The impact knocked Ed down and he slid along the road while the cyclist flew over the top of him. We stopped a passing jeep, put Ed in and took him to the base hospital. He was fortunate no bones were broken but he was bruised and his face was slightly disfigured which would require plastic surgery. Ed said he couldn't write to his parents about this accident because it would be too embarrassing to tell them that he had been struck by an English cyclist and ended up in hospital. After a couple of weeks of rest and rehabilitation Ed was as good as new."

Occasional road accidents with vehicles were almost inevitable for men conditioned to use the right lane. Not long after arrival at King's Cliffe, John Woods and Sam Horning, two 62nd drivers, were told to take a 2½ ton truck and go north to collect some equipment. Driving along a twisty country road and rounding a sharp curve they were confronted with six large horses on the left side and an English lorry on the right side. In avoiding the horses Woods braked and swung the truck to the right, hitting the English lorry in the side and causing substantial damage, the driver being pinned inside. By the time Horning and Woods had reversed and got out of their truck several men had arrived on the scene. One of the Englishmen was heard to holler 'Get a rope.' Horning looked at Woods nervously and said, 'Red Dog, do you think they are going to hang us?' The rope was needed to fix to the lorry door and jerk it open so the driver could get out.

King's Cliffe airfield had been grass-surfaced, laid out in 1941 as a satellite for nearby Wittering. The following year three hard runways were put down and extra accommodation erected and this work was still in progress when the 56th arrived. With little else to do, men of the 41st Service Squadron helped the English contractors in putting down a cement base for a hangar, while others were sent on courses to study British aeronautical hardware. Pilots had a frustrating time waiting for P-47s to be delivered. Most days there were lectures by RAF personnel on intelligence, evading capture, aircraft recognition, indoctrination in the use of UK maps, navigation systems, flying control, etc. With no aircraft to fly, a lesser piece of transport was used to simulate formation tactics and expend youthful energy. Gerald Johnson:

"We didn't have very much to do. They issued each pilot a bicycle and we had all kind of races and stunts. On one side of the flying field there was a kind of big ditch beside the road with a little pathway. Too narrow for two people to walk across and there was water at the bottom of this ditch. We would have a formation of three bikes in a vee, the idea was to follow the leader's movements. Well the leader would suddenly make a quick turn onto this path and the other two trying to follow him would end up in this ditch. Great sport. It was a lot more fun after we'd been to the bar."

While the winter weather occasionally dropped to freezing level the temperatures were never as low as those experienced in a North American winter, yet to most of these young men there was a greater chill. 'A cold damp atmosphere that really got to you.' For some the introduction to wartime Britain and its winter weather brought a mood of depression: Sylvester Walker committed his feelings to his diary: "I like this country and people less all the time. This is the worst weather I have ever seen, the wind never stops and it rains every other hour and is cold between. The mud is knee deep everywhere." Some bright days and a better understanding of the British would modify Walker's opinions in weeks to come.

If there was no call for outside duty men stayed in their billets or the social meeting places that had been set up. With, usually, only one lecture a day the rest of the time was free. John McClure:

"A favourite pastime was poker, and the actions of two 62nd pilots in separate ways illustrate the game's attraction and pitfalls. Connie Saux grew up on the wrong side of the tracks in New Orleans and learned how to play cards in the casinos. A house dealer hired Connie, and in handling cards, he was about as street-wise and card-wise as the most effective croupier could be. He always had money in his pocket, and he loved to get in a card game where he would fleece anyone. When he joined the outfit at Bradley, I got to talk to Connie a couple of times. A question arose when he joined us as to who would room together; Connie got paired with Harry Coronios. Connie and Harry were extreme opposites in experience and temperament. Connie discovered quickly how innocent Harry was, and I noted that Connie knew he couldn't take advantage of 'this stupid kid'. Connie started to nurse-maid Harry: 'Don't do this, don't do that.'

"When the poker games began Connie never entered one with his friends. He knew that if he couldn't win a game, he would buy it. Some of the guys thought that Saux was unsociable. I advised him to tell the outfit's card players that he was a professional player. Connie finally agreed that he would sit in on games as long as he never had to handle the deck of cards. He promised he would not touch the cards. 'Someone else can handle my deal. I am out,' he said. Under this promise, he played a little poker with the gang. Watching the games, Harry Coronios decided to join in. One time Harry won some money and thought he was a poker player. Saux complained that he had 'raised'Harry but could not tame his gambling desire. Saux asked permission to sit in a game with Harry and to take his money. Saux would buy the pot only when Harry had some money in it. Saux thus took every cent Harry had, and Saux would lend Harry money to put more into the pot. Each time his aim was to teach Harry a lesson about gambling. He got two months of Harry's paycheck with this plan.

"One night he foreclosed on Harry, telling him he played his last poker game and that he owed Saux two month's pay. Saux went up to the pay table with Harry for two months running so that Harry would learn how much he had lost at poker. Saux made Harry beg him for money for a coke. However, Saux had given Harry's money to me for safe-keeping up to the day when he took Harry into the post office and made him send his folks a postal money order. 'You still can't have a coke,' Saux told Harry, and made him quit playing poker. Harry obeyed his friend."

Neither man would go home.

The immediate restrictions to base were soon lifted and passes given for men to explore the countryside and local towns. The nearest of any size was Peterborough, some ten miles to the east, which many found disappointing and typifying the drab state of wartime Britain. The American authorities were anxious to promote good relations between their people and the British, cautioning about the severe rationing and shortages of many commodities that existed. This did not stop some enterprising GIs taking advantage of the situation. Marty Stanton:

"Our rations included cigarettes for the smokers. Some didn't smoke so Hank Greenberg bought them from the guys. At Peterborough he sold them to anybody in town until a couple of policemen arrested him. No tax was paid on our cigarettes. Hank got six months for that and we never saw him again."

With too much spare time on their hands boyish pranks were commonplace, fun at the expense of others, 'Letting off steam.' Each flying officer was issued with a .45 Colt revolver for personal defence if forced down in hostile territory, although it was for each individual to decide if he wished to carry the weapon. With access to guns some could not resist the temptation to fire them. One such was the exuberant 2nd Lieutenant Richard Allison who, being a late night man, frequently entered his barrack hut in which seven other officers were billeted when all were asleep. Allison could not resist announcing his arrival by switching on the light with a shout and a blast of his 'forty-five' into the ceiling of the wooden hut. As the activity was repeated on several occasions, the other occupants of the hut planned to forego their slumbers and lie in wait for Allison's return ready to blast a fusillade of shots into the ceiling the moment he stepped in the door and switched on the light. However, Allison was apparently tipped off as to the plan and waited until the others had tired of their intentions, fired a few shots into the ceiling in boredom and retired. Whereupon he burst in to repeat his usual annoying performance. The ceiling of this hut became well perforated.

For Hub Zemke there were more pressing matters. Provided with a large Wolseley limousine as a temporary staff car by the RAF, he was driven the sixty-odd miles south to VIII Fighter Command headquarters to see Brigadier General Hunter. Like most establishments provided by the British for a headquarters location, that of VIII Fighter Command was a large country mansion. Bushey Hall near Watford, once a wealthy

family home, provided elegant accommodation for the staff officers. The
contrast with the mud and damp of King's Cliffe was not lost on Zemke.
From an audience with 'Monk' Hunter and senior officers Zemke learnt
that although shipments of P-47s had arrived in the UK priority was being
given to the sole operational Eighth Air Force fighter group, the 4th. As
this group, originally formed from American volunteers, had combat
experience under RAF Fighter Command its pilots would be the first to
take the Thunderbolt into action. The 56th would receive a few P-47s
as soon as possible and would engage in gunnery practice on RAF
ranges. Initially operations would be in conjunction with RAF Fighter
Command.

Having established his contacts in VIII Fighter Command Zemke
returned to King's Cliffe, frequently pressing by telephone on matters that
concerned getting the 56th into an operational state. It was tentatively
understood that when operations started these would be on a group rather
than individual squadron basis. At no time since the early days had all
squadrons been based together and there was little day-to-day contact
between individual squadrons that were on the same base. In consequence
both pilots and ground crews were far more indulged with their squadron
than the group as a whole. Zemke strove to build a group identity, to get
the men to focus any unit pride as much on the group as their squadron.
As the group figurehead he would have to be the catalyst. Regular
circulation among pilots and ground personnel had been part of his
philosophy since taking command, but the men saw only a CO with the
necessary military conduct. Zemke reasoned he had to show a lighter
side, something that would help his popularity with the enlisted men in
particular.

In his youth he had taken up boxing, first as an amateur, then semi-
professional and in 59 fights he lost only two. It helped build self-
confidence, although the extent of this sport was kept from his parents.
When a US Special Services officer arrived and endeavoured to enlist
men at King's Cliffe to box in a London Albert Hall tournament, Zemke
entered as Corporal Billy Mills. The subterfuge was necessary because
officers were not permitted to take part in such activity and most certainly
not a group commander. Zemke knew that his participation would leak
out, helping morale and his standing with the enlisted men when they
heard that 'the Old Man' was a sport. Having not been in a ring for eight
years he had some reservations about being able to win his bout against
an unknown opponent. At the event the other boxer proved an able fighter,
yet Billy Mills won on points.

Hub Zemke was the only child of a Bavarian couple who came
through US Immigration at Ellis Island, New York, early in 1910 and
settled in Montana. His father was a railroad man, but his mother aspired
to see her son have a good education, which he did. His father introduced
his son to hunting pursuits, while his mother encouraged gentler interests
such as the violin. At Montana State University Zemke joined the Reserve
Officer Training Corps which, liking the discipline and organisation

involved, encouraged him to seek a military career, being accepted for Army Air Corps cadet training in 1936. Conscious of his background he was determined to succeed in what, pre-war, was something of 'a gentleman's club'. A fairly strict observer of military conduct, he was his own man. He would listen to other opinions if rarely seeking advice. Once having made up his mind on some matter he was hard to convince otherwise. While this facet of his character was probably a natural defence of self-confidence, those who persisted in a disagreement were often confronted with an apparent aggressive obstinacy. Passable in his own command, occasionally Zemke's firm conviction on some matter was maintained with those of higher rank when it would have been wiser to desist. Affable and with a wry sense of humour, his behaviour was to some extent deliberately restricted by what he believed were the demands of office. But he had no close friends.

Added to the complexities of bringing the group to operational readiness, Zemke was hindered by having men in his command, some in key positions, struck down with respiratory illness. Exposure to the damp environment of an English winter, where coughs and colds were commonplace amongst the indigenous population, meant that many men arriving from North America were hit. Loren McCollom, 61st Fighter Squadron CO, had pneumonia for most of February. Of average height with a lean serious face and receding hair, 'Mac' was intelligent, determined, well liked and respected by his pilots and enlisted men. A sociable if refined individual, he was a few weeks younger than Zemke. At this time Zemke considered the most dependable of his squadron commanders to be Philip Tukey of the 63rd who, at 25, was also the youngest and had been with the group since June 1941. Heavy set and handsome, Tukey was a good administrator, running a reasonably tight unit, despite the excesses of some of his junior officers – albeit that he was not aware of all their escapades, such as poaching deer. Across the A1 highway from Wittering was the mansion of Lord Burghley surrounded by parkland in which deer grazed. With the aid of a Thompson machine gun the carcass of one stag, acquired by clandestine activities, was secretly roasted on the far side of the airfield.

On 25 January there was great excitement at King's Cliffe; five Thunderbolts had arrived and most pilots hoped for a chance to fly. Zemke decreed that until these aircraft had been checked over and the required modifications made no one was to fly them. He made the mistake of adding that anyone who did would be fined £5 (20 dollars), then a sizeable sum. Owing to necessary radio modifications and the transfer out of several to the 4th Group, it was another two weeks before any aircraft were ready. By 10 February Zemke had still not given permission so Captain Merle Eby, 61st's Operations Officer, took donations from several people and put £5 on Zemke's desk to enable them to fly the first completely ready P-47.

A few days later Zemke was asked by Ajax (the code name for VIII Fighter Command which came into common use) to go to the 4th Fighter Group base at Debden to advise on operating the Thunderbolt. On arrival he found a pessimistic attitude towards the fighter. In comparison with the Spitfires the 4th was flying, the P-47 was lacking in rate of climb and manoeuvrability. In short, the pilots thought it too large and heavy to stand a chance against the Me109s and FW190s they were up against. Faced with this negative outlook Zemke sent for two of his most experienced flight leaders, Bob Wetherbee and John McClure of the 61st and 62nd respectively, who spent a few days at Debden advising dos and don'ts to both pilots and ground crews. Three accidents, one fatal, did not help the 4th pilots' acceptance of the Thunderbolt. It was plainly to be a reluctant conversion.

Zemke had also learned that a third fighter group, the 78th currently based several miles north at Goxhill, was being equipped with Thunderbolts. This group had arrived in England the previous December flying P-38 Lightnings only to have all aircraft and most pilots taken to replace the losses of operational P-38 groups in North Africa. The 78th was also receiving P-47 trained replacement pilots from the USA. To provide the 225 aircraft needed to give all three groups their full complements would take several weeks at the current rate of assembly and delivery. In an effort to speed matters up it was agreed with Ajax that a number would come from the docks to be re-assembled at King's Cliffe by the 56th ground crews who had the necessary engineering knowledge. The major components arrived in wood boxes approximately 36 feet long by 8 feet wide and high. As they were double skinned and weather-proofed, the ground crews sought to use the empty boxes as shelter cabins at the exposed aircraft dispersal points around the airfield. Zemke approved and asked Colonel Lawrence Brower, the 33rd Service Group CO, to support his request to retain a number of the boxes for this purpose. When a few days later it was reported to Zemke that none of the boxes remained, confirmation was sought from Brower who maintained that his duty was to return the boxes to an air depot as originally required. There had already been some friction between Zemke and Brower over what the former thought was the service group commander's reluctance to co-operate fully with the combat group. The box business inflamed Zemke who requested an audience with General Hunter to complain about Brower and the lack of response from Ajax staff to many of the 56th's needs. Driven down to Bushey in the Wolseley, dubbed the Sex Machine, because other officers used it to collect girls for station dances, Zemke was more than frank with the general, who did not take kindly to being so addressed by a subordinate. As in their first meeting, Hunter passed Zemke's complaints over to senior members of his staff rather than dealing directly with the problems.

One day Zemke received a telephone call from Lt Colonel Bob Landry, Personnel Officer at Ajax, asking him to take on a USAAF officer who had been flying with an RAF Polish-manned Spitfire squadron. Captain Francis Gabreski from an American Polish family had been commissioned in 1940 and served in Hawaii until volunteering for service with an RAF Polish fighter unit to gain experience of operations in

Europe. Zemke, pleased to have the officer, felt his pilots could benefit from Gabreski's experience. Assigned to the 61st Fighter Squadron, his coming did not please everyone, however. By this time the squadron pecking order was well established with the positions of flight leaders and operations officers filled. The new arrival, a captain with combat experience, was a threat to these positions. All McCollom could do was to appoint Gabreski as an Assistant Operations Officer, a rather nebulous position. Gabreski was conscious that his reception was cool, even more so when, after Zemke had aired his views, McCollom made Gabreski B Flight leader and moved 1st Lieutenant Dick Allison from that position to element leader. The one pilot who warmed to the 24-year-old, lean, sharp-featured Polish American was the genial Gerald Johnson. "I felt sorry for him the way he was cold-shouldered at first."

At the end of February 1943 each squadron had around a dozen P-47s and it was arranged with the RAF that much needed gunnery practice against towed targets would be conducted over ranges. Llanbedr on the Welsh coast was used but the weather was appalling with little opportunity to fly, so the RAF provided the use of Goxhill, near Hull and Matlaske in Norfolk, on the eastern side of the country. Seven aircraft, ferried to Llanbedr and temporarily based there, were used by a succession of pilots. Accommodation was in requisitioned farm cottages where one sport was driving sheep into some slumbering pilots' bedrooms. In poor conditions on 27 March an American-operated Lysander target-tug crashed into the sea south of Penthos, its demise attributed to the ill aim of one of the P-47 pilots. Only one of the two-man crew was rescued.

On 10 March, while several of the pilots were away on gunnery practice, nearly fifty members of the British and American news media descended on King's Cliffe to view the Thunderbolt, the presence of which in the UK was until then supposedly secret. On this same day the 4th Fighter Group introduced the type into operations with a sweep over the coastline of continental Europe. Sweep was the RAF code term for a fast in-and-out flight by a formation of fighters aimed at engaging enemy fighters in combat. During this debut pilots found radio communication was drowned out by noise, an ongoing problem since VHF (Very High Frequency) radios were installed. John Brady, technical inspector for 56th communications:

"VHF installations were required for long distance communications. At first, in the States, a stub antenna was required to be installed midway on top of the fuselage but it did not prove sufficiently strong to withstand the pressures of abrupt manoeuvres and broke off. Once this was solved a problem had begun to manifest itself with electrical interference to radio communications which was first thought to be easy to solve; it was not. The normal practice of tightening all connections, shielding certain wire leads and proper grounding of all shields was of little success. The problem existed in all P-47s once fitted with VHF radios. It became such a priority that factory engineers were attached to the group to assist and provide advice in trying to solve the problem. It was determined that all electrical components of the engine, particularly the magneto, distributor and spark plugs were the sources of the noise. After several months of trial and error, a solution was worked out. A completely new design of electrical harness and spark plug wiring was developed to eliminate the interference."

The Thunderbolts went to war with broad white bands painted round noses and tail surfaces, type identity markings advised by the RAF. The only other radial engine fighter in north-west Europe in numbers at that time was the Luftwaffe's FW190. The white bands would identify the Thunderbolt as friendly and lessen the chance of it being mistakenly attacked as an enemy.

If the 4th Fighter Group pilots were none too enamoured with the Thunderbolt, the 56th had a renewed confidence occasioned by being reunited with the type. Many of their 2nd lieutenants, not having flown other fighter types, were quite prepared to go along with manufacturer's and air force's hyperbole that the Thunderbolt was the fastest and best fighter in the sky. Tactics and formation training continued apace and the sheer exhilaration of flying these powerful machines often got the better of young pilots whenever opportunity allowed. Bunny Comstock:

"I had a friend in my hometown of Fresno who I learned was now based at Shipdham with the 44th Bomb Group, a B-24 outfit. Occasionally when I was on a training flight or air test I'd go over and beat the hell out of the place. One time I got an invitation to a dining-in and as a 2nd Lieutenant I thought this was just great. So I flew over, intending to stay the night. During the evening Colonel Leon Johnson, the group CO, stood up and acknowledged that there was a P-47 pilot present and also that he was the one who had been wakening everybody up early in the morning by buzzing the field. He proceeded to reap me off in very nice fashion. He told me in front of all these people that when we fighter pilots started giving his bombers protection, which we had not done at that point, 'I will be glad to open the hangar doors and let you fly through. Until that time you stay away from here.' Which I did until three weeks later, March 27th, when on a local flight I decided I'd land and see my friend, but after I landed I looked at my tailwheel and saw it was flat. I weighted my options of trying to take off with the bad tail wheel against confessing my sin that I had landed at a foreign base without permission. I chose the honourable way out, called Wittering and told them where I was. So they sent a tail wheel over by Wayne O'Conner. When he got there he informed me I was in deep trouble at home.

"The Major was waiting for me and he was breathing fire. I knew I was in trouble. So the tail wheel is replaced and Butch jumps in his Thunderbolt and is taxiing past me while I'm cranking up, and as he goes by he gives me the finger and laughs; he thinks the situation hilarious.

But I'm looking a bit further and there's a little British Oxford training plane just pulled out from near the control tower and it is right in his path. As I wasn't hooked up to the radio yet I kept pointing, but Butch was so busy making faces at me and putting his finger up he didn't see the Oxford and chopped it right in half. The nose end went up and the rear down. It just crumpled in the middle. It didn't hurt anybody but it was utterly destroyed. By this time my engine is running and as I go by I wave at him and give him the finger. I got to the end of the runway, ran my engine up and wasn't getting enough power. But feeling the sooner I got away from the place the better, I threw the turbos to it, got more power, but it took me a long run to get off. When I landed at Wittering and taxied in my crew chief said, 'What happened to your airplane?' I said, 'I got a flat tire' He says, 'I don't mean that. What's happened to the left side?' When I got out I saw that a hole about three feet wide had been burnt in the fuselage. The problem was that the waistgate had closed, a mechanical defect, and the pipe that took the waistgate gasses back to the turbo had broken and the gasses had been up against the fuselage and burned this big hole. So I reported in to Major Tukey, saluted and looked properly contrite. He wanted to know where O'Conner was and I was delighted to tell him that he had chopped up an Oxford at Shipdham. With that Tukey just about went into orbit. He was so mad at O'Conner he forgot about my misdemeanours. When O'Conner got back he was fined and restricted to base, the latter not being any problem as O'Conner had a WAAF who used to crawl in through the window of his room at night to visit him."

6 Operations Commence

On 24 March group personnel were warned of an impending change of station. Hub Zemke was informed this was to be Horsham St Faith, close to the city of Norwich. A visit with the group's Piper Cub liaison aircraft found a permanent RAF station much after the lines of Wittering with substantial brick buildings, individual rooms for officers, and good messing facilities. Zemke and his cohorts were pleasantly surprised. Moreover, accommodation was such that for the first time under his command the whole group would be based on one station. To enforce the group's role in the air, for the first time, on 5 April, Zemke led a combined formation made up of serviceable P-47s from each squadron to the new base. There is a story that when the RAF flying control officer logged each pilot in by name he remarked that the list looked more like one from the Luftwaffe than an ally, near a quarter of the names being of German origin.

It took a day or two to move all equipment from the relinquished bases into Horsham St Faith. Meanwhile an inspection of King's Cliffe facilities brought complaints from the RAF of removals and damage. Not least was their discovery of bullet riddled ceilings in a building on the former 61st Squadron site – the result of Allison and compatriots' high spirits. Zemke had McCollom identify the culprits, fine and restrict them to base for two weeks. Such punishments could hardly be deemed severe for this and other excesses of the pilots. As one of those who was often in trouble concluded: 'Hub didn't hammer us too much for some of the things we got up to.' Zemke had long reasoned that a commander had to turn a blind eye to such activity if a team spirit was to be built. As another miscreant observed: 'I believe if he had been a 2nd Lieutenant instead of our Colonel he'd have been whooping it up with us. There was a wild guy in there that was never let lose.'

The airfield was sod but well drained, an advantage being that instead of taking off in staggered pairs as the concrete runways at King's Cliffe had demanded, it was possible to get flights of four airborne together from a squadron line-up. Landing on turf was smoother but it had its drawbacks. Gerald Johnson landed on wet grass, causing him to overrun the airfield boundary, tipping the P-47 up on its nose and trapping him in the cockpit until the tail was lowered. For punishment:

> "I had to put a British pound in a glass jar on the Officers' Mess bar each
> week for a month: it was marked 'Lt. Johnson's propeller kitty'. Any

pilot could use this money to buy a drink by placing a note in the jar with his name on it and the statement: 'I will never damage an airplane I fly.' To my knowledge at the end of the month there were four British pounds in the jar and no notes."

At the new station there was an expectancy of operational commitment amongst all ranks, especially pilots, that was soon fulfilled. Two days after arriving Zemke received orders to take a flight of four Thunderbolts to the 4th Fighter Group base at Debden. Zemke's personal aircraft was held and serviced by the 62nd Squadron adjacent to the hangar line and he decided to take its CO and two flight leaders. At Debden they provided one flight of a combined Thunderbolt formation with the 4th and 78th Groups. In the late afternoon of 8 April they flew a high-altitude sweep of nearly an hour's duration over the Dunkirk area and saw little but clouds. Zemke, Schilling and Captains John McClure and Eugene O'Neill remained at Debden for further operations but inclement weather intervened and it was five days before another mission was flown. On the morning of the 13th the four pilots took part in another sweep over the French coast but Zemke had oxygen supply failure and had to abort (turn back). In the afternoon McCollom and Tukey brought a flight each to join Zemke's flight over Debden and fly as a squadron formation with the 4th Group on the second mission of a fine day for another quick hop across the Channel at 30,000 feet. McCollom had selected Captains Eby and Renwick and 2nd Lieutenant Leslie Smith. Tukey picked Captains Dyar and Adrianse and 1st Lieutenant Mahurin. These pilots flew what was then acknowledged as the 56th's first combat mission. Not that there was any combat involved but the mission served chiefly to familiarise the 56th pilots with the enemy-held coastline and mission procedures. These introductory operations were under RAF Fighter Command control, and would be until VIII Fighter Command had gained sufficient experience. Understandably, the USAAF adopted the same basic operational procedure as the RAF and initially British controllers monitored and handled radio communications for these missions.

Like RAF fighter squadrons, those of the 56th were each given a two-syllable code word for radio identification: initially the 61st used Shaker, the 62nd Harbour and the 63rd Moisture. Flying the standard four-plane flights, the three and later four that made up a squadron formation were verbally identified as white, red, blue and yellow. The aircraft within a flight were Leader, Two, Three and Four for radio talk. Thus, for example, 'Shaker White Three' would identify the aircraft flying in the No.3 position of the leading 61st Squadron flight. Each pilot had an individual two-digit number, which coupled with the squadron call sign, was generally only used in seeking a radio homing or air/sea rescue services, for example Shaker 30. Several code words were used for different actions or conditions but radio communication had always to be kept to a minimum for when one pilot in the group was talking the others could not transmit. The standard flight formation was like the finger tips of a hand, hence the name 'finger four'. In the van the leader, who would do the shooting, had his wingman, who would protect his leader, staggered back on his left. The so-called element leader, the No. 3, flew on the right side of the flight leader roughly parallel with the leader's wingman. The element leader's wingman, whose job was to protect his leader while he did the shooting, was staggered further back on the element leader's right. The position of the element could change in a cross-over manoeuvre. A flight formation was flown fairly close on the climb out and return so that in passing through cloud aircraft within a flight remained in view. On approaching enemy territory a squadron spread out its flights in line, and the aircraft of a flight in a loose string of pairs to allow maximum manoeuvrability if engaged with the enemy. These formations were advised by the RAF before the group came overseas.

The pilots were soon using RAF terms and jargon such as 'drink' for the sea, 'deck' for ground surface – although it came to be used for low flying close to the ground, 'prang' for an aircraft accident. Soon VIII Fighter Command would add its own radio transmission code words to those common to both air forces. 'Oranges' for weather conditions, 'pills' for fuel amounts, 'ha, ha, ha' for crossing the enemy coastline, 'angels' for height, and so on. Some would later be changed.

In the exploratory missions aircraft flew at high speed in enemy airspace so as not to be at a disadvantage if surprised by the Luftwaffe. Climb-out from base to enemy-held territory was made at a rate of 1,000 feet per minute and speed of around 180 mph Indicated Air Speed, increasing to 210 IAS in enemy air space. The 56th's pilots had been cautioned by RAF veterans in lectures about the prowess of the enemy, both prior to coming to the UK and during the days at King's Cliffe. It was explained that through intelligence sources, chiefly the so-called Y Service, the monitoring of enemy radio and wireless traffic, the disposition and strength of opposing forces was known fairly accurately. When Hitler turned against the Soviets in June 1941 three Luftwaffe Jagdgeschwader (fighter wings) were left in the west, JG1 defending the north-west area of the Reich, JG 26 the Low Countries and the Pas de Calais and JG 2 the rest of the French Atlantic seaboard. A Jagdgeschwader was usually composed of three Gruppen (groups) operating independently, and each Gruppe had three Staffeln (squadrons) at this time with a strength of twelve to fourteen aircraft each. There was much movement and fluctuation in strength although the overall strength of the Jagdverband (fighter force) in the west was around 200 aircraft.

British fighter development lagged behind that of the Germans in 1941-42, and although RAF Fighter Command believed it was holding its own in aggressive cross-Channel operations, designed to bring the Luftwaffe fighters into combat, the truth was that RAF losses were nearly three to every enemy fighter shot down. Apart from the fact the predominant British fighter model, the Spitfire V, had an inferior high altitude performance compared to the later Me109 and FW190 fighters, the Luftwaffe only had need to intercept when at an advantage or when bombers were present. The RAF intrusions were also handicapped by having to face the blinding sun from whence the enemy often chose to attack. The standard form of Luftwaffe interception, if able to hold surprise, was to descend from high altitude, open fire, roll and dive away. The Spitfire IX levelled the performance differences but this mark was in short supply when the Thunderbolt appeared on the scene. Twice the size and weight of a Spitfire or Me109, slow to accelerate and climb, there were misgivings about how it would fare in combat with the more agile Luftwaffe fighters. Trials against the RAF's captured FW190, then considered the best of the German fighters, showed that the P-47 had an inferior performance below 15,000 feet. At twice that height advantage passed to the P-47 which was faster. The outcome brought recommendations to stay high and speedy when in enemy airspace.

Although USAAF fighter units had been operational from the UK since the previous summer flying Spitfires, all except the 4th Group had been transferred to North Africa when the Allies invaded in November 1942. The Eighth Air Force, committed to daylight bombing operations, was now looking to the three P-47 groups to give support. The self-defending B-17 Fortress and B-24 Liberator formations were proving more vulnerable to enemy fighter interception than expected. The Eighth would have preferred the longer ranged P-38 Lightnings to escort the bombers but other theatres of war had priority. The P-47 had a thirsty engine, consuming the 300 US gallons carried in an hour at full power. Average duration for the early mission was around an hour and a quarter and by the time the Thunderbolts had climbed to 30,000 feet this only allowed penetration over enemy-held territory of a hundred miles. Their early operations brought some engine troubles at high altitude, in fact, Lieutenant Roger 'Herky' Dyar's failed on his first mission. Fortunately he had sufficient altitude for a gliding descent to belly-in near the Kent coast at Deal. During following missions other pilots experienced engine troubles which were eventually traced to incorrect correlation of throttle and supercharger controls. However, neither the operational problems faced, nor the RAF's polite scepticism about the Thunderbolt's chances in combat, did much to dampen enthusiasm amongst the neophyte fighter pilots.

The third mission for 56th pilots, on 15 April, was the first from 'home plate', Horsham St Faith. Twenty-four Thunderbolts for another sweep and the first opportunity for another 14 pilots to fly their firsts. Gerald Johnson:

"So comes my first mission and I'm scheduled to fly Hub Zemke's wing. All the airplanes are lined up on the grass at Horsham to take off a squadron at a time in formation. I was in the cockpit of my airplane at least ten minutes beforehand. Going over everything, thinking about everything. All of a sudden there goes 'Start engines.' Primer, start switch, prop turning. Wouldn't start. Other engines are starting, and here

I am sitting there: 'I'm going to miss the first mission. What's wrong?' We didn't use check lists in those days. Then I suddenly realised I hadn't turned on the fuel! So in great haste, I go through the starting procedure and taxi out straight to the other side of the field where the rest were lining up in formation. I didn't say anything over the radio but just went straight to that lead airplane and no sooner had I pulled up beside him than he began take-off. The sweep was pretty uneventful. When we got back there was a lot of talk. After all, we had crossed the North Sea for the first time, seen the coast of continental Europe for the first time, and I had learned it might be helpful if I put together some kind of check list of what one had to do to get started."

This mission filled the Officers' Club, with those who had not taken part eager to hear from those that had. 2nd Lieutenant Paul Conger, whose engine had faltered so that he lost altitude claimed to have seen three FW190s pass before him and fired his guns. Conger was considered a tough, rough character by other 61st pilots. Kind, generous and fearless, he was bedevilled by an arrogant streak ascerbated by his liking for alcohol. As with the previous operations this one was re-flown verbally by the participants for many hours at the bar.

Another high altitude sweep, this time over the Low Countries' coast, was flown on the 17th and four days later another to an area further north; both were uneventful as far as contact with the enemy went, if fraught by mechanical and equipment failures for a few pilots. Zemke had set out to lead all of these first missions but for the next, on 29 April, he stayed at the base and gave the enthusiastic Dave Schilling the task. Once again it was a high altitude sweep over the Low Countries. In the late afternoon 36 aircraft were despatched with Schilling leading the 62nd Squadron and the 61st flying top cover. Climbing out over the sea, Schilling had passed 20,000 feet when he found his radio was not functioning correctly. Standard procedure in such circumstances was to indicate abandonment of leadership by waggling wings so that the element leader would know to take-over. The proud Major did not think this failure warranted his giving up his first group lead and continued in the van climbing towards landfall at Blankenberge. When at about 28,000 feet and some ten miles from the hostile coast, his leading flight was suddenly attacked by a dozen FW190s of 6 and 8 Staffeln of JG 26. What followed was the usual confused state of an air battle as recounted by pilots involved; an action that only lasted a few minutes is said to have seemed a half hour battle. What is known for certain is that the aircraft of Schilling and his element leader William Garth were hit by cannon fire and Garth's spun down. Schilling evaded downwards and was attacked again. The two other 62nd flights became scattered in trying to turn towards the enemy. Captain John McClure seeing a P-47 below with enemy fighters coming up on its tail, dived to intercept. Following, Lieutenant Charles Harrison, his wing-man, broke away when his aircraft was hit, as was McClure's as he closed and fired on the enemy. Harrison made it back to Horsham St Faith with bullet holes in fuselage, propeller and ailerons and a 20 mm strike in the left flap. McClure did not return. Luftwaffe pilots claimed three victories, apparently believing Schilling or Harrison had also gone down.

Back at Horsham St Faith Zemke had monitored some of the radio traffic and knew all was not well. The 61st Squadron arrived home in formation but the other two squadrons were scattered and several aircraft unaccounted for, until word was received three were down at Gravesend and one at Earls Colne airfields. Major Schilling was, understandably, not showing his usual nonchalant persona. Marty Stanton:

"I was assigned to help Lou Voss who was the armourer on Zemke's plane so I usually worked around the hangar near where his plane was parked. When Schilling returned we could see the door on one of his plane's ammunition compartments had been blown open by a 20 mm hit. He got out of his plane and was more than a little excited. First he wanted his plane repaired and said something like he was going back to knock hell out of those bastards. Then he came across and told us to get our plane ready. Voss got on one wing and I was sent up to the other to put the guns in. While this was going on Zemke came along and calmly talked Dave out of going back. Later he and Dave called us into the hangar and talked for about half an hour on the ammunition that the Germans had and what we had. I think it was to let Dave cool down, take his mind off what happened."

What happened was that in the 56th's first clash with the Luftwaffe two Thunderbolts had been shot down and it was not known if the pilots survived, although Garth was seen to bale out. This was the second time Garth had taken to his parachute, having escaped from a collison on 1 March following a crash with a P-47 of another group while training at Goxhill. When all intelligence had been gathered and reviewed Zemke was a vexed man. Schilling's failure to relinquish the lead when his radio malfunctioned brought him severe censure from the group CO as well as diminishing Zemke's trust in Schilling for some time. In a scolding critique the failure of other leaders to call the 61st top cover down and the lack of air discipline featured large. The confidence of some pilots had been severely tested. Bunny Comstock:

"Gordon Batdorf, the epitome of a fighter pilot, he couldn't wait to get started. This was the first mission for both of us and we got into a scrap just inside the coast of Belgium. Two Focke-Wulfs came up behind Batdorf who panicked, pulled up and snap rolled it, spun it down and recovered and came home at a thousand feet. Batdorf was never the same, no longer a hot-shot Charlie."

7 The First Victory

For the determined Zemke the happenings of 29 April were more frustrating than demoralising. It made him more the stern CO, pursuing better performance from his men. Word that the two pilots lost had both survived as prisoners of war lessened the blow a little, but air discipline had to be improved. Matters were not helped by what happened on the mission of 4 May. This was the occasion of the group's first Ramrod, code word for bomber support. The 56th's P-47s were to provide escort for Fortresses returning from an attack on a target at Antwerp. Zemke led, but had radio troubles, so he transferred the lead to McCollom. Enemy aircraft were seen harassing the bombers but efforts to intercept resulted in a tragic accident. Gerald Johnson:

> "When they landed I noticed my squadron commander, McCollom, jump out of his airplane without any hesitation. Didn't look at anybody, say anything to anybody, ran into the hangar office. A long time later I learned he had shot down an airplane, a Spitfire. Loren McCollom was such a serious man. You would never have thought he had any fun in his life. He was totally dedicated and to be the person who did this was nearly more than the guy could handle. I guess that after he had attacked and disabled the aircraft he closed and saw the marking on it."

Ground personnel believed McCollom had downed an FW190 and command did not correct this rumour in order to maintain the upsurge in morale brought by the group's destruction of an enemy aircraft.

From pilot reports it was clear the standard of aircraft recognition had to be improved. The pace of air combat often allowed only a fleeting glimpse of other occupants of the sky. Canopy glare and the restricted outlook from the cockpit also played a part in faulty identification. Some men never excelled at aircraft recognition. There were other lapses, more through inexperience than lack of air discipline. Lieutenant Walker Mahurin, he of the big smile, was leading one flight in the 63rd Squadron. Spying five FW190s far below, he wheeled over and dived calling his flight to follow. Rushing ahead of his three followers he went too fast, for, just as he was about to attack, his Thunderbolt was severely jolted by hitting compressibility. When Mahurin tried to roll out of his dive, he stalled and wound up fifty feet below, staggering right across the noses of the FWs he had set out to slaughter which were firing on him from 150 yards. One 20 mm hit his right wing, the concussion throwing him from a vertical left bank to a vertical right bank. Somehow he got away and hightailed for home feeling very sheepish and believing he had made a fool of himself. A lesson had been learned: a 7,000 feet power dive was courting compressibility and loss of control. To maintain control a good pass at an enemy aircraft was about 2,000 feet, preferably from up sun. Mahurin gathered the nicknames The Sparrow and Shinny, but that which adhered the longest was Bud. A happy, unaffected individual with self-effacing ways, he had become one of the most popular pilots in the 63rd.

Training was intensified, both on the ground and in the air. Some cocky pilots thought they already knew all there was to know about formations and combat manoeuvres. Zemke thought otherwise and had every serviceable aircraft in the air on training flights whenever opportunity and weather allowed. The importance of a wingman keeping with his element leader and continually watching out for attacks from the rear was strongly emphasised – clearing the tail. If a rear interception was impending the immediate action was to break into a 180-degree turn and face the enemy, head-on fire having a lesser chance of scoring hits. The close battle formation was abandoned. While providing individual pilots with manoeuvrability for attack it had the drawback of enabling an enemy coming in from the rear to pick off one aircraft after another, as had happened on the 29th. Instead, individual aircraft of a flight were flown in a more spaced form of the 'finger four' and more in a side by side line. There was also instruction on power settings, for it had been found that low engine revolutions and high manifold pressure (air pressure boost from the supercharger) saved fuel and could extend duration to an hour and three-quarters or more.

Zemke led the next few missions himself for disapproval of the 56th's performance from higher command fell on him. It was in the nature of the man not to take criticism lightly, to nurture his hurt. This brought about a lack of trust in his squadron commanders. The Colonel – the general upgrading of ranks in the Eighth Air Force found him promoted to a full colonel early in May – believed that the standing of his group would only be enhanced by shooting down some of the enemy and the sooner the better. There was a heightened determination to succeed. The aggressive Zemke did not yet have equivalent skill in air fighting to those he had displayed in the boxing ring. Another escort for B-17s attacking an Antwerp target took place on the 14th when a number of FW190s were seen approaching the bombers. Zemke ordered the pilots of his flight to follow and dived to attack. After much manoeuvring and firing at two different aircraft Zemke thought he had hit and despatched the last. Review of the gun camera film on return to base showed the enemy to be far out of range and probably never even hit. During this interception the No. 4 man of the flight, 2nd Lieutenant Robert Johnson, decided to go after an FW190 he saw, although the enemy quickly disappeared. He returned to Horsham St Faith to receive a reprimand for leaving his element leader, Bob Wetherbee. Flying as a wingman was not a happy post for an action seeking pilot.

Although the group flew 17 missions in May, all but three led by Zemke, there was still no decisive action. On the last day of the month another aircraft was lost over enemy-held territory in particularly tragic circumstances. The group put up its largest number so far for a sweep over the Low Countries. Zemke rotated his leadership from squadron to squadron to show no favouritism and on this occasion was heading the 63rd. The No. 4 in his White flight was 1st Lieutenant Pat Williams and soon after crossing the Belgian coast Williams' P-47 was seen to roll over and enter a near vertical dive. He did not return and was listed missing in action. It was later learned that he had crashed at Moorsele where the Germans had buried him with full military honours. The suspected cause was oxygen failure which rendered Williams unconscious. On earlier missions other pilots who had experienced difficulties with the oxygen system identified the problem in time. Regularly monitoring the oxygen supply was essential at high altitude but attention was, understandably, often directed elsewhere in hostile airspace. Accidents were an expected if not accepted part of flying but fatalities thus incurred often hit the emotions harder than a combat loss.

Vertigo induced by flying in extensive cloud claimed several lives. On Easter Sunday Lieutenant John Coenen, bringing a P-47 back from Burtonwood after modification, was trapped in a towering thundercloud. Realising the aircraft was out of control at a lowish altitude he just managed to escape before it plummeted into a hillside at Chapel-en-le-Frith. With his parachute canopy damaged by the hasty exit, Coenen fractured two vertebrae in the following impact with the hillside, injuries that kept him in hospitals for four and a half months. Richard Allison, the perforator of ceilings, also apparently fell victim to vertigo on 5 June while in cloud, losing his life when his P-47 crashed into the sea. Setting off on a cross-country exercise, he was going to visit a friend to tell him about his wife giving birth to a son. Apart from this tragedy, few 56th aircraft were involved in accidents, even minor, during its first weeks on operational status.

Of some amusement to his fellows was the outcome of Dick Mudge's escapade on 31 May which rated as accident. Pilots were permitted to use the group's L-4 Cub for authorised liaison flights, if the legitimacy of some flights did not bear investigation. Mudge, an extrovert character, set off on an authorised trip having invited a Red Cross girl to occupy the rear seat. During the flight Mudge impressed his passenger with the versatility of the little aircraft, first by dodging in and out of the barrage balloons over the port of Lowestoft and then by boasting it could be easily landed on a football pitch. The story goes that the girl enquired if it would be possible to land in a very small field they were passing, whereupon Mudge dived down, swept over some trees and landed. What he had thought was a meadow turned out to be a long stemmed grain crop. Moreover the field was surrounded by tall hedgerow trees and even if it had been a meadow the Cub could not have been flown out. Of course, the base was informed of an emergency landing due to engine trouble, although the engineers who came to dissemble the aircraft and haul it back to Horsham St Faith by road found no engine fault. However, complaints were received from the balloon barrage operators and Mudge's punishment was restriction to the base for a week and being not allowed to go flying by himself for a month. The irrepressible Mudge was no stranger to reprimand, having been in trouble a few weeks earlier for unauthorised landings elsewhere and using a closed runway.

VIII Fighter Command appreciated the pressures on group commanding officers and early in June Zemke received orders to transfer one of his squadron commanders to group headquarters to take up a newly created position of Flying Executive Officer. Much after the fashion of the set-up on an RAF fighter station, this spread the leadership load and the Flying Executive would share the mission leadership requirement. Zemke selected Loren McCollom whom he considered the most committed to furthering success in air fighting. 'Mac', a quiet, calm individual, had already shown sound qualities of leadership with the 61st Squadron. Schilling was full of ideas and popular but his behaviour during and immediately after the April 29th debacle had left Zemke with doubts. Zemke found no fault with Phil Tukey's leadership of the 63rd other than he felt 'Tuke' lacked an aggressive outlook. Having informed McCollom of his new position, Zemke discussed who should take over command of the 61st. Seniority in rank and length of service were the normal considerations for command advancement and while Merle Eby and Bob Wetherbee were the next in line, both Zemke and McCollom felt that Gabreski, with his greater experience in combat flying, should get the job. This naturally did not go down too well with the original 61st complement that trained on the Thunderbolt and 'Gabby', as Gabreski had come to be called, continued to experience something of a cold shoulder on social occasions.

During May the group had received additional aircraft to bring its complement up to the authorised strength of 25 per squadron, this allowing what became the standard squadron mission formation of four four-plane flights. Pilot strength had been increased with the first so-called replacements, John D. Wilson and William H. Jansen, who arrived in April, and another eight in May. With illness and transfers, in addition to accident and combat losses, squadron pilot strengths hovered around the 25 mark and the cry for more pilots was a familiar one from Zemke heard at Ajax. With near equal pilot and aircraft numbers each man could have an assigned aircraft on which he was permitted to inscribe his name and those of his ground crew, neatly on the left side of the fuselage in the vicinity of the cockpit. The popular naming of aircraft was also allowed, at first in small neat lettering on the engine cowlings, soon to be followed by flamboyant embellishments with motifs or representative art. In the 61st Squadron one flight named each of its Thunderbolts after Snow White and the Seven Dwarfs characters, while the 62nd had its squadron and flight leaders' aircraft marked as characters from the popular newspaper strip cartoon Lil'Abner. Wives' and girl friends' names were also popular to bestow on aircraft where a photograph of the adornment would be sent home to the loved one. Several aircraft had more than one name applied. It became popular to have a caricature of the assigned pilot with an appropriate epithet painted on some cowlings. At last, on 12 June, a long sought after victory symbol in the form of a German cross marking was painted on the cowling of a 62nd P-47 called Little Cookie.

In the two months that Thunderbolts had been committed to operations, the 4th and 78th Fighter Groups had sustained losses but had several victories in air fighting. All the 56th could show for the same period was a few probables and the destruction of two RAF aircraft. Zemke could only reassure his pilots that their time would come and on the 12 June mission it did. McCollom led a 48-plane formation on an 80-minute late afternoon sweep of the now familiar Belgian and northern French coastal areas. McCollom heading the 62nd went in at 20,000 feet, far lower than the usual altitude for such operations, and the flights of the squadrons were spread out more abreast as was the practice on penetration. Near Ypres a Staffel of FW190s was seen about 5,000 feet below and Major Schilling, placed in the best position, took his flight down. The enemy saw the attack coming and evaded, so that Schilling's fire had no apparent hits. Captain Walter Cook, leading one of the other flights, saw that four of the Focke-Wulfs had not dived away like the rest but appeared to be manoeuvring to attack the P-47s and apparently did not see Cook's flight, up sun to the enemy. Cook took his men down and himself lined up on the rearmost Focke-Wulf, holding his fire until within 300 yards. His first burst hit the fuselage but prop wash (turbulence) caused his P-47 to veer slightly and the bullets ran into the left wing resulting in a large puff of black smoke. The explosion was in the FW's ammunition bay, causing a piece of the wing to separate. Thereafter the enemy was seen to spin down into the clouds. As the pilot took no evasive action it was suspected that he had been killed by Cook's fire. Assessment of the gun camera film confirmed Cook's claim of destroying the FW190. This first true victory for the group gave an uplift to morale and even more so after the following day's action.

Colonel Zemke, leading a morning sweep and over the same area near Ypres, saw a dozen FW190s about 7,000 feet below climbing north-west. Ordering the first two flights of the 61st Squadron that he was leading to follow, he approached the enemy formation unseen and shot down two before his presence was known to the other enemy fighters. Second Lieutenant Robert Johnson, flying the No. 4 position in a flight that was not called down, saw the enemy below, peeled off into a dive and successfully attacked the leader of the enemy formation. This was in direct contravention of the rule that a wingman always stayed to cover his element leader. Likewise an element leader held his position in a flight and followed the flight leader unless ordered otherwise. On his return to base Johnson received some harsh words from Gabreski, in whose flight he was flying and even harsher from Zemke, although Hub was conscious of not wanting to dampen an aggressive spirit. Nevertheless, this was the second time Bob Johnson had erred in 'jiggering off by himself' and having destroyed an enemy aircraft was no reason that he should not be reprimanded for his lack of air discipline.

Another weakness in air discipline this mission highlighted was persistent radio usage. Only one pilot at a time could transmit on the group's exclusive radio channel. Pilots were told to only make radio calls on important issues keeping transmissions short and to the point. There was a tendency for some pilots to ignore this instruction, vital in the heat of battle, and so preventing leaders from issuing orders. Zemke also recognised his own error in not calling down the rest of the 61st Squadron to attack and during a review of the mission he emphasised that while one squadron should always remain as top cover for the others, squadron and flight leaders should use their own initiative if there was an opportunity to attack. Both these successful interceptions of the enemy had been where the group had good altitude advantage over the enemy formations and had also been achieved with a varying degree of surprise. Altitude, advantage and surprise were the assets for success in air fighting.

8 Norwich Neighbours

Although the squadrons of the 56th had been brought together at Horsham St Faith and operated as a group, both pilots and ground men generally continued to socialise within their respective squadrons. Zemke had to some degree deliberately isolated himself in order to avoid becoming too 'buddy buddy' – as he put it – with his other command officers. He noticed, however, that they now tended to avoid his company, so realising this would have an adverse effect on group solidarity he ordered that squadron commanders and senior executives should sit with him at mealtimes. Among the three squadron COs the most strongly squadron-orientated was Dave Schilling who one contemporary likened to 'a happy king of a happy kingdom'. Generally popular with the enlisted men of the 62nd, he maintained that popularity by an easy manner with them. He savoured their approval, yet his egotism was a natural part of his personality and not contrived. Once settled in at the new station he set up a party where his officers would play host to the enlisted men for what he termed "the biggest jamboree". Schilling made the following quote before the event which reflects on his laconic language: "A bunch of the boys were whippin' it up the other night and the topic changed from women to the fact that we were having a blow for the boys. Without any argument we all decided that we should do honours. The blow therefore is on us. We'll all be there."

Some officers were not long in establishing contacts among the local population. Lawrence Brower, the service group commander, got to know a nearby member of the aristocracy and was invited to visit his home. Schilling was also in the forefront of exploring the local institutions and striking up associations. The series of small lakes and miles of linking waterways in the area known as The Broads caused some amusement. Learning of the popularity among the British of motor cruising and sailing on these waters, it was not long before Schilling rented a houseboat at Wroxham, which served more as a location for wild parties with local girls than river cruising. There was some disquiet among junior pilots in his squadron who found themselves barred from these events.

While the group endeavoured to serve its purpose in operations, the elevation in living standards that Horsham St Faith provided impressed both officers and men. Marty Stanton, mechanic:

> "The mess at Horsham St Faith was a beautiful place. It had steam kettles
> for cooking. When they cooked pork chops they were looking like they

weren't cooked but they were good. They had Englishwomen who would go down on their knees and scrub the mess hall. Outside the base there was a fish and chip shop. We had good appetites and frequented that place. We would walk into town, drink in the Conservative Club and go to the theatre. I can tell you we were a happy gang."

While most had good barracks many men still found the English climate uncomfortably chilly. Nothing was sacred in the cause of keeping warm, even in April and May. John Sipek:

"We were always on the lookout for something to burn in our fireplace. One afternoon I noticed a civilian crew repairing the tarmac road on the base. They used a huge steam-driven roller to level the road. When it got late in the afternoon one of the workers loaded the boiler with large chunks of coal and banked the fire with some ashes. It was dusk when the workmen left so I got a couple of buckets, a shovel and scooped all the big chunks of coal out that I could. Some of them didn't start to burn yet so we saved them for later and put the rest of them in our fireplace in our room. This mid-evening requisition would provide us with a couple of warm dry nights. We saw the boss of the repair crew the next morning and he was pretty upset because there wasn't any fire in the boiler so no steam. This meant they couldn't use the roller until they built up a good head of steam. The boss told the worker that he probably didn't bank the fire properly."

US Government materials were equal game for 'requisitioning' as those of their ally. Donald Trudell, 33rd Service Group:

"By the time we had settled in at Horsham St Faith our uniforms were getting pretty raunchy having been worn since leaving the States. Some of the flight line crews procured some 100-octane aviation fuel in jerrycans and we proceeded to do a mass cleaning process. We dipped our olive drab wool jackets, blouses, caps and trousers in this raw fuel and they came out clean as could be. The clothes were hung out on lines behind the barracks until the smell of raw gasoline was gone. This could have been one hell of a mess if a lighted cigarette had been misplaced in the area but nothing happened. We did get our uniforms clean and nothing was said about it. We didn't repeat the operation after considering what the consequences could have been."

For most enlisted men this was the first opportunity to investigate a large British urban conurbation. Evening passes were aided by the provision of a so-called Liberty Run service of trucks, departing Horsham St Faith at 7 pm and leaving a central point in Norwich at 11 pm for the return to AAF Station 123, the official US designation. The people of the city were used to foreign troops and were already familiar with Americans whose numbers were increasing. Friendships were made and 'the bloody Yanks' generally liked. Inevitably there was youthful mischievousness amongst the newcomers. John Sipek:

"One evening a group of us were off duty and took the liberty run trucks into Norwich. This was our first trip to town and after a couple of warm beers we started grouping around in the blackout looking for a cinema. We lined up at the end of a queue that we thought was for a cinema but was for a theatre. Big spenders, we purchased seats close to the stage. When the performance began and the main curtain opened a very fine mesh curtain remained that filtered the performers who looked like nude female dancers. Due to the dim lighting and the mesh curtain it was difficult to see the performers until some intellectual GI turned on his flashlight. In a few seconds the whole place was illuminated as other GIs turned on their torches. The main curtain was closed immediately and the manager came on the stage. He told everyone that he was shocked by this exhibition which he said was in poor taste. He said the group had performed all over the British Isles and this was the first display of bad manners they encountered. He warned everyone that the performance would be cancelled if there were any more displays of this nature. My buddies and I left at this time so I have no idea what happened when we left. There must have been a large number of GIs in the theatre judging by the amount of light from the torches. Most of us carried a torch at night."

There were more stupid acts, usually induced by too much alcohol. Joseph Froncek, 62nd mechanic:

"One of the boys and I went pubbing on a day pass. After a few hours we wandered around the middle of the town where women were shopping and many prams were outside buildings. The devil told us to do a little swapping from one carriage to another. So one child was taken out of one pram and exchanged with another. We then ran like hell."

Drink was a common refuge made easy by the number of public houses and bars found in every English town in those years.

At first the taste of British beer brews was not popular with Americans used to a lighter, lager type. They found that beer was stronger in the UK and its effect quickly went to many heads. Several US servicemen had never taken to beer-drinking until coming to Britain and were even less able to deal with its effects. Alcohol became the succour and weakness of several officers and men, causing ongoing problems for both British and American authorities. Bunny Comstock:

"Our mess sergeant was a fellow by the name of Trusko. A very good mess sergeant and Hub Zemke stole him from the 63rd and made him the Officers' Club mess sergeant. Trouble was Tresko liked his alcohol. There was a bombed-out block with a big water tank used by the fire service in Norwich, and one night when he was loaded Tresko decides he was going to go swimming at 3 o'clock in the morning. Bare-assed: not very smart. It was cold. The bobbies found him out there and they called the MPs. There was barbed wire all the way round it. He wouldn't come out. So they got the CO who came down and said, 'Sergeant, this is Colonel Hubert Zemke. Get out of that goddamn pool.' Tresko came out. Tresko would go up and down the promotion ladder like a yo-yo. Alcohol was his problem which always led him into trouble. But a great cook."

A predominant interest of those on pass from Horsham St Faith, as with many servicemen away from home, was the opposite sex. Americans had an advantage in smart uniforms, and accents which British girls associated with Hollywood glamour, as its movies dominated the British cinema screens. It was the Americans who changed the general meaning of the word sex, which as far as the British were concerned meant only gender at that time. An enlightened view of the situation is that of Robert Carnachan, a maintenance officer:

"My friends and I grew up with the 'Madonna' and 'whore' picture of women. Nice girls 'didn't do it'. Those girls that did and were known for having sex fell into the whore category with us. Any popularity that they might enjoy was predicated on the hope that they would succumb on the first or second date. It might have been peculiar to me and my friends, but we did not discuss sex with each other. If any of us were not virgins by the time of entry into the Services, I certainly didn't know it. Perhaps it was because we had been brought up with middle-class standards which, I understand, are more puritanical than those of the upper and lower classes. I am sure that many of us came to Britain as virgins and had our first sexual experiences there. While our middle-class mores and respect for 'good girls' had kept us from seducing the girls we knew at home, knowing we would still be seeing them in the future, the girls of Britain were here today and gone tomorrow. In spite of our background, the sexual drive of the young male was still there and not to be denied if given the opportunity.

"On the other hand, the young men of Britain were largely away at war in other lands. Many of the young women were working in war plants and living away from their parents and home neighbourhoods. They were missing the normal male companionship they would have experienced in peacetime with boys they had grown up with and would continue to know in later years. This left a void that the young Americans could fill. Now I'm not alone in remarking about the difference between the way American and British men treated their women. Perhaps it was carried down from the early days of our country when there were more men than women, as the men were the first to emigrate from elsewhere. In any event, American men, on the whole, were more sensitive to the wants of women and did more courting than was typical of the young

British man. They were more likely to give a girl flowers and gifts than their British counterparts, and to treat her with more respect. As a result, the British girl away from home and the American boy, also away from home, were more likely to engage in sex than would have been the case if they were both living in a stable permanent neighbourhood. Of course, there was also the unstable wartime, which historically leads to greater births as a genetic drive to make up for losses suffered."

Norwich also gave the ground staff of Station 123 their first introduction to hostilities. During the previous year Norwich had been subjected to two sustained night raids by the Luftwaffe in which some 300 people had been killed, over 1,000 injured and large areas of the city laid waste. Air raid warnings were a frequent disturbance during the night when the Americans arrived and usually, as nothing much happened, they came to be largely ignored. That is, until one night a stick of five bombs was dropped on the base, missing a barracks and the officers' quarters but doing no harm. On another occasion a number of Luftwaffe bombers gave Norwich another pounding and GIs helped the local police and fire service in rescue and fighting fires.

9 Hard Times

The last full week of June 1943 was a troubled time for Hub Zemke. On the Monday morning he was notified by Ajax to prepare to move the 56th to a newly constructed base named Halesworth, 25 miles south-east of its current location which was wanted for upgrading for bomber use. To say the least, this was an annoyance when the group was nicely settled in and fully committed to combat operations, so he decided to take the L-4 Cub liaison aircraft used for communication flights and have a look at Halesworth. It turned out to be typical of the new bomber airfields that could be seen sprouting up all over this part of England: concrete runways and taxi tracks and utility buildings. After landing and a conducted tour of this still incomplete station by the RAF officer in charge, the Colonel was not a happy man. The obvious question was why could not the bombers go to Halesworth and the 56th stay where it was? An approach to Ajax to get the order changed was unsuccessful as Horsham St Faith had been scheduled for rebuilding as a bomber base before the 56th had moved in. What was more, Halesworth was only available for use by fighters until a new bomber group arrived from the States, forecasting yet another move for the 56th.

The following day, during support of two new B-17 groups on an introductory mission to Antwerp, the Colonel got into a turning fight with an FW190 which he had attempted to intercept at lower than usual altitude. This proved to be a salutary lesson in the marked performance superiority of the enemy type at under 10,000 feet, and one that might have had a serious outcome for the P-47 involved had not both its pilot and that of the Luftwaffe fighter decided to break off the contest at the same time.

Next day breakfast for some householders along the Cromer road opposite the airfield was interrupted by whistling bullets. A 61st Squadron P-47 being serviced had a gun-firing mechanism malfunction. Fortunately no one was hurt by the fusillade, but such happenings did not help relationships with the British. Zemke's stalwart Ground Executive Officer, 40-year-old Major Stanley Swanson, had the task of dealing with damage to civilian property. Then, true to the agreed pattern of mission leadership with 'Mac' McCollom, who led a sweep on the 24th, the Colonel took out another the following day only to encounter swelling cloud formations, which caused abandonment of the venture; the group's aircraft put down at various airfields on return because of the murk.

It was McCollom's turn to head the mission on the 26th, a Ramrod, which usually meant that enemy fighters would be active. The 56th was to provide withdrawal support for a force of Fortresses that was to bomb a target near Paris in the late afternoon. To increase range and duration over enemy territory the Thunderbolts put down at Manston near the south-east coast to refuel. A force of 49 Thunderbolts took off from Manston at 1812 hours and climbed out to make landfall over Dieppe; McCollom was leading with the 63rd at approximately 25,000 feet. Some forty minutes after take-off the B-17s were seen to be under attack north of Rouen. The 61st Squadron, at around 24,000 feet, was then surprised from above and a confused battle ensued. Gerald Johnson:

"German fighters: there are a lot of them and they are higher than we are. I'm watching them and they are coming around and we are sitting ducks. I can't wait any longer so I called 'Break Left'. So my flight breaks left and we went around and met them head-on. Got out of this mess and tried to find somebody to shoot at but couldn't see anybody. I remember thinking where the hell have they all gone, they were here seconds ago. The people who were in my flight, they're all gone, I'm by myself. Finally I begin to see stragglers around. A lot of conversation on the radio with people sounding as if they were scared to death. Then I saw a P-47 heading back to England with a Focke-Wulf on his tail; shooting at him. The P-47 is flying straight and level. I'm a little higher, I roll around, come in on the Focke-Wulf. Just as I'm about to open fire he sees me, breaks off, but I'm too close and I shoot and get hits all over and he breaks into a fireball. The P-47 that was being shot at seemed okay, so I turned back into France to try and find another German to shoot at. But I don't find any and according to my fuel gauges I'd better be heading back. So I'm one of the last fellows to land. It turns out that the airplane I saw being shot up was flown by Bob Johnson. He had already told this fantastic story about how the German pilot had come up alongside, and so on."

Indeed, 2nd Lieutenant Robert S. Johnson's story was exceptional. He was flying the No. 4 position in Shaker Yellow flight, which Gerald Johnson was leading, when his aircraft was hit by cannon shells. One burst hit the rear of the cockpit canopy shattering a left-hand window with a splinter hitting Johnson in the left forearm and demolishing most of his watch. Another fragment ripped the oxygen mask from his face, scraping across his nose. Instruments were damaged and a severed hydraulic line sprayed fluid into the cockpit. The Thunderbolt fell into a dive, and fearing it was beyond control Johnson released his safety harness and tried to jettison the canopy. It would not budge, even when in desperation he stood up and put his feet against the instrument panel putting his full weight on the canopy. Trapped, he overcame his fear, regained control and after a few anxious moments found his P-47 stable enough to head out towards the Channel. Reaching Manston he touched down successfully, but ended with a ground loop. Rescuers found that the 20-mm burst behind the cockpit had twisted up metal so that to release Johnson the frame had to be forced. The P-47 had taken damage from at least three cannon shells and several rifle calibre bullets. According to the severely shocked Bob Johnson, a German pilot had flown alongside the crippled P-47 as it flew back across the Channel and saluted him before turning away. From times and location Gerald Johnson was convinced that the FW190 he shot down was that which shot up his namesake's P-47. He heard Bob's story and said nothing, although he thought that in the excitement Bob had let his imagination run away with him concerning the chivalrous German pilot. No such incident was reported from the German side.

Bob Johnson's was not the only shot-up aircraft that made it back to Manston. In the surprise attack Lieutenant Justus Foster's P-47 took 20-mm hits, leaving a gaping hole in the right wing and cutting the hydraulics. Foster, recovering from the resulting spins, nursed the cripple across the Channel for a wheels-up landing. However, three P-47s in the 61st formation did not return, those of Captains Bob Wetherbee and Merle Eby and 2nd Lieutenant Louis Barron.

The other two squadrons had suffered less severely in the surprise interception. Oscar O'Neill:

"We made rendezvous a little late and a little low, so we had to pull up. We lost air speed because the timing was bad. We did a 180-degree climbing turn to pick up our position on the bombers coming out. As we did we put the sun on our tail and we were attacked. Our squadron didn't lose any flight commanders but the others did. My No.3 got shot up pretty bad but he got back, we were Moisture Yellow flight and had to take a lot of evasive action. It was pretty much a one sided thing."

Yellow 3 was the third Johnson in the group, Ralph. His P-47 was hit by a 20 mm and the hydraulic system damaged. With an escort Johnson flew back to Horsham St Faith where only one landing gear leg would come down and Ralph was unable to retract it again. Zemke took off and flew alongside to try and advise on actions to shake down the other leg but these aerobatics proved futile. As it was too dangerous to land with only one wheel down, Zemke told Johnson to fly to the coast and bale out over the sea. This he did successfully and was quickly picked up by air/sea rescue 400 yards off shore near Great Yarmouth.

The 63rd lost Captain Roger Dyar, last seen diving into cloud. Lieutenant Charles Clamp's P-47 was badly shot up, ".... the burst hitting my turbo-supercharger. There was then a series of three more explosions in the rear of the fuselage, the last of which exploded on the floor of the radio compartment. A 20 mm broke through into the cockpit, a fragment piercing my left arm just below the elbow." Clamp managed to make Manston where investigation revealed that his P-47 had received five 20-mm hits and between ten to twenty from rifle calibre bullets in fuselage, wings, tail and even the propeller.

When all had been accounted for, the tally read four P-47s shot down, one abandoned (pilot saved), three with severe battle damage (later repaired) and seven with minor. Credits for combats with enemy fighters using the established cipher was 2-1-5: two destroyed, one probably destroyed and five damaged. The Luftwaffe claimed eight P-47s shot down and three probables and lost only one FW190 to action with Thunderbolts. On both sides the claims and credits given were double that of the actual figures, illustrating that even where gun camera film was available, review of this could often lead to faulty assumptions. The main assault on the 56th formations had been by II/JG 26, the Gruppe known in the Allied camp as the 'Abbeville Boys'. They had claimed seven destroyed and three probables, two of the destroyed claims made by their leader Hauptmann Wilhelm Galland, brother of the famous ace Adolph Galland. The tactics employed were those used so successfully over the past two years with altitude advantage and surprise against RAF fighter intrusions. More or less the same tactics that had been used in the few successes the 56th had achieved.

That evening it was a subdued gathering in the Officers' Club at Horsham St Faith. It would have been more so had it been known that all four pilots lost had been killed. Someone did remark that back in the States Dyar had often joked about a visit to a fortune-teller who told him he would die with a bullet in his chest. For the time being the hope was that they had escaped to become prisoners. Charlie Clamp and Bob Johnson had minor wounds which would bring them their nation's award for battle injuries, the Purple Heart, the first in the 56th. The devil-may-care attitudes that had persisted with some pilots disappeared. The mission was fought over and over again verbally at the bar as alcohol soothed nerves. Gerald Johnson: "The losses this day got to me a little. I dreamed about the Focke-Wulf I shot down that was a mass of flames." Pete Dade, who took the liaison aircraft down to Manston to collect Bob Johnson, reported that Bob was so badly shaken up that he did not know if he wanted to fly again.

It cannot have been an easy night for Hub Zemke. To add to his troubles, in the morning he learned that the British police had reported that enlisted men had got into a fight at a nearby village hall and wrecked the place. Major Swanson was left to deal with that while Hub gathered his pilots for a long critique. Obtaining a clear picture of what happened was difficult as there were conflicting statements resulting from the obvious confusion. Opinions were many but what the situation had amounted to was summed up by the worn cliché, being in the wrong place at the wrong time. Based on RAF experience, VIII Fighter Command required close support of the bombers. This may have been the best way to deal with enemy interceptions when flying agile, fast accelerating Spitfires but clearly not with Thunderbolts. Zemke and his senior pilots agreed that it was desirable for the P-47s to be at 30,000 feet when shepherding bombers, or at least 5,000 feet above them as this would lessen the chance of being 'bounced'(surprise attack) from above. Zemke had already complained to Ajax about the poor climb and acceleration of the P-47 and the need for a fighter with better performance in these respects, only to be told no replacement type was scheduled. From what little experience had been gained by the 56th and the other two groups there was agreement that the Thunderbolt was best used in diving attacks, then by using the momentum of the dive to recover to higher altitude. Descending to lower altitudes put the type at a distinct disadvantage against the enemy types. Although duration was critical in giving support to the bombers, fuel economy should not over-ride the need to maintain high speed, 250 mph minimum when in hostile air space. Above all the debacle of 26 June underlined yet again the need for better battle co-ordination between squadrons and radio discipline.

If morale took a dip among the pilots of the 56th it was short-lived. When up against the ropes it was in Zemke's nature to be even more determined to conquer; the defeat of that June day did not appear to affect his confidence one iota. It brought a tougher stance with intensified training both in the air and on the ground. In fact, flight training was such that VIII Fighter Command queried why the 56th's aviation gasoline consumption was much higher than that of the other groups. A more critical eye was turned towards pilot ability and confidence, for there was evidence that some men were showing signs that they were not suited to fighter operations. The Colonel would listen to the ideas of others and take up those he thought had merit, but once having made up his mind he was inflexible, perhaps too much so. His officers learned the hard way that one did not persist in argument with Zemke or it would unleash an angry rebuttal. This stubbornness was in part a natural element of his character and in part a deliberate act to maintain the authority of a commanding officer. His attention was also focused on the ground men, particularly the maintenance crews. Abortives, the term for aircraft abandoning a sortie through mechanical or equipment failure, were being experienced on too many occasions. Engineering officers were lectured on tightening up maintenance procedures, albeit that most of the abortives were due to equipment failures. Zemke had made a practice of visiting ground crews, day or night, when they were at work to learn first-hand their problems and judge for himself the standard of work. Initially seen as a lack of faith in those specialist officers whose task it was to oversee the work of ground men, it became accepted that the 'Old Man' might show up anywhere.

Squadron commanders were also encouraged to talk with their ground men. Schilling had always had more contact with his squadron's ground personnel in that an interest in engineering and making gadgets often took him into the machine shops. Ground men occasionally suggested ways of improving aircraft components or servicing equipment and were permitted to try their ideas. Following suggestion of using the Thunderbolt as a fighter-bomber two men in the 61st designed and built a bomb rack to attach under the fuselage and carry two 300-lb bombs. It was given a flight testing by Bob Wetherbee two days before he was shot down.

Added to Zemke's troubles was the unwanted move to Halesworth for which orders were received that it would commence in the first week of July. Delay occurred while the largely Irish work force of the airfield builder removed the large amount of clay soil adhering to the concrete perimeter track. Many domestic sites spread far and wide in fields to the south of the airfield had yet to be completed and some tented accommodation was necessary. For the most part both officers and men were accommodated in Nissen huts, the curved corrugated sheet steel structures that predominated on wartime-built airfields in the UK. Dave Schilling had his eye on the abandoned farmhouse and buildings of High Tree Farm, just off the north-west side perimeter track. With Zemke's permission he took this over for 62nd Squadron offices and ready-room, employing the energies of his officers to renovate the house, including one room for a laboratory for the photographic enthusiast Tony Carcione. Ten loads of manure were removed from a former cattle shed where a bar was being constructed. Outbuildings were gradually repaired for squadron stores and repair shops. A notice affixed to the farmhouse door proclaimed Schilling's Acres. Among the other properties taken to make Station 365 was a large Georgian mansion known as Holton Hall. This became the group's headquarters building for officers and as it had three stories and a dozen bedrooms some of the staff were accommodated here, those on the upper floor sharing with a colony of bats.

A standard British Air Ministry bomber airfield, to so-called Class A standard, Halesworth had a 2,000-yard long concrete main runway and two intersecting auxiliaries of 1,400 yards. The encircling three and half-mile long perimeter track met all runway ends and spaced around the airfield were 50 concrete parking stands for aircraft. While this kept the P-47s out of mud when wet weather set in, taxying required zigzagging for pilots to see ahead over the large engine cowling and keep from wandering off the 17-yard wide track. With a runway width of 50 yards it was no longer possible for the four 'planes of a flight to take off together with the prospect of more precious time taken to launch a mission. This was partly solved by making use of two runways. It was safe for two P-47s to take off side-by-side, although staggered, each pilot watching his side of the runway edge. The next pair would start their take-off run when the pair ahead were half way down the runway, and so on until the whole 16-plane squadron was airborne. Meanwhile the second squadron had marshalled on one of the other runways to begin its take-off after the first squadron was airborne. While the second squadron's aircraft were taking off the third squadron would marshal on the runway used by the first, ready to roll the minute the second was airborne. In this way the complete group formation could be in the air in six minutes, although it generally took several minutes longer.

One advantage at Halesworth was being only some seven miles from the coast whereas Horsham St Faith had been 21. These extra few miles could mean three more minutes in enemy airspace and a greater opportunity to meet the enemy. VIII Fighter Command insisted that protecting the bombers and minimising their losses was the primary mission of the fighters. Even so, this came down to a matter of numbers for fighter leaders, the numbers of enemy fighters shot down. For the determined Zemke six credits for enemy fighters against nine of his pilots lost on combat missions was not a very promising showing when the other two groups who came new to the Thunderbolt had a better score. Any immediate opportunity to improve the 56th's lot was hindered by VIII Fighter Command ordering the group to take on responsibility for the air defence of the East Anglia area US airfields. To this end one squadron at a time was detached to operate from RAF Fighter Command air defence airfields in southern England for short periods for tuition in air defence procedures. As a result the 56th was only able to commit two squadrons to most July combat missions. In addition, a fighter group recently arrived from America, and equipped with P-47s, was to start operations early in August from a neighbouring base, Metfield. It would be the 56th's task to assist the new group, the 353rd, and provide air leaders for its introductory missions. All this engendered a suspicion among the 56th leadership that General Hunter and Ajax viewed them as the ne'er-do-wells of the command, and this was reinforced by word that auxiliary fuel tanks to extend range were to go first to the 4th and 78th Fighter Groups. This could in part have been due to Zemke's derogatory comments about these tanks when inspecting an installation at VIII Fighter Command's technical station at Bovingdon. The tanks, rated as 200 US gallon capacity, were designed and intended for ferrying P-47s over long distances. A bulbous moulded composition attached to the underside of the fuselage, the tank affected both performance and trim. While offering an extension of range they could not be used in high altitude flight as fuel would not draw from them much above 20,000 feet owing to the decrease in atmospheric pressure. Obviously, if intercepted while still carrying these tanks the P-47 would be at a considerable disadvantage, so they would have to be jettisoned on entering enemy air space. Bovingdon was working on smaller pressurised tanks, which could be taken to higher altitudes, but these were still some weeks away from operational use.

The need to extend the range of the Thunderbolts became an important issue with Eighth Air Force. Even if, as believed, the B-17 Fortress gunners were bringing down large numbers of enemy fighters during their missions into occupied Europe and the Reich, bomber losses were rising. The B-17 force had more than doubled in the spring and was still being reinforced, only to be countered by more Luftwaffe fighter units being placed in the west for defence. Disquieting were British intelligence estimates that raised doubts about the supposed attrition of the Luftwaffe fighter force. While many Eighth Air Force bomber commanders still believed the self-defending bomber concept viable others were less convinced. Most were apt to dismiss any aid forthcoming from fighters as so far negligible.

Meanwhile, experiments with fuel economy had confirmed that reduced engine speed with high manifold pressure (boost from the turbo-supercharger) while slowing the rate of climb could extend duration by ten to twenty minutes. The only drawback was that with a reduced rate of climb the formation would be at a lower altitude when crossing into enemy airspace and thus be at greater risk to being bounced from above. However, it had been noticed that with the increase in B-17 numbers the Luftwaffe had chosen to ignore the escort fighters and concentrate on attacking the bombers.

Two of the men who went down during the 26 June debacle were experienced flight leaders and the third, Wetherbee, had been Assistant Group Operations Officer. The Group Operations Officer, Captain James C. Stewart, worked with the field orders (mission orders), setting up route, timing and other operational matters as required, plus notifying squadron Operations Officers of pilots and aircraft numbers and incorporating these details into the mission plan. He was also responsible for training flight schedules. The Ops Officer needed to be a pilot who could bring his knowledge of combat operations to the job. Hitherto the Group Ops Officer had been allowed to fly missions of his choosing but, apart from the loss of his experience, if he was shot down and captured, there was a possible security risk. Eventually Zemke decreed that the Group Operations Officer must not participate in missions and should be grounded for six months. The Assistant Group Operations Officer was also subject to the same restriction. The new Assistant Group Operations Officer of the 63rd was Captain Lucian 'Pete' Dade. Competent and pleasant, Dade was one of the conservative seniors within the 63rd, a group that included Tukey, Burke and Goodfleisch. Unfortunately, their more military code of conduct began to create a social gulf between them and the more exuberant members of the squadron, leading in turn to rumblings that their leaders were staid and unaggressive in combat.

Apart from his own administrative requirements Zemke now had to deal with a fighter wing organisation placed in the chain of command between fighter groups and Fighter Command. Because of its purpose, operational control, Zemke and other fighter commanders saw it as an unnecessary organisation but it eventually took over some of the work formerly carried out by Ajax.

In the last week of July 1943 a high pressure area gave blue skies over north-west Europe, permitting the Eighth Air Force to launch Fortresses on missions to targets mainly connected with the German aviation industry. Taking advantage of good conditions for visual bombing, the expectation was that the Luftwaffe would be up in force to meet these assaults. Zemke and his men hoped that they would have an opportunity to improve their score. Yet success still alluded them despite two missions on some days. On the 28th news came that the 4th Fighter Group made use of the 200-gallon 'belly' tanks for the first time extending their duration by more than 30 minutes. Flying further inland than ever before they surprised German fighters and claimed nine. Early next morning a telegram was received stating that the famous Great War American fighter ace Captain Eddie Rickenbacker would visit Halesworth with General Hunter at 1340 hours and address group personnel. Before the expected dignitaries arrived a field order was received requiring a sweep over the Low Countries. During this mission a 62nd Squadron flight went down to investigate bogeys (code for unidentified aircraft), but finding Spitfires proceeded to regain altitude. In the climb, with loss of acceleration in speed and manoeuvrability, the flight made an inviting target for high-flying Me109 pilots, who shot down Lieutenant Bob Steele and badly damaged the P-47C of his leader, 1st Lieutenant Voorhis Day, causing the main gear to collapse on landing. Tony Carcione, the photo enthusiast, element leader in the same flight, became over-excited during the combat, continually shouting over the radio blocking other transmissions, a sin for which he was duly admonished on return. Others were forcefully reminded that when one pilot in the group held down his radio button to speak others could not transmit. For Zemke the loss was another example of the vulnerability of the Thunderbolt when flying slow and low. Steele was seen to bale out, but when his visitors arrived Zemke was disinclined to mention yet another pilot gone for no success. From an improvised podium, civilian suit attired, Rickenbacker provided stirring words on American prowess and the enemy's failings. For many of the listeners his assessment seemed a long way from the reality that the 56th had experienced.

10 Winning Ways

The Fortress 'blitz' of late July was rounded off with bombing factories at Kassel on the 30th, a fine day of clear skies. The 78th Fighter Group, making its first use of 200-gallon drop tanks, this day reached the Dutch/German border. Again the Luftwaffe was caught off guard and the 78th returned with a record score of enemy fighters, of which 16 were 'confirmed'. The 4th Fighter Group, also in action, claimed five of the enemy. The 56th, still with only two squadrons available, was given the job of seeing the bombers out from Holland and got into a fight with Me109s. The 61st Squadron saw most of the action, and once again it was Yellow Flight that was attacked. Second Lieutenant Jack Horton, one of the squadron's first two replacement pilots, was shot down, while 1st Lieutenant Milton Anderson's P-47, 'the tail-end Charlie', was extensively damaged but made it back to Halesworth. He was saved by Captain Leroy Schreiber who shot down the Me109 firing at Anderson's P-47. Schreiber had only flown his first two missions with the squadron the previous day, and before that had had one introductory mission with the other two squadrons earlier in the month while assigned to group headquarters. The problem was similar to that faced when Gabreski joined the group: the rank of captain was due a flight commander's post at least. There were no such vacant posts and initially Schreiber remained without a squadron assignment. Before obtaining an overseas posting to a combat zone, he had been an instructor. A likeable individual, Schreiber showed considerable modesty for on this occasion he also claimed an Me109 probably destroyed, but examination of his gun camera film showed destruction which had this claim reassessed as a confirmed 'kill'. A third Messerschmitt fell to the guns of Joe Powers. Viewed as a volatile character by his squadron mates, Powers was said to have Indian blood in his veins.

Schreiber's success was also the second occasion a 56th pilot had been credited with two enemy aircraft shot down on one mission. He had been flying Gabreski's personal Thunderbolt, while the 61st Squadron CO was confined in the US General Hospital at Redgrave Hall. The previous week Gabreski and Ralph Eastwood, the squadron adjutant, had taken the L-4 Cub and flown to Steeple Morden to visit Everett Stewart who had arrived there with a new P-47 group. Gabby and Stewart had served together in Hawaii at the time of the Japanese attack. When swinging the propeller to start the L-4 to return, the engine backfired and a blade struck Gabby's right hand, nearly severing his little finger. After getting him emergency treatment Eastwood drove the injured pilot to the major hospital where surgeons were able to save the finger, although thereafter it could only be bent at the knuckle. With Gabreski in hospital Captain Donald 'Doc' Renwick, C Flight leader, became temporary squadron CO.

One 62nd Squadron P-47 failed to return from the 30 July mission, that of Lieutenant Robert 'Smoky' Stover. With a battle-damaged aircraft Stover had nearly made it back to England only to be drowned after baling out from the stricken fighter. The cold North Sea would take many pilot lives. Claims of three for the loss of two were not an inspiring result and it is probable that the true German loss was two rather than three. Claims of both sides would continue to be suspect and it is doubtful if any individual pilot's score can be confirmed as completely true. The assessment of gun camera film shots could be inaccurate, for aircraft that appeared doomed sometimes survived while claims of probably destroyed were occasionally made for aircraft that were lost. While public relations would willingly proclaim the success of pilots by their credited totals, individuals' scores were not indicative of the air war situation. What really counted in the fighter-fighter battles was the overall attrition. However, individual prowess was good for public morale. Everyone liked a hero and the US press in particular made much of fighter pilots' personal scores. The fighter ace attained glamour status and the pilots of the 78th Fighter Group were accorded that attention after this day's battles.

In early August 63rd Squadron, returning from detachment with the RAF, gave the 56th Group once more its full complement. The air defence role was not called upon and all attention was now towards giving the Fortresses as much support as possible. A consignment of 200-gallon ferry tanks arrived at Halesworth for fitting. Attachment to the four mounting points was difficult and on being filled with fuel some tanks were found to leak. As these bulbous additions to the airframe affected flight characteristics pilots were sent up on test flights to gain handling experience. Captain Walker 'Bud'Mahurin was on such a flight during the morning of 11 August when he spotted a lone B-24 bomber. Liberators, rarely encountered at that time, drew Mahurin's curiosity and he formated alongside to take a closer look. As he pulled away and went under the four-engine bomber's wing the Thunderbolt was caught in turbulence, drawing the rear end up into a propeller which sliced into the tail. Damage to the B-24 was not critical and the crew was able to land it safely at home base. The Thunderbolt was a wreck, however, and Mahurin had to take quickly to his parachute as the collision occurred at around 1,000 feet. Mahurin suffered shock but had no physical injuries. His ordeal was not over for on return to Halesworth he had to face the wrath of the group commander who knew that this incident would only further reduce the 56th's standing with VIII Fighter Command. In caustic terms the flight commander was told he should have more sense than to do such a stupid thing. For the needless destruction of a $104,000 aircraft Mahurin was given the choice of a courts martial or a $500 fine, although Zemke knew full well the errant captain would take the latter.

Zemke was always selective in bestowing punishments. This was because he appreciated that the timid had no place in a fighter cockpit. A recognised aggressive spirit was not to be dampened. Miscreants might be firmly chastised and that would be the end of it. Next day Mahurin was back leading a flight on the first mission with the so-called drop tanks. These provided a duration of two hours but disappointingly the extended range did not provide contact with the enemy. Neither did the additional endurance improve the group's success on the next two raids when drop tanks were used. On the 16th it was galling to have no worthwhile contact with the enemy while the 4th Group claimed 18 shot down over Paris for the loss of one. And the 56th lost another pilot. When George Spaleny's engine stopped he held the P-47 in a long glide attempting to start it. Unsuccessful, Spaleny prepared to bale out, calmly announcing over the radio: "I guess I won't see you guys for a while. I might as well put my affairs in order." He said there was £10 in his trousers in his barracks and this was to be apportioned among officers from whom he had borrowed while on a trip to London. As no parachute was observed before his Thunderbolt was seen to crash it appeared Spaleny had been killed. A few weeks passed before it was learned he was a prisoner. Later that day, however, Zemke received a call from Ajax telling him that the CO of the new 353rd Fighter Group had been lost. Until a new CO was appointed McCollom was to go to Metfield to lead the newcomers as an important operation was expected on the morrow.

It transpired that the Fortress missions of 17 August 1943 would result in one of the milestone operations of the Eighth Air Force. In a maximum effort, one force attacked the Schweinfurt bearing factory returning to the UK, while a second went to the Regensburg Messerschmitt plant and then turned south to fly on to land in North Africa. The 56th was scheduled to support the departure of the latter force and after refuelling meet the return of the Schweinfurt bombers. Clear skies were forecast. Unfortunately, the heavy morning ground fog was not and this severely delayed the despatch of the bombers based further inland destined for Schweinfurt. The mists also posed dangerous take-off and form-up conditions for the Thunderbolts, particularly as pilots had not previously flown in such conditions. Zemke, unaware of the destination of the bombers, contacted Ajax to get permission for a delay, only to be told there could be no postponement. Despite being able to see little further than the sides of the runways and each element having to climb through the mists for some 5,000 feet before coming into the clear, there were no accidents. Fifty Thunderbolts were in squadron formations and on their way within twenty minutes. Enemy fighters were seen gathering to attack the bombers and though none were shot down their attacks were mostly dispersed by the Thunderbolt interceptions. For the first time the 56th was able to stay with the bombers to the German/Belgian border, some of the aircraft being airborne for two hours, ten minutes. But the 200-gallon tanks that made this possible proved troublesome. Two broke away soon after take-off while others would not easily release. There was also a tendency for the released tanks to bang against the underside of the fuselage.

Zemke led his second mission out mid-afternoon with 51 Thunderbolts. Drop tanks were shed at 20,000 feet north-east of Antwerp, followed by a climb to 27,000 feet during which a few Me109s bounced the 61st Squadron, although it was able to reform and continue on course. The bombers were not seen when they reached the scheduled rendezvous point, so Zemke ordered an orbit. It was three minutes before the Fortresses were seen to the south near Eupen and another two before the 56th was positioned over them, the 63rd above the leading formation box and the other two squadrons protecting the rear. The bombers were already under assault from numbers of enemy fighters, employing their common tactic of attacking head-on, diving away and then climbing to pass the bombers and turn in for another frontal pass. Although the rate of closure limited the exchange of fire and accuracy, the Luftwaffe considered the B-17 more vulnerable to strikes in the frontal area and their defensive fire less intense.

The group was immediately embroiled in combat, particularly the 63rd as most enemy attacks were concentrated against the leading bomber box. Although it was sometimes difficult to spot the enemy fighters below many of their passes were successfully intercepted. The pressure on the 63rd was such that Zemke moved the other squadrons forward. The battle lasted a half hour until the group was relieved by other Allied fighter units in the Antwerp area. When the last Thunderbolt had put down on Halesworth and pilots had been interrogated, it appeared some twenty enemy aircraft had been shot down, which was later resolved into 15 confirmed, three probables and four damaged. Three of the group's pilots failed to return, but the losses did not dominate Officers' Club conversation that evening, as for the first time the group could claim a major success in air fighting.

The most notable accomplishment was that of 63rd's 1st Lieutenant Glen Schlitz who was credited with three FW190s. As he later recounted to the newsmen, his operational experience had hereto not involved firing his guns:

"I just made 35 milk runs. Finally I gave up. I made up my mind I just wasn't going to get a chance – and then it came just as I had visualised it and the whole plan unfolded without my even thinking about it. We entered Holland and proceeded south-east to look for the bombers. We spotted them over Liège, flying in perfect formation. We made our turn and were circling over them. At first they looked like flies on a window pane. But when we closed I spotted about 30 FWs making head-on passes at them. I broke away from my flight and headed down, but two of the FWs turned up to meet me head on. Believe me, it doesn't take long to close in under that set-up. I opened fire on the leader at 400 yards and let him fly through my fire. That was the last I saw of him. I pulled up to the right and started to circle, when I spotted four FWs flying in a string at my level. I was sure they didn't see me so I eased in closer. The two end men broke away leaving me the number two straight ahead. I closed to 300 yards and opened fire. At 200 yards I could see my bullets lighting up a half-box pattern on his left wing, cockpit and engine. The pilot slumped over his controls and the plane headed down in a tight spin, with pieces flying off and smoke trailing. I looked about and saw the FW leader slightly above me. I slid over and opened fire at 300 yards with a burst of four seconds. I watched his right wing break off. His ship took a crazy pull to the right and started down. I would like to have watched him but the sky looked like a show the Ringling Brothers would have put on. I was very much interested in living just about then. I circled to find our bombers and turning into the Forts I was about four o'clock from them. This placed me on the tail of the two FWs. I started to close on the rear Jerry and opened up at about 250 yards. The bullets continued forward along the fuselage to the engine, which burst into flame. His ship dropped its nose and that was the last I saw of him. I glanced back on my left and saw four FWs screaming past me. I thought of following them but right ahead of me was an Me210, so I decided to take him on. I moved into about 100 yards and as he started a slight dive I opened up. My left guns stopped, then my right ones. I called my wingman and told him to get up front and start shooting. Just then I looked back and two FWs were coming at me from above and behind. I broke for the deck. They followed and punched several holes in my wings. Much to my relief they broke away about two miles from the coast but not before I clipped a high tension wire with my prop. I couldn't find any of my gang so I headed for home and the nearest base I could find. My gas was almost gone."

'Bud' Mahurin, with a bigger grin than ever, had redeemed himself by being responsible for two of the group score. Gerald Johnson had also shot down two of the enemy and shared in the destruction of another. There were some misgivings over the losses. 'Bunny' Comstock:

"I was flying element leader in Sy Burke's Blue flight. I saw two 109s coming down, called them in, and Sy in his usual way said let them go. The 109s had their bellies to us so they obviously didn't see us. I watched them and at about 6-8,000 feet below they levelled off behind two P-47s. As soon as I saw them level off I just left, because knowing Sy he would have told me to get back in formation. Before I got there the lead 109 had shot Sugas down. Sugas had a nickname of Elmer. His wingman was my friend George Compton. They must have seen me coming because they left Compton alone, turned right and started to dive about 600 yards in front of me. I followed them down and I took a shot at the lead man. I hit him in the left wing, about three feet in from the tip and it appeared I may not have done enough damage. But then a second or two later the wing came off and this guy started to roll to the left. He was rolling so fast I knew he was not going to be able to land it. I was low enough so climbed and picked up Compton and brought him home. I was fined £5 for breaking formation. I was quite bitter about that."

Comstock's sentiments reflected a common disquiet that existed with those element and wing pilots of an aggressive nature regarding the conduct of flight and squadron leaders. Decisions not to engage enemy aircraft were viewed as lack of enthusiasm rather than a leader's judgement of the situation and adherence to good air discipline.

Arthur Sugas was killed, as were the two missing 62nd pilots, Voorhis Day and his wingman Robert Stultz. It is believed these two fell victim to enemy fighters while they were intent on chasing a twin-engine Me110. The Luftwaffe lost 27 fighters that day, but some fell to the Fortress gunners. Following its losses on the 26 June mission the 61st Squadron dubbed itself the Avengers. They were avenged because seven of the fighters were from the Luftwaffe Gruppe that had caused those losses, II/JG 26. Included was its leader Hauptmann Wilhelm Galland, who by now had 55 victories, and was shot down and killed probably either by Mahurin or Schiltz.

Any satisfaction Zemke may have had from the performance of his men on the 17th was to be tempered by a call from Ajax the following day. He was informed that Loren McCollom was to become the new CO of the 353rd Fighter Group and would not return to the 56th. Zemke protested to no avail that when the effort put into building an efficient fighting unit was beginning to pay off, to be robbed of his key man was an undermining action. He also realised that command of a combat group was a prized position and McCollom certainly deserved this assignment. Who to replace him as Group Flying Executive? Tukey or Schilling? He did not make a decision immediately and led the next mission himself. The Fortresses went late afternoon to bomb airfields in the Low Countries and the 56th was in a good position when Luftwaffe fighters approached the bombers. With the sun and surprise to their advantage the group's pilots had another successful battle, being credited with nine enemy fighters with only one loss to themselves and that believed not to be due to enemy action. Lieutenant Glenn Hodges, flying wingman to Bunny Comstock, reported loss of engine power in the vicinity of Breda. Radioing that he was going back to base, Comstock also returned to escort him. Soon thereafter Hodges' aircraft appeared to lose all power and was put into a long dive. For some reason he did not bale out and put the aircraft down in the waters of the Oosterschelde estuary. Ditching (slang for a forced water landing) a fighter usually resulted in loss of life but Hodges was fortunate in surviving to become a prisoner. The original combat complements of the squadrons were gradually being whittled away, and three days later two more pilots died when soon after take-off for a training flight Don Tettemer, a replacement, collided with his element leader, the gambler Conway Saux. Too low to bale out, the aircraft crashed into fields near Sotherton Corner hamlet.

The successes of 19 August brought the group its first ace and the third in the Eighth Air Force. This was Captain Gerald Johnson, although a later reassessment of his credits deprived him of this honour. In acknowledgement of this unofficial accolade, the group borrowed an idea from the RAF in bestowing a hidden embellishment to uniform. Johnson's Class A jacket was despatched to a London tailor to have a scarlet lining inserted although through problems incurred Johnson never got to wear it before the practice was discontinued. Zemke saw this as another means of raising group pride and morale, which were now both beginning to climb. He also had come to a decision on appointing a new Flying Executive. Typically, it was something that Hub mulled over for some time, carefully assessing the two able squadron commanders. Tukey was a good leader and a stickler for air discipline. Schilling was generally popular with all ranks in his squadron, had shown aggressive leadership and was full of ideas, even if he had a tendency to act on these before careful review. Schilling was given the job; the decision was made on aggressive leadership in that Zemke thought Schilling more likely to gain victories with the group than Tukey and victories were the building blocks of success. Ironically, Schilling would not have been disappointed if the job had gone to Tukey: "Dave would have been happy to stay with his squadron. He was a king with a kingdom and he enjoyed the adoration." As it was, his personal P-47 remained to be serviced by the 62nd Squadron and Schilling would spend more time with his old command than other units on the base. 'Pappy' Craig became the new 62nd CO and to increase the squadron's combat leadership the promising Captain Schreiber was transferred from the 61st to take over a flight.

On 23 August Schilling became Yardstick for the first time for a Rodeo (fighter sweep) over the Low Countries; Yardstick was the group leader's mission call sign whoever was leading. The following day Zemke was Yardstick for a Ramrod which saw three FW190s claimed for no loss; the victors being Jones, Schreiber and Gabreski, the first for the 61st CO. Ajax still demanded close escort for the bombers but Zemke and his cohorts were now firmly convinced that to minimise frontal attacks on the Fortresses, one P-47 squadron should be sent five to ten miles ahead of the leading bomber box to intercept enemy fighters before they made their passes. In fact, the group was already splitting squadrons into sections of eight with one ahead of the bombers, although this was not emphasised in mission reports lest a reprimand was forthcoming from Ajax on the need to remain close to the bombers.

This was the last mission where the 'bathtub' drop tanks were employed. Hereafter a bomb shackle was installed under the forward fuselage in preparation to take the so-called 75-gallon drop tank. Made of pressed steel sheet, teardrop-shaped, these were smaller than the 200-gallon bathtubs and had less effect on performance and handling. Their main advantage was that fuel could be drawn at high altitude, as the Bovingdon technicians had devised a system of pressurisation through utilising the exhaust of the instrument vacuum pump. The first use of these tanks came on the last day of the month, when there was much trouble getting them to release.

Although the developed proficiency of the group was now paying off and the 56th was having a better showing against the enemy than the other P-47 groups, there were still days when it took the most punishment in contacts with the Luftwaffe. On 2 September Zemke was leading an escort for bombers seeking airfields in northern France. A lower level of cloud frustrated their efforts while the escorting Thunderbolts had to fly under another layer at high altitude. While the 63rd Squadron was in an orbit over the rear of the bomber formations a Staffel of Focke-Wulfs emerged from the clouds above and attacked the two leading flights, shooting down the Thunderbolts of Walter Hannigan and Wilfred Van Abel, plus damaging those flown by Zemke and John Vogt. Zemke had his supercharger put out of action and made it back to base; Vogt was pursued by his attacker who presumably ran out of ammunition. With cannon shell splinters in his leg, Vogt managed to nurse the crippled P-47 back for an emergency landing at Eastchurch. FW190s of II/JG 26, which had been responsible for the 26 June rout and suffered retribution on 17 August, were the victors. The following day the tables were turned with four FW190s claimed for the loss of Hiram Bevins, who crash-landed to become a prisoner.

Bevins was the twenty-first of the original combat pilots to be lost. With transfers out for one reason or another, 27 pilots, equivalent to a whole squadron complement, were gone. Some individuals were too aware of their mortality, others less so, imbued by the confidence of youth that 'it always happens to the other guy'. Each squadron had a Flight Surgeon, a doctor who monitored pilots and could recommend grounding if they detected an overly nervous disposition. For the most part pilots hid their fears, easier once the group was in the ascendancy, leading the other groups in victories obtained flying Thunderbolts. There was no greater stimulant than besting the enemy. The championing of aces also had the effect of boosting the desire to achieve such status. The emphasis was on fighting as a team, air discipline in following squadron and flight commanders' orders, wingmen following their element leaders and regaining altitude after carrying out a diving attack. A fighter pilot was an individual who had to be self-reliant. His world was the confinement of a cockpit with restricted vision below and to the rear; of incessant engine noise which the muffing of ear pieces dulled, only to have the high pitched whine of enemy radio jamming superimposed; and a constant need to keep scanning the sky, particularly to the rear. The tedium was exhausting, the more so as the radius of action was increased; it was pushed to an endurance of 2 hours 40 minutes on 27 September when British-made cylindrical paper/plastic tanks of 108-gallon capacity were used for the first time to bring the bombers home from Emden. Five enemy fighters were credited as destroyed for the loss of one, Harry Dugas, another original.

Once again it appeared that the Luftwaffe had not expected to see P-47s so far from England. Lieutenant John 'Fat Boy' Coenen, who had spent many weeks in hospital following a bale-out on Easter Sunday was on his thirteenth mission since return to combat. Despite his back pain two Focke-Wulfs fell to his guns. The Flight Surgeon decided that sitting in a cockpit was detrimental to his injury and he was taken off operations, eventually returning to the USA. Another victor, catching the enemy fighter unawares, was Wayne O'Conner:

"I pulled up in a chandelle (high speed climbing turn) to the right and saw an Me109 starting a tail attack on the Forts. I peeled down on him and gave him a shot burst from 500 yards. I held my fire until I was directly astern of him at 300 yards and started firing again. This time I saw strikes on his tail and wing roots. I kept closing to about 50 yards, where I ran out of ammo'. As I pulled up to miss him, his canopy flew by beneath my left wing. I slid over him missing him by about 75 to 100 feet. I could see the pilot slumped over to his right. His helmet was gone and I could see blood covering the left side of his neck and shoulders. Evidently the engine had been hit as his prop was windmilling very slowly. As I watched he slowly rolled over and went into a spin. It was the damnedest sight I ever saw."

It proved a worrying sight for O'Conner. Mostly with the speed of combat the fate of an enemy pilot went unseen and most thought it better that way. It didn't pay to think about the enemy being another human being. 'Butch' O'Conner was jovial, loved dogs and supposedly a real Casanova. It was reckoned that his girls could not have been too particular as Butch frequently pervaded an unsavoury odour. Whether this was an unfortunate affliction or just poor hygiene no one ever established.

Looking for good news, Eighth Air Force public relations put the group's first claimed ace, Gerry Johnson, under the spotlight. A journalist reported him as: 'Well built, he wears his uniform with a sort of Robert Taylor elegance – without giving it a thought. He has crisp dark hair whose slight wave bothers him – and, his pals, say the girls hereabouts. His clean cut features are masked by a very warm, almost olive complexion ... remarkably sharp eyes.... not the least cocky or conceited.' It was arranged Johnson should go to Duxford on 4 September to meet, along with the Eighth's other two ace fighter pilots, General Arnold, the Army Air Forces' chief who was visiting the UK. Afterwards Johnson was sent to London where he joined Mahurin and together they were taken to Buckingham Palace to meet the Queen and have tea with the two young princesses. While both men were so honoured the real purpose of this exposure was good copy for the newspapers in the United States.

Gerry Johnson was reckoned to be the best shot in the group which was not surprising in view of his study and practise of sighting:

"I spent a lot of time with my plane. I had the crew raise up the tail with the nose towards another aircraft about 200 yards away, which I thought was a good firing range. I'd sit in the cockpit, look through the gun sight, and try to get the size of the airplane fixed in my mind so I would know when I saw a Focke-Wulf or Me109 in the sky how big it should look through the sight. Even though they were a bit smaller, I'd have a pretty good feel of when one was in my range."

The group was about to lose Major Philip Tukey, the 63rd CO, who was ordered to report to VIII Fighter Command HQ to take the post of an Operations Officer. 'Tuke' did not want to go and Zemke, not wanting to lose him, made these views known to the Assistant Chief of Staff at Ajax, Colonel Burns. In his usual forceful manner when upset, Zemke complained again about what he saw as the proselytising of the 56th's best men, particularly when the group was getting into its stride. This time his forceful plea met sympathy but no more than the possibility of Tukey returning to the 56th at a later date. In his annoyance Zemke commented that Ajax was a bigger threat to his group than the Luftwaffe.

11 Work and Play

Zemke recognised the confidence of ground staff was essential to the success of the group and that therefore, they should know about any success the 56th had and understand the air war situation as far as was permissible. At Horsham St Faith he had arranged for the local pilot radio transmissions to be broadcast on the Tannoy loudspeaker system adjacent to the hangar line. Every now and then ground personnel, particularly mechanics, would be gathered in a hangar and given an account of operations by a pilot or someone from headquarters. The purpose was to motivate men in appreciating the group's endeavours and thus build morale and esprit de corps. The ground crews' lot could be exhausting, particularly when missions were flown daily, often entailing working in inclement weather with no protection out on the widely dispersed aircraft hardstandings.

Frank Gyidik, a 63rd crew chief, details an average day:

"We were roused up at a dark hour in the early morning by the CQ (Charge of Quarters). If there was time we walked to the mess hall for breakfast – coffee, powdered eggs, toast; if not we'd eat later when the mission was gone. We would board the 'lorries' that took us out to our hardstands where the planes were located. At our P-47s we would take off the canopy cover and then walk round the plane to see if there was anything that didn't look right. First pull the prop'through several times to move the oil that may have collected in the bottom of the cylinders overnight. Then climb up into the cockpit. Calling out 'Clear', the starter was energised and the engine started. Next stop would be to run up the engine to a certain RPM [revolutions per minute] and check both the right and left magnetos. As part of the pre-flight the flaps were checked both up and down, as were all the other control surfaces to see they moved okay. The engine oil and hydraulic reservoirs were checked to see they were still full. Then the radioman would check the radios. If the guns had been fired the day before they would have been taken out to clean and check. If so, the armament man would put them in, then look them over and see that all bays were full of ammunition. The oxygen boys would come by and fill the tanks, making sure the system was working. The gasoline truck would come to my plane and all others to top up tanks. Then we would wait for the pilots to come to their individual planes.

"On the arrival of your pilot you would help him put on his parachute, check to make sure he had fastened all the buckles on his parachute harness, boost him up on the wing root as the pilot used the steps on the side of the plane. We would do this because of the bulky parachute pack. Once the pilot got into the cockpit and sat down I would straighten his shoulder straps and watch as he buckled his shoulder straps into his seat belt and tightened them securely. Also made sure he plugged in his radio lines and connected his oxygen tube to the outlet valve. Once he was securely in his seat and all connections made I would ask him to check all the controls, especially his rudder pedals for full travel. Then we would engage in small talk to ease the tension I was sure he had before the coming mission. Just before engine start time I would get off the wing, tapping him on the shoulder just before I left. I don't know why I did this unless it was a tap of confidence for the mission.

"At one airdrome we rode the left wing as they taxied down the narrow perimeter track, because they could not S-turn enough to see what was ahead of them. Once they got in position on the runway I would slide off the wing and after take-off walk back to our hardstands where we would either read, play ball, or just sweat it out until our planes returned. Sometimes we'd put a canopy cover in a belly tank box, crawl in there and make up for the sleep lost when having to get up early. When the mission returned to base and flew over we would count each squadron. You would stand by your hardstand when the aircraft came by and look to see if the guns were 'smoked' – blackened barrels, a sign they'd been fired. If they were smoked you would hold up your hand with one or two fingers up; by this we meant did you get one, two or more. Sometimes the pilot would signal with one or more fingers, sometimes the thumbs down sign. When your aircraft had taxied in and parked, up on the wing you'd go to assist the pilot in unhooking everything while asking him how it went. If your pilot wanted to talk you would carry on with the small talk, especially about the performance of the aircraft. Once your pilot is picked up you go all over the aircraft for battle damage. There were numerous special inspections at set number of hours. One regular check that was important was the Cuno oil filter for any metal chips in the screen. Metal chips in the screen meant trouble with the engine. If everything was okay, the 'plane would be bedded down for the night. Canopy and pitot tube covered. Then we'd head for the barracks."

Often when there was a problem with their aircraft a ground crew worked late into the night. Most pilots may have been assigned a particular aircraft and probably bestowed a nickname on it, but on average it would only be available for his use for around two-thirds of his total missions. Ground crew chiefs were more justified in seeing the aircraft as theirs and that the pilot was somebody they lent it to – a view engineering officers encouraged. To further imbue a ground crew with pride in their charge much was made of any turn-back from a mission because of a mechanical or equipment failure traced to poor maintenance. Ground crews were well aware of the trust a pilot had to have in their work and endeavoured to convey reassurance. When a pilot whose aircraft they had serviced for several weeks or months failed to return from a mission the ground crew were often affected. Ed Lanham, 63rd Assistant Crew Chief: "I crewed Walter Hannigan's plane. He was shot down September 2nd. A very gentle, friendly person. It's a difficult feeling of loss. You wonder about his family, his friends."

The ground men came to be the perpetuating entity of the group, for pilots were transitory. Apart from those lost in combat or accidents some were transferred to other units for various reasons, a few because they were not suited to flying fighters. Transfers were not limited to other organisations in the UK, a few men went back to the USA for special assignments. One such was Harry J. Chancey who had joined the 61st Squadron as an operations clerk at Bridgeport in 1942. Favouring becoming a fighter pilot, he applied with his CO's blessing to undertake air cadet training and passed the necessary acceptance tests. However, when the 56th Fighter Group had been alerted for overseas movement in November, Chancey chose the option of a postponement so that he could remain with his squadron. At Horsham St Faith Chancey decided to complete his cadet entrance requirement and with Major McCollom's approval a perfunctory review board was set up with the result that Chancey was accepted for aviation cadet training. His orders sent him to Liverpool where he sailed for New York on the *Ile de France* but not before encountering military police suspicious of a private whose papers said he was bound for the ZI (Zone of the Interior), military jargon for the USA. Chancey failed to become a pilot and was commissioned as a bombardier in June 1944. The *Ile de France* brought him back across the Atlantic, this time for service in Italy where he flew 33 missions in B-17s with the 97th Bomb Group. Unlike Chancey, a few men who applied for aviation cadet training had no intention of becoming pilots and simply saw this as a way to return to the USA.

There were some 20 ground officers and enlisted men for every pilot on the station, for in addition to the combat group and the service squadron there were a number of other support units. One was the 1126th Quartermaster Company responsible for sustenance. Fresh vegetables came from local British sources. Most meat was frozen and from the States. Fresh eggs were augmented rations for pilots only; everyone else had powdered eggs. Bread came from local bakeries. There was a 14-day menu rotation at the three mess halls. The food was far superior in variety to their severely rationed British neighbours and it was not long before canned fruit or meats were being traded for fresh eggs and poultry at local farms, albeit that this was a contravention of rationing as far as the British authorities were concerned. The 56th had not been at Halesworth many days before complaints were forthcoming from the local police that some men were hunting with guns on local property. Rabbits, of which there were plenty in the fields of Suffolk, were prized by the locals as an additional source of meat to supplement rations: poaching 'Yanks' were not popular. Ed Lanham: "A stray dog joined our outfit. He would run a rabbit into a hole and we could usually reach in and pull it out. Then that night we would go over to the officers' mess where the cooks would give us butter and it wouldn't be long before we were frying rabbit. We ate so many rabbits we were asked to give a donation to the farmer as we were eating a source of his income." Most farmers were pleased to see rabbits caught as they destroyed their crops.

With an evening pass the chief places of interest were the public houses which, apart from the beer, were the main social centres for males in the country towns and villages. They quickly became an attraction for many GIs. Angelo DeCarlo, 1126th QM Co:

"At first I was assigned to salvage detail, which meant going around the base picking up odds and ends, trash and all that stuff. We would load it up in the morning, drive to Norwich and dump it in a sort of landfill site, stop at the Horsham St Faith base and eat lunch, then drive back to Halesworth. What the First Sergeant and the others in command didn't know is that we'd stop at some of the pubs, drink and play darts until they closed up at 2 pm or whatever time it was, and then head back to the base."

And there were plenty of pubs, most villages had one and some two or more. About all that could be found to drink at these hostelries were a few types of beer – seemingly flat to most American palates – or so-called lemonade and ginger beer, fizzy and non-alcoholic. But mild, bitter and stout soon became a popular escape from service life, so popular that on one occasion some GIs acquired a whole wooden barrel of the stuff, probably by unorthodox means, and proceeded to carry it back to the base. After two military policemen were observed searching men at the main gate, the beer barrel was deposited in an adjacent pond with a view to retrieval after dark when the 'Snowdrops' (military police) had departed. Unfortunately, those who waded into the pond that night were unable to locate the barrel and later attempts also failed. The little town of Halesworth was a mile west of the camp and had several pubs. While many GIs found the locals sociable some took British reserve as unfriendliness. Master Sergeant John Brady found that when sitting by himself with his beer in a Halesworth pub he would be aware people were looking at him. When he looked at them they looked away. This happened on more than one occasion and made him feel so uneasy that he gave up going into pubs. Other GIs preferred to seek out village dances or just explore the rural countryside around the Halesworth base.

A cycle was essential transport and ground crews, mechanics and other key men who had some distance to cover on the airfield to reach their place of work were issued with these machines. The non-essential tasked men had to go out and buy from the locals who did a good trade in second-hand bikes. The bike became the imaginary fighter for many of the young aircraft mechanics, pedalling along the winding country roads at speed with noisy gaiety: David Hubler, 62nd flight chief:

> "Zemke thought it would be a good idea to let the ground crews listen to
> the radio conversations of the pilots. This was broadcast on the tannoys.
> Zemke's call sign was Yardstick and he would draw breath between Yard
> and stick. Men who went to the pubs at night would joke about this and
> mimic Zemke with a long drawn out Yard… stick as they rode their
> bikes: 'Yard-stick here. Break left!' The voice pitch of the pilots went up
> when they were in trouble."

So-called clubs were established on the base to provide recreational
facilities for enlisted men, where they could relax off duty. The American
Red Cross set up Red Cross clubs on Eighth Air Force operational
stations. Staffed by two uniformed American girls the Red Cross
provided coffee, coke, doughnuts and other familiarities of American
living for enlisted men. The Special Services Officer, Captain Alfred
Mellor, had the task of organising entertainment on the base and got
together men who played musical instruments to form a small band that
they called 'The Jivin' Yanks'. Its main purpose was to entertain at special
functions, mostly on-base parties or dances although it also performed on
more serious occasions. One such was the official transfer ceremony of
Halesworth from the RAF to the USAAF on 19 August. This took place
by the flagstaff in front of the group headquarters building and did not go
as smoothly as the participants would have wished. Angelo DeCarlo,
saxophonist:

> "I was in the front row of the band at the change-over ceremony. When
> Zemke saw the two GIs running the Stars and Stripes up the pole upside
> down I could see him talking through his teeth to bring it down, trying to
> get the men to stop without shouting at them. We'd started to play the US
> anthem but we stopped when they brought the flag down and then started
> again when they ran it up the right way. I'll never forget the expression
> on Zemke's face when he saw it going up the wrong way. He never
> chewed anyone out afterwards. He came over and thanked us for
> attendance."

Officers also had the use of cycles for personal transport round the base
while those in command positions had the use of jeeps. The ex-civilian
cars provided by the RAF for the group CO were replaced by US-made
staff cars used for both official and social journeys. Officers generally
made for the more up-market hotel bars leaving the village pubs to the
enlisted men, although many only patronised the Officers' Club on the
base, apart from three-day passes when London was the attraction. Those
who did range out in the local area soon recognised that Britain had a class
system that was not necessarily allied to wealth. The humble agricultural
cottage with a well for water and bucket sanitation made a stark contrast
with the huge mansion that might stand in adjacent parkland.

The most enthusiastic roamer when off duty was Major David Schilling who often explored new avenues of friendship with the British. A meeting with some Royal Navy officers led to ventures out on the North Sea in motor-torpedo boats, which Zemke thought rather foolhardy in that Schilling was possibly putting himself in unnecessary danger. Then Schilling met Andrew and Britter Venneck; the former was from a wealthy and titled family owning the large Heveningham Hall estate some five miles south-west of the base. Schilling learned that shooting game birds, pheasant and partridges, was a popular country sport commencing on September 12th each year. Wartime had led to 12-bore cartridges only being available for pest control in Britain and sporting activities were curtailed. The 56th had ample supplies of this calibre cartridge used in skeet shooting (catapulted targets on a range) thought to improve pilots' aim. Thus Schilling, supplying the ammunition, was invited to bring other officers to participate in bird shoots.

Fighter pilots, loners in one situation, were gregarious in another. Physical isolation and confinement during missions led to an eagerness to mix with other pilots in the squadron ready rooms or the Officers' Club when back at base to discuss operations and 'hangar fly'. Officers' Club evening gatherings were often rowdy with the exuberance of young men fuelled with alcohol, as this was an easy relief from stress. At times some would drink too much until intoxicated to the point of extreme drunkenness. One such was Joe Powers who tended to become belligerent. On one occasion he took a swipe at the group CO, but Zemke took no action; Powers was an excellent combat pilot. The Flight Surgeons kept an eye out for heavy drinkers and occasionally warned the bartenders to try and restrict the amount some men drank. Whisky, rationed to three bottles a day in the Officers' Club, was not available until after 5.45 pm. Dave Schilling regularly frequented the Officers' Club bar when on the base and although he did drink heavily at times he could 'always hold his liquor'. Zemke rarely stayed long in the Officers' Club, part of his deliberate policy not to be placed in a situation where he would become too buddy-buddy with his pilots. The enlisted man who tended the bar, Private First Class Ray 'Tex' Chapman, observed that the Colonel did not drink much. "He takes a glass of sherry once in a while or a glass of beer, but he seldom empties it." Addressed on the subject by a visiting officer Zemke responded, "Hell, I get as drunk as anyone." He was not believed. Self-discipline plus a natural resilience ruled with Zemke; and he was absorbed with his mission.

Indulging in what was termed fooling around was another relief from the stress of combat flying. Practical jokes abounded. A not uncommon expression at the time among these young men, if one did not agree with something said was 'Oh bite my ass.' In a friendly argument with fellow pilot Jack Brown, Walker Mahurin expressed his disagreement in this way. Whereupon Brown wrestled him to the ground and did just that. 'Bud' had teeth marks on his buttocks to prove it. Some individuals excelled at practical jokes and others were entertaining raconteurs. Joe

Curtis, a 61st pilot who had a troubled time on missions, was renowned for his flow of anecdotes. 'You could always rely on Joe to make you laugh.'

Inevitably various degrees of personal friendship and animosity arose between individuals but this did not affect operational commitments among pilots. The ground complement was comprised of a much wider section of American society ranging from the illiterate to the sophisticated in the same units. There was also more disenchantment with rank and command in some quarters: some of the men in the ground elements were incompetent and lacked leadership and discipline, including some of the officers. Some were obnoxious. The 41st Service Squadron had not been happy with its commander for some time so when there was an opportunity to 'get back at him' it was taken. John Sipek:

"One evening while I was on charge of quarters duty it became very boring and uneventful, so I did a little rummaging around through papers on the desks of our squadron orderly room to find out what was happening. I also searched through the papers of our beloved squadron commander, Major James D. Osgood's desk. There was an open gift box on his desk with a beautiful Ronson cigarette lighter and according to a note this was a birthday gift from his wife. About that time some of my buddies came in to keep me company. I cautioned them not to disturb anything and if they did to replace everything the way it was. One of them noticed the lighter and in checking it out discovered that Osgood hadn't put any fluid in it yet. He volunteered to make a TO change to the lighter so that it would never light and no one except us would know why. I was a little sceptical at first because I would be responsible if anything could be traced to my tour of duty. He persuaded me not to worry that all signs would lead the Major to believe it was a defective lighter. My buddy took the lighter and filled the fluid compartment with carbon tetrachloride which he obtained from a fire extinguisher in one of our trucks. He then poured out the excess fluid and screwed the cap back on the fluid compartment. Everything was wiped clean and then placed back in its original position.

"During my scrutiny of the desks I came across a stamp that was used by the officer who censored our photos. I asked my buddies if they had any photos they wanted me to censor? They hurried back to their hut and returned with a load of pictures. The rear of each photo was imprinted with the stamp which showed 'Passed by US Censor. Not for publication.' We sure censored a big pile of pictures that night without rejecting a single one! A few days later while in the mess hall a couple of orderly room clerks were overheard discussing the problems Major Osgood was having with his new cigarette lighter. According to them he had tried everything but couldn't get it to light. After he filled the compartment with lighter fluid and repeatedly pressed down the button there was plenty of spark but no light. One of his brainy assistants suggested it might work with 100 octane aviation gas so he sent him out to fill it with gas. It wouldn't work with aviation fuel either so he gave up. Our buddy who was a member of the fire crew knew his business when he said it wouldn't light after he made the TO modification [TO stood for Technical Order, the essential instruction for any modification to military equipment]."

Officially no pets were allowed on a US military establishment but authority turned a blind eye. It was not long before dogs and cats were to be found on most domestic sites. There were also attempts to make pets out of British wild creatures. Men of 62nd's hangar crew discovered what they called a miniature 'porcupine' in their hangar. The hedgehog immediately rolled up in a protective ball, spines extended. After attempting to make the animal open up by dipping it in a puddle it was taken to dry out by a stove. For two days no movement was observed but not a little amusement was caused by the hedgehog finally succumbing to the temptation of powdered egg placed nearby. The animal was then named Thunderbolt and considered a squadron pet until one day it disappeared, obviously to hibernate for the winter.

12 Combat Ascendancy Continues

By the end of September the 56th's standing by the yardstick of assessment as Zemke considered it was near equal to that of the 4th Group, 52 victory credits against 53, while the other 'original' Thunderbolt group, the 78th, had 49. The numbers game was given to fluctuations through reassessments of gun camera films by the controlling fighter wing and VIII Fighter Command, but Zemke saw the group scores as a further means of imbuing his pilots to achieve, building a competitive spirit. From the poorest standing in the command his group was going to show it was the best. Zemke knew better than anyone, however, that the old adage of being in the right place at the right time, was paramount to progress in this deadly business. The air fighting already experienced had shown that the principal element of success was surprise. The turning combat and gladiatorial dogfight had no place in this battle with Focke-Wulfs and Messerschmitts; the Thunderbolt was a dive, destroy and away fighter.

October 1943 saw a leap in the 56th's fortunes. On 2 October it started well for the two 'wheels' of the group. During another 500-mile round trip to support bombers at Emden little enemy opposition was encountered. However, Zemke surprised and shot down a FW190, his fifth victory, while Schilling, leading the 63rd Squadron, at last had success, shooting down a FW190 and Me109 from a small formation. These were Schilling's first victories in 52 missions and earned him congratulations at the Officers' Club that evening. Two days later unit pride soared for with 16 more credits the 56th was now way out in front of the other groups. Fifty-four P-47s took off with a mission to provide withdrawal support for Fortresses attacking targets in the Frankfurt area. For the first time each aircraft carried one of the sheet-steel British-made 108 US-gallon drop tanks, which provided 50 minutes of flight before being released some ten minutes before rendezvous with the bombers near Düren in the Ruhr. Range was extended to near 260 miles from base, and again the Luftwaffe was evidently taken by surprise. As the 63rd Squadron, led by the Group Flying Executive, arrived to cover the last box of Fortresses they saw some 3,000 feet below a large number of twin-engine Me110 fighters approaching the bombers from the rear. With the sun to their advantage, the Thunderbolts turned and swept down on the Messerschmitts from their rear; their approach was unseen and in a few minutes 14 had been despatched. ZG76, the decimated unit, had not anticipated American escort fighters so far inland. The group returned to Halesworth without loss; there had been almost three hours between engine start that morning and the last aircraft landing back. Walker Mahurin, shooting down three, achieved ace status; Schilling added his third, while Lieutenant Vance Ludwig, the element leader in Schilling's flight, also claimed three Me110s. Ludwig had previously flown 47 missions, mostly as a wingman, and told the news reporter:

> "The greatest day of my life.... We spotted about 30 Me110s trailing the bombers and keeping perfect formation. The order was 'let's go' and we went down on their tails. Three out of the four of us in my element got on them and down they went in flames. We came back up but had to queue to get another shot at them. We dove down again and this time my Jerry tried evasive action, but I got in a deflection shot and he went down too. My third one was tougher. His rear gunner was firing tracers at me and they were zipping right over my head. I dropped below him to get out of his range and then came up fast. My first burst must have got the gunner because he didn't fire after that, and a moment later the Nazi went down, too."

The seemingly boastful statements to the press were akin to the after-mission Officers' Club bar sessions, where success was aired much in the manner of a game bird shoot or animal hunt. The fate of enemy pilots shot down did not feature large in this talk and feelings for a fellow human rarely. A combat pilot could not allow himself to think on this aspect of a victory. The destruction of enemy aircraft was the primary goal and aggressive intent should not be weakened by sympathy. There could be no dwelling on the thought of having killed or maimed. This was war and it was kill or be killed. Ludwig's victories on 4 October would be his only successes: a few weeks later he became the victim of a Luftwaffe fighter pilot. Two other credits went to 61st Squadron pilots that day, one being a recently arrived replacement flying as a wingman, 2nd Lieutenant William Marangello. At the bar, when asked about his success he exhibited a dry sense of humour, casually responding that he shot the Messerschmittt down because he wanted to get home and the German was in his way. Marangello was another pilot not long for this world.

Withdrawal support for Fortresses on 8 October provided interception of the FW190s attacking them and brought the 56th credits for five of the enemy shot down. One P-47, unseen to fall, failed to return. There was some battle damage and Captain Ray Dauphin was wounded by shell splinters. The victories put the 56th comfortably ahead of other groups. Zemke spurred his men by suggesting a goal of a hundred by Christmas. At lunch next day somebody joked that it should be a hundred by Sadie Hawkins' Day and that the Luftwaffe wives be warned to start looking for new husbands. A syndicated comic strip in American newspapers was *Lil' Abner* featuring a mythical hill-billy location called Dogpatch inhabited by wild mountain men and women. This popular strip, by artist Al Capp, was one of three run regularly in the daily *Stars and Stripes* newspaper published in the UK by the US authorities for their military personnel. Dogpatch folklore held that on Sadie Hawkins' Day the eligible womenfolk had the right to marry any single male of their fancy they could catch, catch being the operative word as Dogpatch men were extraordinarily disinterested in matrimony. This appealed to Schilling, and as Zemke approved he let his public relations officer advise the newsmen that the group was intent on shooting down a hundred enemy fighters by Sadie Hawkins'Day, 6 November. Although unit designations were secret and not used in news reports, no restriction was made on identifying a particular unit by linking it with the commander's name. Thus the published word of the 'Zemke group's' boast, apart from appearing over-ambitious, presented something of a challenge to other fighter groups. But primarily it was a challenge to 56th pilots and a spur to esprit de corps, to make the men feel that they were now the best outfit in VIII Fighter Command.

With some dissatisfaction in US government and military circles at the Eighth Air Force's progress in its daylight strategic bombing campaign, General Eaker decided to send a small team back to Washington to explain achievements, difficulties and methods of operations. For this he wanted the best of his combat commanders. Major General William Kepner, who had replaced Hunter as the head of VIII Fighter Command in late August, contacted Zemke and told him he was to return to the States to give presentations on fighter operations. This order was met with horrified protest by Zemke in that the 56th was now really getting into its stride and to remove its commander would surely upset the teamwork. Kepner consoled him that this was only for a limited period. Zemke, realising he could not defy generals however objectionable he found the order, obtained a promise that when he returned he could resume command of his group. Brigadier General LeMay, Eaker's most promising bomber leader, was to be in charge of the party and Zemke was instructed to meet with him and learn his requirements. LeMay, whom Zemke had known in earlier service, instructed him to prepare an explanatory lecture on fighter operations. So engaged, Zemke was unable to participate in some of the early October missions.

Zemke also had to think about command of the 56th in his absence. Dave Schilling was the obvious man, but although Schilling was showing excellent air leadership in his position as the group's flying executive, Zemke harboured misgivings about leaving the group in his hands. This resulted from Schilling's habit of coming up with ideas which he was enthusiastic to pursue, some of which were good but many far from soundly thought out. Schilling, in his pleasant manner, would assail Zemke with these ideas; Hub listened but rarely committed himself to any he thought worthwhile there and then. There was this lingering doubt that in his absence Dave might embark on some foolhardy enterprise if he was in command. Zemke recognised Schilling's general social popularity and while he also liked his second in command and laughed at his jokes there was the thought that this popularity might induce squadron commanders to be less inclined to question any of Dave's plans. In trips to Ajax in connection with return to the ZI, Zemke talked with Colonel Robert Landry, a staff officer known for many years, and suggested he might like to take command of the group during his absence. There was also the thought that as the 33-year-old Landry was a staff officer the promise made to Zemke of return to the 56th was more likely to be kept than if a younger man took over temporarily. Landry was taken with the proposal and, with Kepner's approval, it was arranged for him to take the CO's position to learn the fighter pilot's trade, while Schilling continued to lead combat operations.

The bombers went to Munster on 10 October and, once more flying at around 30,000 feet, the pilots of the 56th were again able to dive on Luftwaffe fighters preparing to attack the bombers. Using proven tactics, the group was able to pick off a number of enemy fighters without loss, but a critical situation arose when short of fuel the Thunderbolts returned to find the East Anglian coastal area swathed in a mist that had rolled in off the sea. With visibility limited to about 400 yards the aircraft put down at any airfield they could find. The 62nd's Jim Jones landed on Boreham, still under construction, wrecking his P-47 in a collision with an earth mover. When information had been collected and duly assessed from eleven airfields where landings had been made, another ten victories were added to the group's total. Dave Schilling shot down an FW190 to become an ace after four consecutive missions and was the hero of the day, soon to display a scarlet lining to his flight jacket. The two Johnsons of the 61st Squadron, Gerry and Bob, were each credited with two victories. Gerry Johnson was also responsible for one of the three aircraft shot down by the group four days later, during the provision of escort for Fortresses involved in the infamous Schweinfurt raid when 60 of them were lost. Weather was poor with heavy cloud, and on return the Thunderbolts were again faced with difficulty in finding airfields with much of East Anglia completely blanketed. The 63rd Squadron was badly scattered and told by Warmsun control to fly west where conditions were a little better. John Truluck became separated and having warned control his fuel supply was near to exhaustion he was told to bale out. His response was, "Who the hell is flying this plane!" He found RAF Northolt and made a safe landing. Later Truluck was informed that General Kepner, present in the fighter wing control room, had been the person who told him to bale out and received a curt admonition. Two other pilots crash-landed when fuel was exhausted.

The weather now turned for the worse with low pressure bringing extensive cloud and a series of fronts, one upon another. Zemke led an abortive escort on the 18th when a huge cloud bank forced the group to climb to 32,000 feet. Beyond they chanced to see a lone aircraft flying north-east several thousand feet below. Because of unclear direction from their leader a whole eight-plane section of 61st Squadron followed Zemke down, six taking turns to pump bullets into the unsuspecting enemy; an over-kill put down to bad communications. In another cloud-filled sky two days later Zemke obtained the sole victory in a mission hampered by enforced short duration. With only 75-gallon capacity drop tanks available time spent defending the bombers was cut, causing the 56th's commander to vent his spleen on Ajax over the lack of 108-gallon tanks. He thought this would be his last mission before return to the USA, for having convinced LeMay and Kepner that a better understanding of fighter operations could be achieved by making a documentary film, Zemke became involved in its production. Poor weather kept the heavy bombers from further attacks until 3 November when three more victories were added to the total, but the group was still four short of the 100 pledged for Sadie Hawkins' Day, only three days away. Removed to VIII Fighter Command HQ awaiting transportation to America, Zemke saw the preparations for an escort mission to be flown to west-central Germany on the 5th. With the Sadie Hawkins Day boast as yet unfulfilled he could not resist influencing the mission planners to schedule the 56th for penetration support of B-24 Liberators going to Munster, a commitment he thought the most likely to meet opposition.

Not to lead 'the show' was more than Zemke could resist; he procured an aircraft and flew to Halesworth unannounced. Arriving as briefing was about to begin he strode up to the podium and told a surprised Dave Schilling that he, Zemke, was replacing him as the mission leader. Colonel Landry had officially taken command of the group a week earlier but did not have the experience to engage in air leadership and was scheduled to fly as a spare although, in the event, he did not participate. Schilling was not pleased by being usurped and grounded for the day, particularly when the group attained six victories to pass the 100 destroyed mark. It was decided that the 100th was the first credit for Lieutenant George Hall of the 63rd who claimed an Me 210 (actually an Me 410). Hall, of slightly smaller build than average, came from a wealthy publishing family. He was later given a silver cup to commemorate the occasion, even if by that time revision of scores made the 100th claim tenuous. That the advertised gamble of a 100 of the enemy falling to the Zemke group by Sadie Hawkins' Day met with success was noted in the press. With some 40 more victories to its credit than any other fighter group in the Eighth – and there were now eight – the 56th was elevated to the elite. Pride was now evident in all ranks, and they now began to think of themselves as 'the best fighter outfit in the ETO'. There was an impromptu party in the Officers' Club that night but the real celebration took place the following evening when the officers gave a party in appreciation of the ground crews 'who made the victory possible by keeping 'em flying'. British servicewomen were invited and there were hot-dogs a plenty. Arrangements were put in hand to have a loving cup presented to Zemke. But the chief architect of the 56th's success went back to London in preparation for returning to the States. That morning Schilling had escorted him to the local railway station and joked "to make sure you catch the darn train".

13 On and Off the Base

Sergeant Robert C. Kirschner, an administrative assistant in the 41st Service Squadron, spent hours typing out payroll submissions for payment to 300 officers and men on an English Loaner portable typewriter. The squadron's office equipment had been lost in the Atlantic when being shipped to the UK. Kirschner was the first man at Halesworth to marry an English girl.

"I met May Lockwood who was a Land Army girl working on farms around the area, rather than go into the military or do factory work. We fell in love at first sight, I at 24, May at 23, and we decided to marry. It took months of letter writing through chain of command and permission was finally granted after our CO, Major Osgood, had a good look and decided I had made a good choice. We married on November 2nd, 1943. We had a beautiful ceremony at Coddenham, Suffolk, May's home village, and Major Wells, who replaced Osgood, was at our wedding. My buddy Gene Hassmorick was best man. The boys from the camp provided plenty of cookies and a cake. The honeymoon was spent in London with May's uncle and aunt. He was a London Bobby. After London we set up a kind of hit and miss get-together until daughter Carol was born in summer of 1944. Then we rented a small house in Coddenham, near Ipswich. The house was an old run-down shelter for farm workers prior to wartime. The old farmer, Mr. Cousins, rented it this way: 'You fix it up or do what need be at no expense to me. I'll take £1 (4 US dollars) per month rent to make it legal.' This we enjoyed together until wife and daughter left to go to the US in March 1945."

Before the 56th Fighter Group and its allied units returned to the USA following the end of hostilities near a hundred of their men would marry British girls, and the majority of these relationships endured. American servicemen had a particular attraction for British women who were taken with the lack of reserve in efforts to charm. The Hollywood come-to-life aura also played a part. On the other hand, many Americans found British girls generally less demanding than the women at home. Moreover, English girls were considered aesthetically shapely. One experienced connoisseur of the female form later expounded that, "You saw more shapely legs in England than anywhere else in the western world."

As with any body of men there were those who sought women for sexual relief and the comparatively well paid GI was a target for prostitutes. In the summer the British police were approached to see off three professionals from London operating in the Halesworth and Southwold area. However there were a few locals eager to dispense their favours for free and a sudden upsurge in gonorrhoea among the enlisted men was traced to two Halesworth girls whose names and addresses were made know to personnel and declared 'off limits'. Dave Hubler:

> "Lieutenant Virgil Durrance was the 62nd Adjutant, such a nice guy; he was called Father Durrance because everyone reckoned he should have been a reverend. He had a notice put up on the bulletin board outside the orderly room that gave the names of women infected with venereal disease. Bradshaw walks up and reads this and says, 'Well damn; this outfit is pickin' up! How about this. Look, they even put up here where you can get pussy!'"

While the natural attraction of the sexes may have been a major force in contact with the indigenous population around the bases, many friendships were made at other levels. The approximate 1,700 men at Halesworth were bound to have a social impact on the sparsely populated villages in the immediate area. Both British and US military authorities encouraged get-togethers in an effort to bring some understanding of each nations' way of life. Several men at Halesworth had the opportunity to undergo specialist training courses at British institutions and in many cases lived with local families. Marty Stanton:

> "I was called in and asked by Smokey [M/Sgt Joe Krsul] if I wanted to go to London to a welding school. I went in November 1943 for six weeks. I could weld steel but aluminium was too fast for me. I lived with a family off Crest Road [NW2]. The family consisted of father, wife with a married daughter and young child. That father was a great one; when the Jerries came over he would go outside and watch until it was all over. My nerves couldn't take that. We used to go to the London baths for our weekly bath. I got to enjoy it. We had our special pub in Neasden and on Saturday Pete Bruno from the 61st and I would go to the dog track. Pete would do good and we would split so I went back to Halesworth with a few pounds."

At this time only half the homes in Britain had a bathroom and working class accommodation was often found primitive by US standards. American servicemen observed the considerable difference in the standard of living between the classes in Britain and with more class distinction than in the States. Sergeant John Brady moved in a higher stratum during his posting to a British establishment:

> "While at Halesworth I was fortunate to be selected to attend an intelligence and cryptographic program conducted at Oxford. I was able to spend several weeks in that interesting, historic area and personally

benefited greatly. The school was very secret. To disguise the activity it was established in two confiscated houses named Harbeton House and Cotuit located in Pullen Lane. I was given quarters in a private house. I was able to gain much personal edification from this experience. Training lasted through ten hour days on cryptography techniques and specifically a fantastic encoding machine which I later came to learn as Enigma. I was amazed at the arrangement of this facility. It was located in the middle of a residential area, people moved around casually all the time, but there was no outward appearance of anything unusual going on. Were this a US facility it would have been surrounded by a guarded fence with identification checks of people's comings and goings. I have one outstanding memory of the burly RAF Group Captain whose favourite expression was 'blithering idiot'. At the time I was not aware of this expletive, but found it descriptive and amusing. It remained in my memory."

While some men were eager to cycle out in the Halesworth neighbourhood, others rarely ventured from the base, finding entertainment in the leisure facilities or just sleeping, reading and writing letters home. Such was the volume of outward mail as the weather deteriorated and men were less keen to move out from their Nissen huts, that the base postal service decreed that letter writing must be reduced. The result of this pronouncement was that men protested this was their right and proceeded to write even more letters in protest until the order was withdrawn. With domestic sites separated from the communal site and recreational buildings by a fair cycle ride, inclement weather deterred men from leaving their barracks. Another pastime that absorbed some men was making models or trinkets. Sergeants Ralph Pesetski and Donald Trudell, 33rd Service Group clerks, made charm bracelets; from silver threepenny pieces bought from a bank and cleaned in an acid solution. The links would then be silver-soldered to the coins so that they could be joined together to form a bracelet with a snap catch. There were a number of versions, single band, double band and a combination thereof. The bracelets sold 'like hot cakes' and it was hard to keep up with demand. Local banks were unable to supply the large amounts of threepenny pieces sought, and probably suspected illegal use of British coinage. Pesetski and Trudell had to go to London to get coins. They also made earrings to match and set up quite a thriving business, as both trinkets were popular presents to send home.

Although the majority of the ground echelon's men had enlisted and not been drafted the building of a group esprit de corps among them took longer than with the pilots. This was in part due to a dearth of information as to the results of the frequent combat activity despite regular talks by pilots and others in authority to bring the ground men into the picture. There was much that could not be told to them for security reasons which naturally resulted in speculation. Rumour ruled supreme and the favourite topic was movement of the group or its units to another UK base, another theatre of war and, more popular, movement back to the USA. There would always be an element who had few interests outside their own welfare. This is well illustrated by the experience of Colonel Landry on leaving the base one wintry day: "I picked up several men in my car and offered to drop them wherever they were going. They didn't salute when they entered and upon questioning them they were not aware of the station commander's name!"

Unit pride had to go hand in hand with a determination to achieve the best and that was sometime lacking in certain elements of the ground echelon in the view of the fighter commanders. Zemke's displeasure with the first 33rd Service Group commander eventually led to his replacement by Major Osgood, the CO of the 41st Service Squadron. Osgood may have been extremely unpopular with his men but he evidently impressed the fighter group hierarchy. There were other changes in ground officer positions as efforts were made to reduce the number of combat abortives related to poor work by mechanics. Robert Carnachan, 63rd Engineering Officer:

"While my predecessor was a very nice guy, he attempted to micro-manage the work of 120 men reporting to him. As a result, the squadron had the worst maintenance of the three squadrons on the field. My immediate objective was to make clear to all the men that each was responsible for his own job. If he had a problem he was to take it up with his superior and, if necessary, with the next higher superior. I was only to be involved with maintenance if it required dealing with other departments of the squadron or group, or the pilots themselves. I was a fresh 23-year-old Second Lieutenant whose only training in maintenance was a 13-week mechanics'course, while a private in Texas. On the other hand, the ground crews of the 63rd had been working with the P-47 since they had first been released to the 56th fresh off the assembly line at Farmingdale. The Line Chief, M/Sgt Creagh, was age 40 with 17 years in the Air Corps and had serviced Major Hap Arnold's P-26 at March Field, California. The Hangar Chief was Master Sergeant Lanier, about the same age with 18 years in the Air Corps. Why would I be telling these men and other experienced crew chiefs and specialists what, or how, they should be doing their job? It was a rough several months at first, but things smoothed out and eventually we achieved the highest percentage of in-service planes of the three squadrons. I had a terrific group of men servicing our planes! A happy result of this was that my work load was not all that heavy and the men's morale rose along with their assumption of responsibility."

There were occasions when the maintenance and repair of aircraft and equipment were frustrated by shortages; when those in the front line at Halesworth were bitter about the bureaucracy and seeming unappre-ciativeness of urgency at supply organisations. An example is the following notation made in group records:

<u>Wings for P-47 model D-10: red tape and plenty of it.</u>
December 23: Air Corps Supply ordered from Wattisham Air Depot a set of wings for a D-10 model P-47 aircraft. The wings were classified 'Urgent repairs required.'
December 28. Wattisham teletype Burtonwood to ship us a set of wings for the D-10 model since they don't have any in stock.
December 29. Air Corps Supply teletype Wattisham that the wings were no longer classified 'Urgent repairs required' but that the classification was changed to 'Aircraft on ground.'
December 30. Wattisham notified Burtonwood on the change in classification.
December 31. Burtonwood teletype Wattisham and Air Corps Supply to say the D-10 wings were not available and that they would be obligated to this station when they were received.
Eight days of red tape and there are still no wings. Supply never seems to run out of red tape!"

Air Corps Supply was the office in the chain of command to which the group engineering officer made his request. Wattisham Air Depot handled all VIII Fighter Command first-line operational repair and modification and Burtonwood was the main air depot.

Shortages were a familiar part of the wartime scene, and particularly so with the hard-pressed British. Many of the domestic needs at USAAF bases were met from local civilian establishments where rationing appertained. As winter took hold so did the demand for solid fuel to bring warmth to the Nissen and Laing hutted accommodation. Because of shortages of coal and coke, orders were issued that no fires were to be lit until 1600 hours each day and removed ashes were to be raked over and unburnt pieces of fuel saved for reuse. The unauthorised use of wood for fires, also banned, went on just the same. Clandestine raids on local woodland kept many iron stove fires burning through the nights. The situation became critical during December when the regular coal wagon failed to arrive at Halesworth railway station. In a desperate move to overcome the situation fires were ordered to burn for only two hours each day and trucks were sent out to obtain coke from Lowestoft gas works and coal from less troubled US air stations in the area. GI ingenuity then turned to electrical heating and the acquisition of electrical fires from civilian sources with the result that in the evenings the sudden upsurge in electrical power requirements often threw out the station overload switches.

Although temperatures were never extreme, the damp chill of the English winter was hard on many Americans, especially those from the warmer, more arid states. The recreational buildings became more popular as the days shortened as, though poorly insulated and heated, a gathering of men added to the warmth. The Officers' Club at Halesworth was a large and long Nissen hut building with a row of pot-bellied coal stoves, an improvised bar and a number of tables; Schilling's was identified as the only one with a tablecloth. An assortment of easy chairs procured from local sources and wall decorations brightened the otherwise austere interior. This building was even more so the on-base gathering point for officers in the evenings. The American Red Cross opened a social centre for the enlisted men early in January 1944. Known as the Aero Club, it had a lounge plus ping-pong and billiards room. Its snack bar was the most popular feature, serving hot-dogs, doughnuts and non-alcoholic drinks.

14 Winter Battles

Following Zemke's return to the USA there was no doubt amongst other 56th Fighter Group officers that Schilling was disappointed in not being given the group command, even though he dismissed this with a joke. Although Bob Landry was the group commander, at first he relied on Schilling's advice for matters outside operational commitments. As decided, until Landry had gained experience Schilling would take the major responsibility for mission leads, alternating with squadron commanders, most frequently with Gabreski. Landry flew on operations at every opportunity, at first in an element slot and then progressed to flight and squadron leadership. Unfortunately he discovered that rapid ascent to high altitude could result in aeroembolism. Owing to their physical make-up some men were prone to 'the bends', and Landry was one of them. On one occasion after a rapid let-down he had to climb back several thousand feet and reduce altitude slowly to gain relief.

Schilling led the Ramrod mission of 7 November when little was seen of the enemy. Flight Officer Robert Sheehan, a recent replacement pilot, baled out over Holland owing to a runaway propeller which caused an engine fire. Sheehan had the distinction of being the first 56th pilot to evade capture and through the resistance network was back in England twelve weeks later. Another Ramrod four days later, with Gabreski making his first group lead, encountered enemy fighters in the clouds with claims of six for one loss. Lieutenant Malcolm Van Meter, a replacement pilot who was at first reported missing was one of the lucky ones. Fuel exhaustion on the flight back across the North Sea had forced him to take to his parachute. RAF air/sea rescue pulled him out suffering from severe exposure and shock, and he would not fly again with the 56th. The group was airborne for three hours that day and several aircraft were critically short of fuel on return. That evening there were complaints about Yardstick not ordering an earlier withdrawal. One pilot who only just managed to make it home was 2nd Lieutenant Melvin Wood, flying as Captain Les Smith's wingman. During a diving turn over the bombers an Me109 made a surprise attack on 61st Squadron's Yellow flight, coming up behind Wood's Thunderbolt and hitting it with five 20-mm shells.

"When first hit the airplane jumped and bucked and the engine stopped. As I was in a vertical dive the engine started again, but was coughing and spluttering and running very rough. I proceeded to the deck at about

Enschede and flew from there to about ten miles out into the Channel on the deck, drawing 54$\frac{1}{2}$ inches of mercury and 2,720 rpm. The engine was very rough, coughed a lot and cut out an estimate of 40 times but always momentarily. As I reached mid-Channel I had cut it back to 30 HG and 2,000 rpm. The engine was much rougher and the vibration intense. Finally I had to cut it back to 23HG and 1,400 rpm. At this speed the vibration was so intense that the pitot tube was vibrating an arc of approximately one foot and the instrument panel four inches. It was impossible to read any of the instruments and I expected the engine to disengage itself from the aircraft at any time. About ten miles from the coast the engine stopped completely when I changed tanks and I finally got it started by priming, turning the emergency fuel pressure clear on and engaging the starter. I landed at my home base with only a couple of gallons of gas."

It is not difficult to imagine Wood's apprehension and stress as he struggled to eke out the fuel with the expectation that the aircraft could disintegrate at any moment. Two 20-mm cannon shells had hit the engine cowling, exploding against the manifold and oil lines. Another exploded in the rear fuselage causing damage to the tailplane and other structure. Two more 20-mm hits severely damaged two propeller blades, the major cause of the vibration. Woods was soon back on operations but the Thunderbolt was deemed too weakened for further operational use and retired for training. The sole loss this day was Wayne O'Conner, a notable character of the 63rd. The Germans later reported he had been killed. He left a pining black mongrel dog named Slipstream, which his family wanted shipped back to the States. This was arranged but when taken to Liverpool for shipment six months later the dog got loose and was lost.

   With a good supply of both replacement pilots and aircraft available, VIII Fighter Command increased the strength of its most experienced fighter groups to enable each to despatch two formations and improve the escort presence for the Eighth's burgeoning bomber force. In consequence the 56th received an additional 30 P-47s in mid-November; its authorised holding was advanced from 75 to 108. In addition to more pilots an additional 33 mechanics were assigned to each squadron to handle the new intake, with many 'old hand' assistant crew chiefs becoming full crew chiefs to meet the expansion. The new Thunderbolts, P-47D-10 and D-11 models, had marked improvements, not least the full plumbing for water injection, which when implemented would allow an extra 300 hp to be drawn from the engine for a brief period and boost performance. Installing water injection equipment on the earlier P-47 models was a difficult task requiring some 200 hours per aircraft. Several of the group's experienced pilots took over the new models and passed their old aircraft for use by newcomers.

   Since the summer there had been interest in using the P-47 to carry a bomb, and Zemke had encouraged this with a view to attacking targets such as enemy coastal airfields on days when the group was not called to fly bomber support. The B7 shackles fitted to the Thunderbolts in late summer for use with drop tanks were actually designed for bomb-carrying. This led to discussions about mimicking the bombers' formations drops. Schilling, keen to pursue this idea, persuaded Landry to approach Ajax to allow an experimental mission. The plan was to borrow the use of a B-24 Liberator and crew from the nearby 93rd Bomb Group to lead a bomb-carrying P-47 formation. When the B-24 sighted and released bombs the P-47 pilots would release theirs, hopefully achieving a good concentration on the target. After practice missions, using a range off the Norfolk coast, Schilling was confident enough to propose to Landry that a trial combat mission could be run; this despite some misgivings among those involved in the practice drops about reducing flying speed to stay with the B-24 and hence their vulnerability to flak. One of the practise missions had resulted in the loss of Harry Coronios, the innocent in the King's Cliffe poker games. His P-47 was one of a four-plane flight that encountered severe icing in letting down through several thousand feet of high cloud. It is supposed that Coronios lost control and perished in the North Sea.

The experimental mission was run on 25 November with the airfield at St Omer/Longuenesse the target. A total of 53 P-47s took off from Halesworth each carrying a 500-lb HE (high explosive) bomb on the belly shackles. The B-24 was late and the joining formations did not have time to become as compact as desired before reaching the target. The Liberator bombardier's release was delayed and as far as could be ascertained most bombs landed beyond the airfield boundary and no damage was done to the military installation. For the pilots trying not to over-run the B-24 with landing gear lowered and one-third flaps, their position was made precarious by intense anti-aircraft fire. After a close burst John Truluck of the 63rd was convinced his P-47 had been hit and the engine was running rough. Additionally flight controls suddenly seemed heavy. Thinking that if the wheels were retracted he might never get them down again if the hydraulic system was holed, Truluck flew all the way back to Halesworth with the gear extended. He had no problem in landing and after parking expected his crew chief, Sergeant Jim Walker, to remark on the battle damage but none was to be seen. Eventually Walker found a tiny splinter hole in a wheel door that would have had no effect on the aircraft's performance. The supposed rough engine and heavy controls were figments of Truluck's imagination induced by fearfulness. Truluck was one of the early replacement pilots in the 63rd. Of average height, lean with angular nose and prominent ears, he was known for a sharp intellect and speaking his mind. A competent pilot, the following day he shot an FW190 off another pilot's tail, and the 56th again furthered its standing in VIII Fighter Command.

That day the 56th was tasked to provide withdrawal support for B-17s coming from an attack on Bremen. Sufficient 108-gallon drop tanks were on hand to provide a good duration. Schilling was to lead and fly with the 61st Squadron. When the 62nd pilots went to collect their parachutes and flight gear from the storeroom Walter Cook found a black cat asleep on his pack. He brushed the animal off and it promptly moved onto Craig's parachute and then Schilling's – although with group HQ Schilling still kept his equipment with the 62nd. After a reluctance to move from the parachute rack it was shooed out through the doorway, not without some curt observations about people befriending animals and letting them roam around. No one made observations about black cats being lucky but the thought is said to have crossed minds.

Climbing to 30,000 feet the bombers were seen to be under attack from the rear by twin-engine fighters employing cannon fire and rockets. The Luftwaffe had a top cover of single-engine fighters to aid the Me110s but as these were involved with P-38s on the far side of the bombers, Schilling let all three of his squadrons enter the fray. In the ensuing battle some twenty of the Me110s went down but not without a dozen of the P-47s sustaining bullet damage from Messerschmitt rear gunners. Lieutenant Byron 'Fats' Morrill's aircraft, hit in the main fuel tank, started losing gasoline at a high rate. Morrill, who was a big man, hence his nickname, had to bale out to be made prisoner, the only loss of the day against the group's claims of 26 enemy fighters. This was a record for one mission for one group up to that time, although the total was later reduced to 23. Four of these were single-engine fighters which arrived on the scene too late to prevent the decimation of the Zerstörer unit, ZG 26, at the hands of the 56th. Captain Eugene O'Neill brought home solid evidence of his kill.

"An Me110 exploded under my fire and pieces of the enemy plane struck mine putting gouges in the leading edge of the left wing and a large piece of control cable, about 20 feet long, wrapped itself around the rudder and horizontal tail surface. I didn't notice at the time as my wingman and I then attacked an FW190 which we thought was about to go after the bombers. After the engagement, on the way across the North Sea to Halesworth, I noticed the stick moving back and forth. So looking around I saw that the enemy's control cable was lifting up and down across the elevator in the slipstream causing the unusual movement. As a result the tail required repairs and changes, but despite all this I still flew my entire tour in the same aircraft. It was a great ship which I named for my wife, the 'Jessie O'. I landed with the control cable still wrapped around the tail and the guys made bracelets for their wives and mine, cutting it in small pieces and soldering on little silver four-leaf clovers cut out of sixpence coins. We sent these little rough bracelets to our wives in the States as souvenirs."

Three of the Me110s fell to the guns of Bud Mahurin's Thunderbolt, raising his score to ten and making him the leading ace of the group.

Gabreski accounted for two but returned with battle damage. Among the other victors were Schilling, Cook and Craig who that evening decided that black cats were indeed lucky. The animal was thereafter encouraged to take up residence in the parachute room, with Schilling providing a soft pillow and a saucer of milk. Sixteen pilots had scored that day and Schilling had all out on the taxiway to link arms in a pose for the public relations camera.

The group's success brought an impromptu party; in fact, there was an upsurge of parties as the days grew shorter and the weather more unpleasant. Under Schilling's influence the parties became a little wilder but Landry did not seem to object. With his genial demeanour Schilling may have hidden personal stress, if so his relief was through fun. It was often sought off base where he continually added to his contacts, not least the opposite sex. Dark-haired, well built and reasonably good-looking, with his charm he was a natural draw to women and the fact that he was married with a family was no bar to indulging his desires. His upper-class friends the Vannecks were often invited to Officers' Club functions and the mutual attraction between the gorgeous Mrs Britter Venneck and Schilling was evident. This did not seem to trouble Andrew Venneck who was known to go up to London with Schilling for joint enjoyment of the metropolis. There were times when Schilling caroused a little too much in the Officers' Club, and times when he was perhaps a little unruly in view of the position he held, particularly when he appeared in a tartan kilt. Captain Eugene O'Neill:

"Coming back by train from London after a leave, Bob Taylor and I got in a First Class compartment and a little later this British officer came in with us. Bob had a bottle of gin in his knapsack and invited this British officer for a drink. By the time we finished the bottle we had become pretty good friends . The 'Brit', a Lt Colonel, was still on the train when we dropped off at Halesworth. He invited us up to his outfit. It turns out he was the commander of a Black Watch regiment battalion. When we got back to base we told Schilling about it. He said, 'Hell, invite those guys down here'. So we did, and they came down in their kilts and we had a party for them. Next thing you knew everybody was so stinking drunk and some of our guys were going around with kilts. We became pretty good friends with them. They were stationed just north of our base."

With the influx of new fighter groups at this time there were frequent demands for experienced personnel to aid newcomers. VIII Fighter Command's strength had increased to nine P-47 and two P-38 groups by the end of November 1943 and IX Fighter Command, the fighter air element of the USAAF tactical air support for the forthcoming cross-Channel invasion of Europe, had many groups arriving or scheduled; one was equipped with the new Merlin-engine P-51B Mustang, which was soon to become operational, initially under Ajax control. The 56th had to part with some ground officers and men on a permanent basis and it was also asked to loan specialist personnel to the newcomers. Brigadier General Jesse Auton, who commanded the 65th Fighter Wing, decided the recently operational 356th Fighter Group at Martlesham Heath would benefit from the leadership of an experienced combat pilot and selected Gerry Johnson, one of the 56th's most competent aces. Johnson was not happy about his orders but was told this was a temporary exchange with one of the 356th pilots and that he would eventually return to Halesworth.

The next few missions saw tough fighting and more losses. On 1 December for three confirmed claims three pilots were shot down, one being Vance Ludwig who had been the first man to have three victories on a single mission. Gabreski's P-47 was shot up by a Me110 which made several rifle calibre hits in the wings and engine, severely reducing power. Lieutenant Norman Brooks, leading the element in Gabby's flight, shepherded his leader to the coast and then encountered trouble with the electrical propeller pitch. He called Yardstick (Gabreski) saying: "My prop is out, I am going down to 10,000 feet and bale out." Gabby asked him his position and Brooks replied, "I am over the continent." Gabby called; "Somebody give a Mayday," (the alert to air/sea rescue), following this with a message to control: "Keyworth 63 is just over Dunkirk. His prop is out. He cannot do anything about it." Then he called Brooks: "Good luck, see you in a week. Thanks a lot for taking me up to the coast. God bless you." At lower altitude the propeller controls of Brooks' aircraft functioned and he did not have to jump. Meanwhile Gabreski managed to fly his damaged aircraft safely across the sea to land at the Wattisham repair depot. That evening Colonel Landry, who had led a flight on the mission, celebrated his 34th birthday.

Another successful mission on 11 December resulted in 16 credits for no loss in combat. The success was marred by the collision of the two wingmen in the 61st Squadron's Yellow flight during a cross-over turn to position for an attack on a formation of Me110s. Lieutenants Larry Strand and Ed Kruer were both killed. On penetrating enemy airspace at 30,000 feet the 62nd Squadron was bounced from above by Me109s which had obviously been detailed to intercept to cause the P-47s to release their drop tanks and thus restrict their range. Fortunately the approach of the enemy fighters was seen and the 62nd turned to meet them. Schilling ordered the rest of the group to continue to rendezvous with the bombers where both single and twin-engine enemy fighters were found to have them under attack. Once again superior altitude, surprise and good air discipline paid off; 11 of the victories were Me110s, the second mauling ZG26 had received from the 56th. Also, for the third time in six sorties, Gabreski's aircraft had been shot up. Since his assigned aircraft had been damaged he had taken over that of Milton Anderson, an original combat pilot, who had recently been transferred to fly for a ferrying unit. Gabby was fortunate not to be wounded as a 20-mm fragment took a piece out of the right rudder pedal.

Colonel Landry progressed to a squadron lead and in this position shot down his first and only enemy fighter, an Me109 on the 11 December mission. He headed the group for the first time on the 20th, when there was the loss of a popular 62nd pilot and an unusually high number of abortives. Eugene O'Neill:

"Bob Taylor was from California. A big old teddy bear of a guy. As we were going through contrails over Holland he noticed the fuel was running real low. Couldn't get rid of his baby and we could see that fuel was siphoning out for some reason or other. I sent him back with my element leader Mike Quirk. He got too low, ran out of fuel some ten miles from the coast and instead of baling out he ditched it. It hit a big swell and went in. Quirk had called air/sea rescue but why Taylor didn't bale out we don't know. Hell of a nice guy. We really missed him. His brother had been shot down on the low-level Ploesti raid in a B-24. Survived although burned. Bob Taylor would kid me about my boots. My wife had given me a pair of Abercrombie & Fitch, a pretty classy place in New York. I used to shine them a lot. Old Bob said, 'Man, when you get shot down I get those boots.' We all think it is going to be the other guy."

Another boost to P-47 performance was forthcoming in late December with batches of the group's aircraft being flown to the Wattisham depot so that new 'paddle blade' propellers could be fitted, a fairly quick task. The first to have been equipped was 62nd Squadron and all first-line Thunderbolts had them by the end of the month. The wide blade propellers gave an improved rate of climb in the rarefied air at high altitude, although some pilots thought they caused some vibration.

No doubt feeling that his time in command of the 56th was limited, Bob Landry made a point of leading all the remaining missions of the year despite the risk of experiencing discomfort at high altitude. On the 30th the group lingered too long in escorting B-17s back from Ludwigshafen. Fred Christensen's P-47 ran dry on approach to Leiston airfield, and elsewhere after 3 hours 10 minutes in the air there was many a 'near thing' for the same reason. At the mission launch that morning Lieutenant Isadore Porowski's aircraft didn't become airborne and went over on its back when the main wheels sunk into the wet ground off the end of the runway. The story goes that Father John McGettigan accompanied the crash crew to the rescue. While they prepared to lift the inverted Thunderbolt, he bent down, scrapped some of the soil away that was covering the cockpit glazing and looked in. He was greeted with: "Don't stand there, you son of a bitch. Get me outa here!" When the rescuers finally lifted the aircraft and released Porowski they asked him if he realised who he had sworn at. Feeling somewhat guilty Porowski walked over to the chaplain and apologised. McGettigan responded: "If

I'd have been trapped in there I'd have used far worse language than that!"

The last day of the year, when the bombers went to attack targets on the French Atlantic seaboard, the 56th flew south across England to provide withdrawal support. Leading Keyworth Red flight was Les Smith:

"We had climbed up quite high, close to 30,000 feet. We were about to make landfall over the Brest peninsula when Marengello, flying Red 4, suddenly aileron-rolled left over me and my wingman and went into a dive. I thought right away anoxia. I told the others to carry on and followed him down, yelling on the radio hoping he'd hear. He never pulled out and went straight into the water. He was an older kid, steady. I liked flying with him."

The overriding problem with oxygen starvation was that the victim did not usually know it was happening until too late. Failure could be due to several reasons, one had recently been highlighted. During a mission Truluck noticed that his oxygen supply was severely depleted and found the setting was Full Rich. The lever should have been set in the Automatic Lean position. Talking this over with his crew chief, Truluck found that when he reached up to operate the engine priming his elbow caught the oxygen regulator lever. He had Sergeant Walker move the position of the regulator control ten to twelve inches forward. When his P-47 was sent to the depot to have a paddle blade prop fitted the aircraft was returned with the regulator control back in the original position and a report went to 56th Engineering about unauthorised placement of the regulator. Truluck had it moved forward again. After some disagreement about this with the 63rd's engineering officer, Schilling called Truluck in and asked him what all the fuss was about. When told, Schilling sided with Truluck and had the control repositioned on his personal P-47. Truluck was asked to write a report on the matter for forwarding to the service command.

The day's action on the year end mission dispersed the group, when the return to England was fraught by extensive cloud. William 'Sam' Aggers:

"I was flying No 4 in Colonel Landry's flight. As we flew north the weather was forcing us to fly lower and lower to stay in ground contact conditions. Eventually the Colonel called all flights to go up through the weather, which meant each flight was on its own flying on instruments. When flying on instruments in flight formation only the leader is on instruments. The No. 2 and No. 3 men fly eyes on the leader and No. 4 man flies watching No. 3. Shortly after going on instruments No. 3 lost sight of the leader in the gloom. This caused him to make some violent moves as he established himself on instruments. In an effort to stay with him my airplane went into a spin. I tried to recover from the spin but there was not enough altitude. As I saw 1,200 feet on my altimeter, I pulled the canopy back and went over the side. Clearing the overcast, I could see my airplane directly under me burning. Luckily it landed in an open field and near Maidenhead and caused no injury or damage. After I landed and wrapped up my chute I was approached by a member of the Home Guard. He took me to his house, gave me hot tea and contacted the local airfield. Following this incident I developed a phobia about flying in weather; couldn't make myself fly on instruments; and if you cannot fly instruments over England where there's weather more often than not your dead. It really upset me because flying was all I wanted. Went through a really tough period until I conquered this fear. Les Smith, my flight leader, took me up and made me fly off his wing through cloud and more or less helped me get over this phobia. He did the most to bring me back."

The danger of becoming disorientated was ever present in the long climbs or descents through several thousand feet of cloud where visibility was often severely limited. There had been and would be many cases of vertigo and spin-outs, some fatal.

Sam Aggers did not get back to Halesworth until next day, as did most 63rd Squadron pilots on the 31 December mission who, off course on the way home, had to land at Exeter and Gatwick in the west and south. These pilots missed out on the New Year's Eve party to which WAAF, ATS, WRNS and other British women had been invited. Because of the late hour arrangements were made to move the officers sleeping in Holton Hall to other accommodation and turn this old mansion over to the girls for the night. They were to be gone next morning and Colonel Landry was not happy about those who were encouraged to linger on late the next day. He felt the regime at Halesworth a little too relaxed and tried to bring more military order. Noting that ambulances were seen frequently on base roads he surmised they were being used for clandestine journeys, presumably because they were unlikely to be stopped and searched by guards. Even Doc Horning, the 61st's Flight Surgeon, had been privy to extracting one pilot's girlfriend from the station this way.

Pressing operational problems arose for Landry as, with the increase in pilot and aircraft strength, VIII Fighter Command was inaugurating the despatch of two separate formations by the group on selected missions. Each formation, to be known as A and B, would have three instead of four 4-plane flights. There was the question of formation leadership, the use of radio communications and additional call signs for the B group formation. The increased pilot complement had led to some imbalance as the inexperienced were nearly as many as the experienced. It was thought among the old hands that the replacement pilots were not so well trained as earlier intakes, despite a few weeks' initiation at the Atcham OTU (Operational Training Unit) base where theatre indoctrination was given. From the receipt of the first replacement combat pilots back in the spring of 1943 they had been given both flight and ground instruction by the

56th before being despatched on operations. Tutors were the experienced pilots on the days when there were no combat missions. Because of misgivings about some of the recent influx, the group had set up its own transitional school with a programme to instruct and test each newcomer. Ideally, each trained for three weeks before being allowed to fly combat.

Probably the greatest problem was the newcomers' limited experience in instrument flying, as Aggers had found; this was essential for negotiating the frequent extensive overcast conditions of the north European winter. Frequently soon after take-off a squadron formation had to climb through cloud for 10,000 or 20,000 feet before breaking out into the clear. In such conditions it was necessary for tight flight formations, the leader endeavouring to keep the flight ahead in view through the gloom and his flight pilots keeping a tight watch on him. Even experienced pilots could become lost in such circumstances. An example of this occurred on 4 January when Postgate Yellow, the trailing flight of 63rd Squadron, set out to provide cover for B-17s coming back from Ludwigshafen. Soon after take-off 2nd Lieutenant Harold Matthews, on his first mission and flying wingman to the Yellow flight leader John Vogt, had belly tank trouble and aborted. His place was taken by 2nd Lieutenant Anthony Cavello, flying as a spare. Emerging from the cloud Vogt saw a squadron formation at some distance, only to find on joining that it was a different P-47 group. Continuing with this formation Postgate Yellow found it was making for the Paris area to escort B-24s. Somehow Cavello, who had been flying with the 56th for three months, got separated and lost after encountering what he believed were three Me109s. He became completely disorientated and way out over the North Sea, ending up, fuel almost exhausted, on a grass aerodrome at Woolsington, a few miles from the coast north of Newcastle, about 220 miles north of Halesworth!

The first A and B group mission was run on 11 January 1944 when the Eighth's bombers carried out a major raid on industrial targets in central Germany. The A group went to give penetration support to B-17s going to Oschersleben and B group took off nearly fifty minutes later to cover B-17s going to Brunswick. The B group, led by Gabreski saw no action. A group led by Schilling saw plenty. It was the introductory mission for 19-year-old 2nd Lieutenant Carl Hayes flying wingman to the leader of Keyworth Blue flight, Captain James Carter:

"I was flying with A group for my first mission. We took off and needless to say I had very ambivalent feelings. A little bit worried, not knowing what to expect. We climbed through overcast to rendezvous with the bombers as planned. We were at about 30,000 feet; our squadron was flying high right on the bombers and I was on the right side. I looked up and saw some 30 little dots, bogeys, and I alerted the squadron. Next thing they had turned into Me109s. I could barely say 'Bandit': I was stuttering I was so scared. The flight leader said tuck it

in and stay close, so I did. I was glued to him. He couldn't have shaken
me off if he'd had to. He went down on two enemy planes and he told me
to take one. This one immediately took off diving for the deck. I opened
fire just before he entered the clouds and saw hits. The flight leader told
me to come on back up. I didn't realise until later that I'd swallowed my
gum that I'd been chewing to keep my ears cleared when this action
started."

Hayes was awarded a damage claim in the A group's total of 12
destroyed, 2 probables and 5 damaged; all were single-engine fighters.
The most notable performance was by 1st Lieutenant Glen 'Guss'Schiltz
who for the second time was credited with triple kills on one sortie. His
account:

"The first batch of Germans I saw included about 75 FW190s and
Me109s. I led my flight of P-47s at the first group of about 20 Me109s.
They were flying tight, but we got in and I shot the leader off first. He
nosed over and I gave him a burst in the belly tank and he blew up like a
firecracker. The fool who was flying his wing just sat there watching, so
I gave him a few bursts too and he blew up. I guess there were more
Germans in one spot that day than I've seen since starting my combat
operations in April. After we broke up the Me109 crowd, I saw a single
Jerry attacking a struggling Fort, so I went down and he repeated what
the others did. I guess good old American calibre point fifties affect them
all the same way. When my bullets first hit this fellow he nosed up,
exposing the belly tank, so I gave him a few there and he blew up."

Schiltz later made passes at two more 190s: "I was going too fast. My
ship slipped right by them without doing any damage."
   Schiltz's wingman was another pilot on his first mission, 2nd
Lieutenant Lloyd Langdon, who commented: "It was more action than I
expected. I stuck on Schiltz's wing like a baby chick to its mother."
Schiltz was reckoned to be a quiet individual by some with a touch of
arrogance by others. Married, his newly acquired P-47D-11 model was
named Pam, for his year-old daughter. These would be his last victory
credits with the 56th.
   The wingman's task in covering the leaders of their element was well
performed by greenhorns Hayes and Langdon. The day's score had been
obtained without loss; once again this was the result of good tactics, in
having one squadron, in this case the 62nd A, at higher altitude to cover
the Schilling-led 61st which was carrying out most of the interceptions.
Good leadership and air discipline had again paid off. With each of the
major successes there was a growing confidence among the group's
seasoned pilots, an increasing belief in their superiority. With the over
700 US fighters now available to provide escort and support for the
bombers the Luftwaffe was near to becoming overwhelmed, despite
concentrating some two-thirds of its interceptors in the west to meet the

American daylight intrusions. As the destruction of B-17s and B-24s was the main objective of the Jagdverband, to some extent the Me109s and FW190 pilots were vulnerable to the American fighter groups which, knowing the enemy's intention, could position themselves in advance to intercept. With the arrival of P-51B Mustangs on the scene, range would soon cease to be the critical factor in escort, for the Mustang had internal tankage giving a radius of action of near 400 miles. With drop tanks it had the potential to go anywhere the bombers were likely to go. So impressed was General Kepner with the Mustang that plans were made to re-equip most of his fighter groups when production allowed. As the most successful group the 56th could have been an early convert but its senior pilots (predominantly Dave Schilling) somewhat heady with achievement, preferred to stay with the Thunderbolt.

Next day, 12 January, the word went round the Officers' Club that Zemke was back. But he wasn't. The situation was confused. Ajax informed Landry that Zemke had returned and that Landry was being re-assigned as of that day to Eighth Air Force HQ. Lt Colonel Schilling would hold temporary command until Zemke arrived. Meanwhile there was a problem, for while Kepner had promised Zemke that he could have his group back it transpired that Hub was being accused of going absent without leave. Apparently, although having written orders to return, Zemke was informed on the quiet that General Hunter, running a fighter training force, was going to arrange for Zemke to be reassigned to his command in the US. This sounded like a desk job to Zemke, the last thing he wanted. Finding a transport aircraft bound for the UK he left in a hurry. Hunter was not pleased and immediately communicated what he viewed as a disregard of orders to the Eighth Air Force command. Zemke pleaded innocence and referred to his written orders and promise of return to his group. General Kepner sent him off to Edinburgh until the matter had been resolved. What occurred was unknown to Zemke until seven days later when Kepner simply told him to get back to Halesworth. It can be assumed as Kepner thought Zemke his best fighter commander that he took Zemke's part with Generals Doolittle (who had recently taken command of the Eighth Air Force from Eaker) and Spaatz, the senior US air force man in the UK. It was rumoured that Hunter considered this a court martial case.

In the meantime Schilling, probably hoping Zemke would not come back to the 56th, consolidated his position by removing Gabreski from command of the 61st Squadron (having put him forward for promotion to Lt Colonel) and transferred to group headquarters with the title of Flight Executive and Operations Officer. The former Operations Officer, Major James Stewart, took over the command of the 61st. Gabreski was not particularly comfortable with this. His relationship with Schilling was cordial but they were completely different personalities with little in common other than being aggressive and skilful fighter pilots. Gabreski was verbose and opinionated, even though his opinions were mostly sound. Deeply religious, he attended Mass with the Catholic chaplain every day and acted as his altar boy. Gerry Johnson:"Gabby wasn't at the bar after a tough mission when most of us were there flying the mission with our hands." On leave, Gabreski mostly went to spend time with the Polish friends he had made while serving with the RAF. True to his fiancée, he had no obvious interest in the local girls. This was in contrast to the popular, charismatic Schilling, who loved wine, women and song, and was out to enjoy himself at every opportunity.

15 George Goldstein's Story

Several weeks, sometimes months, passed before the fate of the group's missing pilots was known. For a few no word was received from German sources and in these cases there was hope that some had managed to evade capture. Lieutenant William Grosvenor, who went down in Belgium on 30 November, was the second 56th pilot to be helped by brave civilians to elude the enemy. The group's successful evaders were few, although many were the attempts to avoid capture. One of the most remarkable experiences in this connection was that of Lieutenant George Goldstein when an uncontrollable propeller pitch forced his bale-out in France on 5 December.

"The last squadron dance I attended I was responsible, with the help of the Red Cross, for bringing in about a hundred girls. One of our boys had too much drink and I was asked to take his place on the following day's mission. I was scheduled for leave and for taking Dauphin's place I was offered a five-day pass instead of a three-day pass. I had a brand new plane but it hadn't finished being slow-timed and the guns hadn't been test-fired, so I had to leave it and take my old plane. It had more time than any other in the squadron. When I took off my prop' was surging badly, I really should have aborted, but to abort was almost a sin. You felt guilty and people looked askance at you. However, when the bombers we were to escort were in sight, I decided I couldn't finish the mission. I called Gabby Gabreski who was leading the group that day. He told me to take my wingman with me. My wingman's name was Kelley and he stayed with me to the coast, but even in manual now my prop' was acting up and I was losing power. Then I got an electrical fire and I had to bale out. I inverted to bale out and hit one of my legs on the tailplane and cut it badly. I was above clouds when I baled out.

"When I got to the ground I had the misfortune to land on a cow. That hurt my back. Farmers who had seen me come down appeared and took my 'chute and some of my equipment away from me. They told me to run. I started to run but until then I didn't realise my leg was hurt and could see blood coming through my flying suit. I headed for a haystack and hid. I stayed there quite some time. I saw a farmer come out to use his privy and when he was inside I went and blocked the door and let him know I was an American airman, I was armed and needed help. He was quick to convey to me he would help me and with the few French words I had he seemed to understand. When I let him out of the privy, he told me to follow him and we went on up to the house. He first looked at my leg, cleaned it up a little and put a temporary bandage on it. He had some soup on his stove and I had not eaten since early that morning and it was now afternoon and he joined me in having some hot soup. He got me comfortable sitting by a wood fire stove in the kitchen, then indicated for me to wait there and he would be back in a little while. It seemed a long time but he finally came back and with him was another man. This other man wanted to see my dog tags and he wanted some identification, made some notes and indicated for me to stay where I was.

"That night the man came back accompanied by another person who was introduced as a doctor. No name was given and he made it known that he was happy to help me as he was Jewish as I was Jewish. He explained that I must not know anyone's name because if I was caught and mentioned names it could mean their death sentence. He cleaned and bandaged my leg. The man who had originally come to identify me let me know he had already heard from London by radio that they were satisfied I was who I said I was and would help me. He said you must stay here with the farmer and you will hear from us soon. That night the farmer put me upstairs in a feather bed and let me know that he had lost his wife several years ago and had nothing to lose; he hated the Germans and would do anything he could to defeat them. I thanked him and went to bed early that night. A few days later I was beginning to get impatient and made this known to the farmer who was befriending me. He said he couldn't do anything until he heard from others. That evening there was a knock on the door and it was a policeman. I thought I was about to be arrested. He was the only one in this little village, which I believe was St Sauflieu, about six miles south of Amiens. He said come with me and that I was being moved to another house. He had a bicycle for me. The three of us set off, the farmer, the gendarme and myself. We went through a village with high walls to this house where there were several couples waiting. They were throwing a party in my honour. They drank to France, to America, to my fellow airmen. They served some cookies, wine and brandy. Eventually the gendarme indicated that I should follow him.

"We went outside in the dark and I followed him on his cycle. We went past some German troops but no one stopped us. I was taken to his house and there I met his wife, an attractive lady. She wanted to make me feel at home. Sat me down in her husband's easy chair and had me put my bad leg up on a stool. We sat and talked for awhile. They spoke little or no English like I spoke little or no French. We were sitting there with dictionaries carrying on something of a conversation. Eventually everybody got tired of this and I was shown to a bed. Next morning I heard the gendarme and his wife talking and him say goodbye and the door close. After a little while the wife comes up with a tray. I told her I would get up and come down for breakfast but she said no I've brought your breakfast up. She sat there while I ate, smiling. I felt kind of stupid because I couldn't converse with her. We seemed to manage to be able to make ourselves understood. It wasn't much of a conversation. She left after awhile, indicating she had something to do downstairs. In a little while she comes back and I had gotten up and started to dress myself. She wanted to help me and did but she was a little more than friendly for someone else's wife. Kept sitting next to me helping to put my clothes on. She indicated for me to come downstairs and keep warm by the fire. It was roughly the middle of December and it was pretty cold out. So I sat by the fire and it wasn't long before she'd finished her house cleaning before she pulled a chair up along side me and had a dictionary in her hand. And she looks up a word and it's 'love'. So I say, 'Yes, I love everybody.' And pretty soon it's clear to me what she had in mind. I told her no we shouldn't be doing anything like that, you're a married woman and I'm taking advantage of being in your house and I can't do that. She was quite persistent to the extent that she was making it clear that if I didn't she could turn me in for the reward she could get for me. She may have been joking but my excuse is I wasn't taking any chances. We made love. This went on for the better part of a week. As soon as her husband would leave she would want to get in bed. And I couldn't wait to get out of this situation because I was so afraid that if her husband came back and caught us in the act I would never see the end of this war. I'd be killed by a friendly bullet.

"Anyhow, one evening when he came home he told me we were going somewhere. Again we got our bicycles and went down the road a bit. He led the way into a field and near a tree there was a small truck with an enclosed body on it. The driver was obviously known to the gendarme. We folded the bicycles, they were the type that folded so one wheel was on top of the other, and they had me get in the back of the truck then they closed the doors. Next thing I knew we were off down the road and soon we were on a hard surface road but I had no idea where we were going. Eventually we stopped at a house and went in. These were friends who I was introduced to and we drank toasts all round. We left and continued on towards Amiens. I couldn't see where we were going but we went over a cobblestone street and when we stopped I could hear a train in the background so we must have been somewhere near a station. It was night and I couldn't see a thing. They knocked on the door and it was opened by a little old lady. I couldn't see in because, as I found out later , there were curtains behind the door that kept out the light. We went in through the curtains. This was Madame Vignon Tellier.

"Madame Vignon Tellier was in charge of the Somme sector of the French underground. She was, I guess, in her sixties, small and rather obese. Very stern on first introductions and apparently all business. But I soon found that she had a heart bigger than you could imagine. She carried an automatic pistol in her apron pocket and after being introduced my gendarme friend and his friend left. She spoke fairly good English, we were able to converse easily and she was most hospitable. She redressed my injured leg. Wanted to know if I'd had any supper and I had not. We sat down and had something to eat. Hot soup, bread. She shared whatever she had but there wasn't much in the house. Next day she introduced me to her grandchildren when they came over. The boy was Claude and the sister Lily. They would come over after school and Lily was a great help in teaching me a little French. We all got along very well. She had a walled-in garden behind her house which gave me a chance to get fresh air. As Madame Vignon headed the resistance in the area it appeared that everything was planned in her house. She arranged for forged documents and knew about all these activities. The Germans had taken her husband away during the First World War and she hated the Germans. I became quite attached to her during the weeks I spent there and came to call her 'Mama Deuxieme' and she really was a second mother. I was anxious to leave but she tried to persuade me to wait for the invasion: 'Let them come to you.' She said she was afraid for me and that if they catch you they will probably shoot you because you're Jewish. She really had an interest in my wellbeing but I told her it was my duty to try to get back. So she planned an escape for me by way of a fishing boat which would rendezvous with a British boat in the Channel. However, the night I was ready to go a message came that the people who had the fishing boat had been arrested. Of course, I was very disappointed. Madame Vignon again tried to persuade me stay but agreed to find another escape route for me.

"One night a man arrived with a manual that showed the cockpit layout of an FW190. He made it known that there was a ground crew engineer married to a French girl who had persuaded him to become involved in letting me steal a plane. He was to pretend that he had been knocked out by me on the taxiway when the plane was on its way to the place it was normally kept in the evening. I was assured that this was genuine. So I familiarised myself with the cockpit layout, where all the controls were. Someone had converted the metric to imperial measures for me. I felt confident to fly the plane. I put everything to memory in a very short period of time. This was right after the Christmas celebration. Madame Vignon had a little party at her house. Her son John who worked in the town and his wife plus their two children whom I knew, they were there. There was also another young lady and a neighbour who was a professor of something. Most of these people only identified themselves by first names. Everybody had brought something and we had a nice dinner, sort of a farewell dinner in my honour. The next night I went with this young lady who came to the dinner on bicycles to this farm near this airport. We checked in with the people there, then she and I secreted ourselves near the taxi strip where this plane was to taxi by slowly and where I was to overcome the mechanic and from that position take off right across the field. We waited and waited and no plane showed up. Finally the farmer where we had left out bicycles, he comes out and finds us where we were hiding under some bushes. He let us know that the plane had not been flown so the mechanic didn't have to service it. The plane would not be going by where we were and there would be no reason to have the plane running.

"We went back to the farm and spent the night and next day we went back on our bicycles to Madame Vignon's. This young lady appeared again on the last night before the first of the year. She said she was spending the night here, supposedly she was going to sleep downstairs but she slipped upstairs and she had put warm bricks in my bed to warm it. When I had gone to bed and the lights were out and Madame Vignon had long since gone to bed, this girl comes up and slips into bed with me. We had an adventurous night. Next day I knew I was leaving. I had some French money in my escape kit and I gave some of it to Lily and told her to buy something for Madame Vignon as a going away present. She came back with some little statuette. Madame Vignon put on her bluff face; it was a statue of Apollo. I had no idea what she was going to get but I told her to get something Madame Vignon would like. I don't know whether she liked it or not but she did put it on display. A couple of days after New Year's Day Madame Vignon gave me my new identification with a photo from my escape kit affixed to it. She coached me on how to handle myself on the trains, to travel in that part where working people would travel with livestock and chickens. Before I had left the train station for Paris, a lady sat next to me. She said something to me and I just nodded, I didn't say anything. But despite my beret and civilian clothes she figured out I wasn't French. I think she guessed I was an escaping airman. She then said to me if anyone comes, sit still and I'll do the talking. Sure enough it wasn't long before the conductor came through with some man in uniform. They asked for identification and she must have said she was seeing me to Paris as I wasn't very well and couldn't talk much. I guess it satisfied them.

"I got off at the station I'd been given which was on the outskirts of the city. I was met by two French ladies, one was small and elderly, the other of average height and younger. They took me to their apartment. The plumbing was the kind where you have to stand on a couple of treadles to do whatever you have to do. We had something to eat and talked a little bit, then I went with the younger lady to her home. We went by the metro and she lived on the fifth floor in an apartment near the Eiffel tower. She lived with her husband, infant baby and grandparents. It was rather congested but they gave me a room that was hidden behind a bookcase. To get into the room you had to get down on your hands and knees to go through a couple of cupboard doors under the bookcase. She let me know that if anyone knocked on the door I was immediately to go close myself in the little room. This went on for awhile. These were lovely people, they were taking a terrible risk having me in their apartment and I knew it. Their name was something like Larmay. They took me to a football game and I went out walking with them and this gave me concern. They said don't worry; we wouldn't introduce you to anybody who would cause a problem. Well, somewhere along the line they didn't know one of their friends because on the day before I was to leave with a guide to go over the Pyrenees into Spain the Gestapo walked in and I was captured. They marched me down the stairs and they took the grandmother with them. When I got down the stairs there was a big black Mercedes. Inside were four women; one of them was the tiny lady I'd met at the subway station. The others I didn't know. One was a very attractive middle-aged lady, probably in her middle forties. She spoke wonderful English and she let me know her husband was a professor, and he was on sabbatical teaching at the University of West Virginia, in Charlottesville. Virginia was my home state. I found this out later because when we were in the car we weren't allowed to say anything.

"We were driven off to a down-town building which had been taken over by the Gestapo. I'm quite sure it was the Gestapo Headquarters. We drove into an enclosed courtyard. The building facing us in the courtyard had verandas on two layers. As we walked up they were interrogating people who were standing nude in tubs of water and they were pouring iced water over them as they interrogated them. I thought to myself, my God, is this what I got to go through? I don't know if this was intended to loosen our tongues but it was a pitiful sight to behold. They took us to a room that had been turned into a cell. No window, a single electric light, and only a peephole in the door. The cell was rectangular and you were out of sight of the peephole if you went down to one end either side. Being locked up with five women was really quite an ordeal. There was one chamber pot and a single cot and absolutely no privacy. Well, the lady who had been to Charlottesville very quickly let me know that this was the last day we would be around and this would be her last chance to make love. She didn't beat about the bush. She wanted to make love one last time before she was executed. The little lady I'd met at the station was busy eating papers she had which were incriminating, and so were some of the other women. I tried to resist this demand to make love in front of these other women. She said they'll turn their heads to the wall. Sure enough, we used the cot and one of the other women was warming up to the idea when they started taking us out for interrogation. They took us one at a time and the interrogations lasted most of the day.

"They had taken my watch from me so we didn't know the time but it seemed we were there a good twelve hours. Then they came and marched us to a bus or van that was made up of separate little cells with a narrow isle running down the middle of the vehicle. My first thought was that they were going to gas us and dump us somewhere. We were driven for some distance to a prison outside Paris. A very old prison (Fresnes) judging by some of the writings on the cell walls. Here we were separated and I was put in solitary confinement. It was pitch dark when I was put in the cell and all I could find was a pile of straw on the floor. I quickly discovered I had visitors in the cell in the way of bugs crawling around in that straw. However, I was tired and I decided I couldn't stand up all night. I had a rather fitful sleep. When I woke up in the morning light filtered in the louvers in the window. Enough that I could see there was a cold water faucet in one corner with an icicle hanging from it, there was also a place where you could relieve yourself. There was no bunk, only that pile of straw. My leg was beginning to bother me. When they brought me a bowl of the soup I asked to see a medic but it was neglected. I did get a bath and I cleaned my leg up the best I could. I also got some exercise in the yard under guard.

"After a week or so they started to interrogate me. At first my interrogator was a military man and the questions and answers were routine and I was even offered a cigarette. After several of these they started to get a little mean. When the interrogator didn't like the answers to his questions he would kick me in my sore leg. I asked again to see a medic and eventually I did get to see a man who gave me some pills that would supposedly arrest the infection. He also gave me a clean paper bandage. After several more interrogations they brought in a dossier on me that showed they knew all about me. A lot was obviously gleaned from newspapers right back to where and when I trained in the States but they also knew a lot about my group and squadron, mentioning what had happened to others that had gone down. They tried to get information on those that had helped me but I didn't tell them anything they did not already know. After that they put me in a cell with two Americans and one British airman. It was good to have company. There were cots and the food was a little bit better. One day we were transferred by train to a Gestapo prison in Frankfurt. Here they put the fear of God into us by parading some prisoners who were so emaciated it was a wonder they could even walk. Perhaps it was to intimidate us.

"Here again I was in solitary confinement but conditions were clean. They tried to get us to do some work. They had us gluing up little envelopes for medicines. As I was determined not do any work for them I glued them together. I got by with this for a few days until they found out where these envelopes were coming from. They came to let me know that if I didn't stop gluing the envelopes together and did them the way they wanted I would get no rations, only water. I put up with the water for a couple of days and decided eating was more important, so I agreed to make envelopes the way they wanted. Again I was interrogated. These people meant business and slapped you around a little bit. I was here three or four days when an RAF night raid set the town on fire. There was a direct hit on part of this prison and the ceiling of my cell fell in. Must have been here for two weeks and then I was transported by bus to Dulag Luft, the Luftwaffe interrogation centre. Here the interrogation was routine and eventually I was shipped out to Stalag Luft I at Barth."*

---

* At the time of writing, George was alive and well and living in Richmond, Virginia.

16 Hub Returns

Hub Zemke need not have had concerns about the leadership of the group under Schilling and Landry for the winning streak was if anything stronger than when he had departed. The aggressive spirit was alive and growing. One of his first acts was to condone Gabreski's move to group HQ and change the name of his position to Assistant Flying Executive. Landry had also brought the service group headquarters together with that of the 56th which made for smoother co-operation. Zemke did not immediately resume leading missions. There had been several changes in operational practice and equipment and he needed to come abreast of these.

Prominent were developments in operational communication control. From mid-November 1943 pilots had direct communication with their Halesworth base in making homing calls, which reduced the radio traffic pressure on 65th Fighter Wing control, then working under the codename Tack Line. Local direction-finder stations were now linked directly to Sturdy, the Halesworth tower. A radio call for a bearing to fly was the only rescue line for a lone lost pilot perhaps a hundred miles or more away over Europe. On extreme range missions the group now put up relay aircraft to pick up transmissions from the group formation to pass to Tack Line. A British radar system, Type 16, offered the prospect of accurate vectoring to enemy formations within 120 miles of the operating station near Beachy Head on England's south coast; this was first used by the 56th on 14 January with indifferent results. Type 16, highly secret and in its infancy, held great promise.

Tactics on bomber escort missions were little changed from those employed before Zemke left except that it was now felt permissible to follow enemy aircraft to lower altitudes in advantageous circumstances. Water injection and paddle blade propellers had given the Thunderbolt improved performance in emergency situations but the type could still be at a disadvantage if intercepted by Me109s or FW190s at low altitude.

To re-orientate himself into flying missions, Zemke began by flying with one of the squadron flights. Landry, not yet having a defined assignment at Eighth Air Force HQ, continued to fly with the 56th, leading B group on 21 January. The only claim and loss was in the A group formation. Keyworth Red flight, led by Captain Leslie Smith, spotted four FW190s attacking Liberators from astern at about 15,000 feet near Rouen. As Smith took his flight down the Focke-Wulf pilots saw him coming and broke left and right. Pursuing one pair Smith called to his wingman, 2nd Lieutenant Dimmick, who was on his first mission, to pull up so that he could keep an eye on him. At about 3,000 feet Smith opened fire as the enemy aircraft began to turn. Unnoticed, another pair of Focke-Wulfs had pulled round behind Smith and Dimmick. Bob Johnson leading Keyworth Blue and covering Red flight, went after the FW190s, calling a warning to Dimmick to break; he did not and was blasted out of the sky by cannon fire. Johnson closed with the aggressor and shot him down at about 1,000 feet altitude. It was learned later that Dimmick was killed. The loss caused Smith, a sensitive man, considerable concern, feeling that he was in some part to blame. "I felt terrible. He was new and I had to look after him. The loyalty to one another." Les Smith was not alone in his concern, for many experienced pilots who lost a wingman were similarly troubled. Experienced or otherwise, a wingman was usually the most vulnerable member of an element in an enemy interception. Another on his fourth mission was lost to an enemy fighter attack out of the sun a few days later. Generally, it took many sorties for wingmen to graduate to element leaders.

After a fairly uneventful mission on 24 January, when Ajax ordered a new tactic involving individual groups patrolling a defined area while the bombers passed through, and a more fruitful outing on the 29th, the following day produced another high score for no losses. The 15 destroyed credits on the 30th took the group's total past the 200 mark. A few weeks earlier it had been proposed at an Officers' Club get-together that the target should be 200 by St Valentine's Day. Someone noticed that 30 January was Roosevelt's birthday and so the 200th victory was dedicated to the President. Another move to wave the flag of success and to note that the nearest competitor in the numbers' game, the 4th Fighter Group, had only just passed the 100 destroyed mark. Bob Johnson and Gabby Gabreski each obtained two victories, as did George Hall and wingman Lloyd Langdon. Bud Mahurin, making his 63rd sortie, claimed a Ju88, and with the Me109 credit from the previous day became the leading VIII Fighter Command fighter ace with a total of 15 victories. Running him close by only one was Bob Johnson. As one of Johnson's victories was his 13th he joked he didn't want it and told Major Wilbur Watson, the group's Air Inspector, that he could have it. This mission was also Colonel Bob Landry's final sortie with the group before departure to Pinetree, Eighth Air Force HQ, from where he later took command of a bomber group.

Although considered by most to be 'a nice guy', Bob Johnson seemed comparatively unrelaxed and rarely smiled, whereas Mahurin had a contagious schoolboy grin and usually appeared carefree. Twenty-five years old, 5 ft 9 in tall and only weighing 133 lb his usual nickname of Bud was frequently replaced with Skinny. Mahurin protested: "Gee! I've been trying to put on weight ever since I got here. I have a glass of beer before meals. I eat plenty bread and potatoes. I like potatoes. But it makes no difference." His father, an architect, died in 1943. His mother was then still alive and he had an older married sister. "When I was twelve I saw

an airplane fly overhead and knew what I wanted. I knew I was going to
fly." At 17 he did odd jobs for a year, a spell in a library and as a clerk in
a grocery store. In 1939 he went to Purdue University to study
engineering to qualify for the air force. "I tried to get in the Air Corps in
1940 but had not the necessary college requirements. So after a few
months' work with engineering firms went back to Purdue." In summer
1942 he learned to fly under the Civilian Pilot Training Scheme on Cubs
and Aeroncas. "I got an extra 24 hours on Cubs by paying seven dollars
an hour." He was finally able to enlist in the AAF and was commissioned
as a 2nd Lieutenant on 29 April 1942.

Bob Johnson had similar aspirations to fly from an early age and his
father, an automobile mechanic, took him on a first flight when Bob was
only two years old. Like Mahurin he did not come from a wealthy family
and it was a struggle to earn sufficient for flying lessons. Bob married in
1942 and his frequently expressed desire was to get back to his wife. Said
to have the sharpest eyesight in his squadron, he had the acquired ability
to pick out far off aircraft from a sky or land background. Some pilots had
this perceptual skill of being able to focus on a distant object that was lost
to others. As fractions of a second counted in this lethal business such
ability with sight was a major asset in combat success, to say nothing of
personal survival. Johnson's comment on this was that a pilot needed
"... good eyes and a good neck to survive. If you haven't these you're a
goner."

The group's passing the 200 mark and Mahurin's new status was
passed to the news media by Eighth Air Force public relations and
brought newsmen to Halesworth for interviews. This began to worry
Zemke for while publicity of the 56th's success helped to fortify the
group's pride, the press now presented the bloody business in which his
pilots were engaged in as a form akin to sports reporting. The
achievements of individual pilots were written up like the scores of ball
games. While he was eager to promote competition with other fighter
groups, seeing challenge as a means to still further build esprit de corps,
he did not like the way the news media projected air combat, even if this
advanced morale with the public. Generals like to boast of their soldiers'
achievements, and this was no less the case with the Eighth Air Force,
particularly as so often the news was grim for its other operations. And
soon VIII Fighter Command realised that publicising the 'Zemke
Group's' success could inspire other groups to greater endeavours. If
numbers of enemy aircraft destroyed were the yardstick of success then
so be it, because destroying the Luftwaffe was their major war aim.

It also gave Zemke much concern that many of the group's most
experienced pilots, particularly squadron and flight leaders, were nearing
the 200 flying hours total that was fixed as an operational tour. On
completion a pilot would be transferred to a non-combat assignment. A
50-flying-hour extension could be obtained but was purely voluntary. In
discussing the situation with his staff, Gabreski mentioned that some of
his Polish friends in the RAF had been retired to desk jobs and were not

Top left: Some of the 56th's first aircraft. A line of hand-me-down Curtiss P-36s at Charlotte, North Carolina.

Middle left: Lieutenant Eugene O'Neill on P-38F 41-2306 at Bendix airport. At the time, early 1942, the 56th expected to become fully equipped with Lockheed Lightnings.

Middle right: The English bulldog 'Buddy', that became the 62nd Fighter Squadron mascot and, in caricature by Walt Disney, the squadron's emblem. Photographed on 10 June 1942 in flying helmet.

Bottom: 62nd Fighter Squadron mechanics – from left to right, John Brannen, James Bunn, Jack Calloway, unknown and James Spears – 'shooting the breeze' outside a barrack building at Bradley Field.

Top left: Private John Sipec clad for engineering work while at Grenier Field.

Top right: Lieutenant Ralph Johnson, one of three Johnsons in the group's original combat pilot complement. Ralph had many close calls, including a dip in the North Sea, but endured to complete his combat tour.

Bottom: Pow-wow beside the King's Cliffe control tower, 10 March 1943. From left to right: Richard Allison, Harold Comstock, three B-17 fliers, Hub Zemke, Goodfleisch and Saux. Allison and Saux were both killed in flying accidents in 1943. Zemke wears black flying suit bought in London while detached to the RAF in 1941.

Top left: A 'finger-four' of Thunderbolts pass the King's Cliffe control tower on a press day on 10 March 1943.

Top right: 'Doc' Renwick leads a flight of 61st Fighter Squadron P-47s over the eastern boundary of Horsham St. Faith on another press day, 26 April 1943. The grass surface at this airfield permitted aircraft of a four-plane flight to take off together.

Bottom: Royalty visit King's Cliffe. The Duke and Duchess of Gloucester, whose private residence was at nearby Barnwell, on the control tower balcony with Zemke, 29 March 1943. The Duke is enjoying a cigarette.

Top left: Captain Donald Renwick (left) and Lieutenant Norman Brooks (centre) chat with Captain Gabreski on return from their flight. Renwick would be the last officer to take command of the group in England.

Top right: Captain Walter Cook, who was credited with the group's first victory on 12 June 1943, poses beside the group CO's personal Thunderbolt.

Middle: Captain Merle Eby and the P-47 in which he was shot down on 26 June 1943. The aircraft was originally assigned to Robert Wetherbee before he became an assistant operations officer.

Bottom: P-47s of the 62nd Fighter Squadron at Horsham St. Faith, 26 April 1943. Nearest aircraft is Ralph Johnson's 'Pud'; the next in line John McClure's 'Lonesome Polecat', one of the first two 56th aircraft to be shot down.

Top: Captain David Robinson, the 'Silver Fox', looks on as some of the 63rd pilots study a map for the photographer. On the right of the picture the squadron's first Flight Surgeon, Joe Sayers, looks over the shoulders of pilots Wilfred Van Abel, Glenn Schiltz and John Vogt.

Middle: German soldiers lower Lieutenant Pat Williams' coffin at his burial, 2 June 1943, Moorsele, Belgium.

Bottom: Lieutenant Gerald Johnson climbs in. Destined to be proclaimed the group's first ace, 'Gerry' would come to head the Eighth Air Force as its commanding general in a later conflict.

Top: Following the official transfer of Halesworth from the RAF to USAAF, the senior officers were photographed in front of the flagstaff. From left to right: Major Abdalah, 33rd Service Group Executive; Major Watson, 56th Fighter Group Air Inspector; Squadron Leader Crocker; Colonel Zemke; Flight Lieutenant Knott; Lt Colonel Brower, 33rd Service Group CO, and Lt Colonel Caffrey, 33rd Service Group Deputy.

Middle: The irrepressible Dave Schilling fashioning some device on a lathe in the improvised machine shop at Hightree Farm (Schilling's Acres). Fashioning hunting knives out of old rasps or files was a favourite pastime.

Bottom: VIII Fighter Command's Brig. General 'Monk' Hunter addresses the 56th gathering on the occasion of Eddie Rickenbacker's visit, 28 July 1943. The World War I ace stands on the podium with Zemke. No. 2 hangar, on the far side of the airfield, is visible through the summer morning haze.

Top left: 'Pappy' Craig, a level-headed stalwart who took over the 62nd when Schilling became group flying executive.

Top right: Eugene O'Neill, one of the most popular pilots in the original 62nd complement.

Middle: The burning wreck of Conway Saux's P-47C 41-6224 in a field at Valley Farm, Henham, the result of a collision in the Halesworth circuit on 22 August 1943. Saux baled out but his parachute did not have time to open properly and he was killed. Don Tettemer, the pilot of the other P-47, was also killed.

Bottom: Doc Horning, the 61st Flight Surgeon, hands out coffee to Milton Anderson, after the successful mission of 26 November 1943. An interrogating officer (out of picture on left) seeks information from Schilling (centre, facing camera), who flew with the 61st and sits with other squadron pilots in their ready room. Gabreski sits on Anderson's right and Marangelo on his left. A tired Norm Brooks sits behind Schilling. Horning used these occasions to look for extreme fatigue or other signs of war weariness among his pilots.

Top left: Captain Gene O'Neill's personal P-47C in which he flew most of his 87 missions. It carried three nicknames, 'Lil' Abner', for the squadron, 'Torchy' for his ground crew, and 'Jessie-O' on the right side, for his wife. Schilling's Acres is in the background.

Top right: Lt George C. Goldstein, who had adventures in France.

Middle: Major Gabreski's right foot was protected by his boot when a 20mm shell fragment struck under the right pedal of P-47D 42-7871, HV:A on 11 December 1943.

Bottom left: Colonel Robert B. Landry, the interim CO at Halesworth. He later commanded and flew with an Eighth Air Force bomber group.

Bottom right: Schilling in the Halesworth Officers' Club in the kilt obtained through partying with the local Black Watch battalion. The lady friend appears to be wearing mens' overalls.

Top: Robert and May Kirschner outside Coddenham village church, 2 November 1943. Best man Sergeant Gene Hammerick, bridesmaid Alice Fuller and Mr and Mrs Lockwood, the bride's parents, also smile for the camera.

Middle: 'Stormy' Sadowski and a typical weather map for a winter mission.

Bottom left: Doc Horning mixes a 'cocktail special' for his boys. Not all the stock in his laboratory was used for medicinal purposes.

Bottom right: 'Cannon Ball' Klibbe: "A great little guy and a fine pilot."

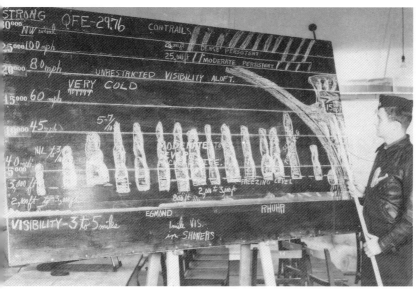

Top: John Truluck and his ground crew at Halesworth. The painting of assigned pilot and ground crew names on aircraft was permitted by the Eighth Air Force.

Middle left: 'Bud' Mahurin (left) shares a joke with Jimmy Doolittle (right), Eighth Air Force commanding general, while Dave Schilling joins in; 14 March 1944.

Middle right: General Spaatz (extreme left) and Zemke discuss P-47 matters on a 61st hardstanding at Halesworth, while Doolittle and Auton (extreme right) confer with Schilling (back to camera), 14 March 1944. Hub's thirtieth birthday.

Bottom left: 'Fats' Morrill was killed by exploding bombs at the site of a B-24 crash. An avid poker player, it is said that as a gesture of respect his friends played poker on his coffin the evening before his burial.

Bottom right: General Kepner congratulates Bob Johnson while Zemke (left) and his deputy Schilling (extreme right) look on.

Top: Harold Comstock was fortunate to escape little harmed when his fuel-exhausted P-47 was crash-landed at Mutford on return from the 3 February 1944 mission. A farmer working his fields nearby came to the pilot's aid.

Middle left: Captain Edward Schumacher, the Group Flight Surgeon.

Middle right: Four of the 61st Fighter Squadron staff. Adjutant Ralph Eastwood and supply officer Edwin Bergquist on left, and Edward Weinberg, Intelligence, and Doc Horning on right. Officer in centre is Captain James McGarrigle who handled public relations. Ground officers were often men in their thirties and forties.

Bottom left: Captain Lawrence Albrecht. The Group's first weather officer.

Bottom right: Captain Clifford Tichenor, 62nd Fighter Squadron's first Flight Surgeon.

Top left: Captain Virgil Durrance in his office at Boxted. Originally the 62nd Fighter Squadron's adjutant but later adjutant for the 56th. A popular officer with all ranks, and one of the longest serving with the 56th.

Top centre: Leroy Schreiber. One of the most respected pilots assigned to the 56th. Lost to ground fire in attacking what is said to have been a dummy airfield.

Top right: Lieutenant Arlington Canizares. His forebears are said to have been with the Conquistadors.

Bottom left: A former farmhouse, Langham Lodge became Boxted's 'Wheelhouse', with a notice outside the drive gate listing the senior group officers who occupied the residence. From left, Zemke, Dade and Watson.

Bottom right: S/Sergeant Albert Holliday looks on as Lt William Gordon straps up in his 'Barbara Ann II', LM:G at Boxted.

Top left: Lt Robert Cherry, ready to fly.

Top centre: Robert Rankin, who earned his place in group fame as the first pilot to be credited with shooting down five of the enemy on one mission on 12 May 1944.

Top right: Joe Powers, considered wild and unpredictable after a few drinks, but an excellent shot at the controls of a Thunderbolt.

Middle: Sergeant J.C. Penrod (left) was the crew chief on Robert S. Johnson's Thunderbolt in the 62nd Fighter Squadron. This photo was taken after Johnson used the fighter to claim his 26th and 27th victories on 8 May 1944 and before the additional symbols were painted on. The tents visible between the pile of 150-gallon drop tanks and a field hedgerow afforded C Flight ground crews shelter from inclement weather.

Bottom: Out of fuel, Lieutenant George Butler had a smooth belly-landing with LM:J on the shingle at remote Orfordness, 4 May 1944. Although little damaged, the inaccessibility of the site saw the aircraft written off as salvage.

Top left: Zemke receives help with his safety straps prior to take-off from Manston, 4 May 1944. Returning from combat he had to put down at the 'lame duck' airfield for repairs to turbo ducting on his personal aircraft.

Top right: Lieutenant Barney Casteel took a 20mm shell in the tail of P-47D 43-25531, UN:A, when bounced by Me109s on 19 May 1944.

Middle left: Warm work for Billy Collins, Frank Gyidak and Merlin Ritter. A few hours later the P-47 in the background was lost along with Sam Lowman.

Middle right: More scuttlebutt: 62nd mechanics listen to prominent flight chief Sgt David Hubler (centre).

Bottom: Zbigniew Janicki, the only Polish volunteer lost while flying with the Wolfpack.

Top left: Arming a P-47 of the 61st at Boxted, albeit posed for the camera. S/Sergeant Robert E. Robischon arms the guns, Master Sergeant James H. McGee and Sergeant A. Koval attach a 500lb GP bomb to a wing rack.

Top right: The 62nd taxies out past No. 2 hangar for a fighter-bomber mission on 15 July 1944. Each carries two 500lb bombs on wing racks and a 150 US-gallon drop tank under the fuselage.

Middle right: Gabby returns to Boxted late on the last day of June 1944.

Bottom left: Six days later a 28th victory symbol was painted on Gabreski's personal aircraft, HV:A. The top scoring USAAF fighter pilot in the war with the Luftwaffe joins his ground crew to record the event. From left to right: Crew chief, Staff Sergeant Ralph Safford, assistant crew chief, Corporal Felix Schacki, armourer Sergeant Joe DiFranza, and pilot Gabreski.

Bottom right: Wendell (left) and James McClure, both 62nd pilots (but no relation). Wendell went down in France on 7 June 1944 after being attacked by FW190s. Sheltered by the French he evaded capture and returned to the UK.

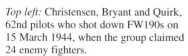

Top left: Christensen, Bryant and Quirk, 62nd pilots who shot down FW190s on 15 March 1944, when the group claimed 24 enemy fighters.

Top right: George Bostwick examines the remains of the tree his P-47 hit on take-off from Boxted, 4 July 1944. It appears to be a part rotten elm stub.

Middle left: Auton decorates Gladych, who wears an RAF uniform with Poland shoulder flash.

Middle right: 'Pat' Knafelz and crew chief Sergeant Carl Boehler on P-47D 'Button Nose'. The symbols are for six locomotives claimed destroyed, and the cross for an enemy aircraft shot down on 4 July 1944.

Bottom: George Bostwick reaches for a generous sandwich in the 62nd Fighter Squadron ready room at Boxted. Enlisted man behind the refreshment bar is Alexander Rajk. Oranges were something the British rarely saw by the fourth year of war.

Top left: Lt William 'Air Boy' Hartshorn, summer 1944.

Top right: By October 1944 most of the P-47Ds in the group were the longer-range models with 'bubble' cockpit canopies. In this 61st formation there is only one high back model (No.4 lead flight), which happens to be the first Thunderbolt without a camouflage finish received by the squadron.

Middle left: 'Get busy for the photographer, boys.' The ground crew of P-47D 44-20626 HV:X at Boxted, 9 November 1944.

Middle right: Well wrapped up. Martin Stanton, armourer, outside one of the tents that provided winter cover for 62nd's C Flight dispersal points at Boxted.

Bottom: Schilling (centre), with a Luftwaffe fighter leader on his left, views Boxted airfield from the control tower roof. It was typical of the 56th's former commander to cause a stir by bringing along an enemy pilot who had been captured on New Year's Day, 1945.

Top left: Mike Jackson. Credited with 8 air victories and 5½ by strafing between July 1944 and February 1945.

Top right: Felix Williamson, last wartime CO of the 62nd.

Middle: The musical talent that led to the formation of dance bands at Halesworth and Boxted. By 1945 'Schilling's Serenaders' were accomplished enough to play at London's Stage Door Canteen in Shaftesbury Avenue. An event arranged by Al Mellor, special services officer. From left to right, first row: Mellor and saxophonists, Bill Gifford, Hose Hernendez, Angelo DeCarlo and Leo Butiste. Second row; Mac Ryan, piano, Lawson Whitlow, bass, Carle Gray and Lou Gruenberg, both trombone. Third row: George Pladis, drums, Phil Foster, guitar, Merle Mowery, Charlie Ball and Merle Woods, all trumpet. Vocalist, John Keeler. Keeler and Butiste were pilots and Woods the 63rd's Flight Surgeon.

Bottom left: Walter Sharbo, credited with the last enemy aircraft shot down by the Wolfpack.

Bottom right: P-47Ms of the 62nd Fighter squadron in their disruptive camouflage paintwork pass over Shooter's Hill, Langham.

Top: P-47Ms pass over Thorrington Street, Suffolk, March 1945.

Bottom left: Lt Edmund Ellis poses beside the three victory symbols on his black P-47M 'Blue Eyes'.

Bottom right: Group CO Pete Dade (left) congratulates Randel Murphy on destroying 10 enemy aircraft by strafing during the 13 April 1945 mission.

Top left: Sergeant R.J. Waggoner, the crew chief of Randel Murphy's 63rd Fighter Squadron P-47M 'The Brat'.

Top right: Tobin Armstrong (left) and Alfred Bolender, the two 63rd pilots who rescued men in a British army vehicle from the river Colne.

Middle: Longest serving pilot with the 56th Fighter Group, James R. Carter. He flew two tours, was credited with eight air victories and was the last of the combat originals at Boxted.

Bottom: Resplendent in red and black paintwork, the 61st Fighter Squadron's appropriated He111. The cipher on the rear fuselage was the initials of the self-appointed crew.

very happy. Why not invite these long-time combat pilots to fly with the 56th? Liking the idea, Zemke suggested Gabreski sound these men out. Many Polish pilots had distinguished themselves in RAF service, although gaining a reputation for being somewhat wild. Gabreski made contact with one of the 'resting' pilots who arrived at Halesworth in a Spitfire IX, parking it near the technical site. While the pilot, Flight Lieutenant Michael Gladych, had gone to see Gabreski a mechanic, zig-zagging a P-47 along the taxiway to move it to a new location, caught the tip of one of the Spitfire propeller's four blades with a wing tip. The damage was reported immediately and the Engineering Officer had Sergeant John Sipek, who had taken a course on British airscrews, examine the propeller. In Sipek's opinion the wooden blade should be replaced and the RAF pilot's home station should be asked to send another over. When Gladych arrived back at the Spitfire and was informed of the accident he took a look and the gist of his remark in broken English was "The prop' still has three good blades. It will get me home." There appeared to be no undue vibration when the engine was run up and Gladych taxied out to take off, which onlookers thought most unwise. Not only did the Spitfire take off smoothly, it was immediately put into a near vertical climb and disappeared into the clouds, only to reappear a minute or two later zooming across the airfield no more than ten feet above the runway. Gladych sold the idea of flying with the Americans to Wing Commander Alexander Gabsezewicz and, apparently without orders, both moved to Halesworth. Following hasty training in handling the Thunderbolt they started operational sorties with the 61st Squadron on 8 February, flying as an element in Jim Stewart's flight on this and several other missions. Gabsezewicz's stay was short for later that month this eight-victory ace was recalled by the Poles and promoted to group captain (Polish airmen used RAF ranks).

On 3 February Major Horace Craig, the 62nd CO, becoming the first 56th man to reach the 200-hour mark, was given the lead of B group. The mission, supporting bombers attacking Wilhelmshaven, produced another victory for Mahurin but on the way home the 63rd Squadron was accosted by Me109s when depleted fuel was at a critical state. Lloyd Langdon, flying as Joe Egan's wingman, had his P-47 run out of fuel while still some 40 miles from England and baled out. Egan did not see him jump or his aircraft go into the sea because of cloud patches, but orbited the spot while calling air/sea rescue. As his fuel situation was desperate, he had to leave, and was just able to make a coastal field at Clacton to crash-land before the engine finally stopped. Langdon succumbed to the extreme cold of the North Sea where life expectancy averaged about three minutes. Joe Egan, an original combat pilot of the 63rd and at 6 feet 3 inches the tallest flier in the group if not VIII Fighter Command, was understandably distressed by Langdon's loss. Such circumstances were again reason for an element leader to ponder if his actions, or lack of them, contributed to his wingman's demise; more so than a loss to enemy fire. Wingmen invariably used more fuel than their element leader in jockeying the engine power input to maintain position.

'Pappy' Craig, a modest and responsible individual, vacillated on whether to take an extension. As one of his buddies said: 'He almost had an anxiety thing about it. He did and he didn't want to go.' During his operations Craig had never had to turn back through a mechanical failure. Craig did leave and Zemke made Schreiber the new 62nd CO. LeRoy Schreiber, from Plymouth, Massachusetts, had spent two years in the US as an instructor. Tall, dark-haired and serious, and whose chief relaxation was listening to popular music, he was the intellectual member of the group, having graduated from Harvard majoring in mathematics. Considered excellent in training pilots he was kept on as an instructor and his first attempts to be released for combat service were rejected. On the morning of a graduation by his pupils Schreiber and some other instructors buzzed the local town repeatedly. His CO gave him papers for overseas service instead of having him grounded. Schreiber enjoyed popularity with fellow pilots in the 62nd, chiefly because of incidents where both he and a wingman had fired at an enemy aircraft, Schreiber had forgone a shared claim to give the whole credit to the other pilot.

For sometime in the regular discussions pilots had with their seniors there had been doubts about the distinctive white bands with which Thunderbolts were adorned for type identity. While the purpose was to prevent Allied pilots mistaking P-47s for FW190s in particular, they also aided Luftwaffe pilots to recognise them. The Me109s and FW190s encountered often had red or yellow noses but never white. Someone suggested that if the 56th painted its P-47s' noses red or yellow the enemy fighter pilots might mistake them for FW190s until it was too late. There should also be the advantage that different nose colours would enable the three squadrons of the group to identify each other on missions at greater range than fuselage code letters could be distinguished. Zemke, taking up the idea, telephoned General Kepner asking permission to change the white engine cowling band to a different colour for each squadron and explained the reasons. It was granted and that night, 5 February, Thunderbolts were taken into hangars for the work to be carried out. The same colours were used as those that had identified the squadrons back in New England: red for the 61st, yellow for the 62nd and blue for the 63rd. For Zemke there was another aspect of this introduction; it promoted the individuality of the group and its supremacy.

At the beginning of February 1944 General Doolittle announced that when not engaged in escorting bombers the Eighth's fighters could range after enemy aircraft wherever they could find them. This meant that enemy airfields could be strafed and aggressive pilots were quick to take advantage of this policy change. Ready to take the offensive down to earth was the ever eager Zemke. On 11 February he took out A group supporting B-17s raiding Frankfurt, his third group lead after resuming operations. During the mission Zemke diverted two squadrons to intercept Me109s approaching from the Liège area where the 62nd managed to shoot down one and damage another before the rest evaded into clouds. Not long thereafter Don Smith called his element leader Les Smith: "Keyworth Red Leader. Look at that airdrome underneath you and the eleven planes down there." Hearing this, Zemke told the rest of the 61st to remain as top cover and took Keyworth White flight down in a wide arc, calling the 62nd lead flight to follow. Hoping to obtain surprise the let-down was made some distance from the airfield and little ground fire was noticed when the P-47s swept in low at well over 300 mph. Zemke fired at a parked Me109 which went up in flames and Schreiber's fire ignited an Me110. Other pilots shot up Me110s but their gun camera film images only had these aircraft adjudged damaged. With enemy defences awakened, Zemke considered further attention unwise and ordered his pilots to regain altitude and make for home as fuel was low. As it was, it became necessary to land at airfields close to England's south coast to refuel before making for home base.

Wing shackles in small streamlined pylons were being fitted to Thunderbolts to allow a drop tank to be carried under each wing and further extend range. The drawback was that although the pylons were relatively small their drag reduced top speed by some 10 mph. The installation was initially done at the Burtonwood depot and it was anything between ten days and a month before aircraft were returned. Meanwhile, the arrival of a supply of 150 US-gallon capacity drop tanks for use on the belly shackles allowed a potential extra fifteen minutes flying time. Initially fabricated in the UK, viewed head-on the 150-gallon tank had a horizontally squashed profile to obtain the necessary clearance from the ground. However, drop tank capacity was not the restricting element of the Thunderbolt's radius of action; it was the aircraft's internal tankage of 305 US gallons. Once the drop tanks were released there had to be sufficient fuel to return to base. Following combat activity and high power usage the supply could be reduced to where only an hour's flight remained at cruise settings. At first the auxiliary tanks had been dropped soon after crossing the enemy coast, but then the practice changed to one where the tanks were retained as long as possible.

After a week of sleet and rain the 150-gallon tanks were first employed on 20 February when good weather with clear skies was forecast for central Europe and the US strategic air forces based in England and Italy were sent on a series of raids chiefly against aviation related targets. This became known as 'Big Week' to the Eighth Air Force fraternity, but it was big not only in the numbers of aircraft despatched but in the scale of air fighting and of aircraft lost by both sides. Major Sylvester Burke had reached the 200 hours limit and 20 February was his last mission. Sy Burke, 26, who had been with the group since December 1941, was not every pilot's favourite leader in the 63rd Squadron; some thought he followed the rules of air discipline too rigidly and passed up opportunities to engage the enemy. He went to a headquarters staff post and was replaced by Major Gerald Johnson, whom Zemke had just retrieved from detachment at Martlesham Heath. Most 63rd pilots thought Mahurin would be promoted and made their new CO, but with Johnson already being a major and an experienced combat leader he got the job. No one resented this, least of all the effervescent Bud Mahurin, as Gerry Johnson was not only dependable and experienced he was genial and happy to be one of the boys.

The mission once again saw the 56th demonstrating its expertise, taking out enemy fighters as they made for the bomber formations to return with credits of 14 Luftwaffe aircraft for no loss. Reaching some 350 miles from Halesworth, the location for their bomber support was Drummer Lake, a prominent landmark that would feature in many future missions. LeRoy Schreiber elevated himself to acehood. Coming up behind a flight of Me109s intent on making a head-on pass at a B-24 formation he eliminated No. 4. The next rocked his wings vigorously and Schreiber rocked his wings back in kind, then calmly shot this Messerschmitt down before transferring his attention to a third member of the flight. Rocking his wings and receiving a similar acknowledgement he despatched this aircraft as well. The remaining aircraft finally realised the two aircraft behind were not friendly and dived for terra firma. It would appear that the enemy fighters, so intent on closing with the bombers, did not realise the yellow noses seen behind were hostile. Next day there was some thought that the red and yellow noses were the cause of an unusually large number of bomber gunners firing at P-47s that ventured too close to their formations, mistaking them for enemy fighters. Bright colours or not, however, this was a well known hazard at any time as the standard of gunner aircraft recognition was generally poor. Again, the 56th excelled with 12 credits for no loss, of which the Polish volunteer Mike Gladych was credited with two.

For the third day running combat produced high claims for no loss, with 15 being credited once gun camera film had been studied and pilots interrogated. This day the 61st Fighter Squadron chalked up its 100th victory, the first US fighter squadron in Europe to do so. There were no losses despite 'a few tight corners where superior airmanship saved skins'. Flight Officer Frank Klibbe having been frustrated in a dive to attack an Me109 at some 6,000 feet, started to regain altitude:

"Having no further business at such low altitude, I began a climbing left turn while looking over my shoulder at what appeared to be my wingman attempting to join in the climb. With a feeling of security I relaxed for a moment, until I was suddenly awakened by a realisation of what I had really seen. Those flashes from the leading edge of this aircraft were not those of a friendly wingman. My only chance was to immediately enter a Lufbery Circle [circling manoeuvre named for its WW1 exponent], praying my opponent would be unable to bring his guns to bear. We were now at approximately 8,000 feet climbing in a tight Lufbery. How experienced a pilot was I up against? How could I gain a margin of advantage when he was already on my tail with speed, position and a host of tactical manoeuvres available to him? I tugged at the stick to tighten my turn. As my opponent came even closer on his first pass, I could see more fire from his guns and ducked my head awaiting the impact of his bullets which I believed at the time was inevitable. Much to my surprise it didn't happen and I continued to frantically pull on the stick to tighten the circle. My engine with full supercharger on purred like a kitten, but sounded equally as weak to me! My oxygen mask under the G forces imposed by my tight turns had by now slipped under my nose, adding further discomfort to my already unpleasant situation. Despite this discomfort, I couldn't bring myself to release a hand from the stick in order to make an adjustment, for any loss of pressure on the controls would only result in a gain for my opponent. I continued in the Lufbery, the throttle pushed forward to the breaking point and the control stick in my belly, as the Me109 again came slicing inside and from above, firing all the way. One slip on my part was all he needed. If I reefed in too hard on the controls I'd stall, placing myself in an even more critical position. On occasions I could feel the first burble of a stall: I must maintain this thin edge of destiny.

"During each attack I instinctively ducked my head, as if to suppress the pain should his bullets rip into the cockpit. By now I was wet with perspiration, and fear and tension were beginning to weaken me as I wondered if I could maintain the strength to carry on. Time was of the essence, although I had managed to hold my own in the Lufbery my fuel was rapidly being depleted. If only someone would spot me, how easy it would be for them to free me from this rendezvous with uncertainty. Then I noticed two P-47s on the deck below me heading east at about 2,000 feet. I began to scream over the radio for help. Even though my oxygen mask interfered with the transmission, I was sure they could hear my plea. Between occasional glances at the Me109 I watched the P-47s continue on course until I lost them in the contrast of the countryside below. Shortly after, I looked upwards and saw four P-47s heading west at about 20,000 feet. I again screamed for help. At least someone heard me as I received a call asking for my position and altitude. How in the hell did I know my position except I was directly below four guys passing overhead. A second transmission wanted to know, 'What's the nearest town?' 'I don't know' I screamed back. 'I'm right below you guys at 9,000 feet.' I didn't realise at the time but to expect help from such vague and unintelligent position reports was asking for a miracle. Despite my pleas for help, I watched the four above fade away in the distance.

"By this time I had reconciled myself to the fact that my survival depended solely upon my own ability and initiative. I began to lose some of my initial fears; we had been in the Lufbery for well over six minutes. My opponent had made no appreciable gain, at least he had not hit me; some consolation. I watched over my shoulder intently as I tried to take advantage of any mistakes the 109 made, offering me breathing space. Slowly I began to widen the gap between us until he was in no position to bring his guns to bear. Finally I managed to secure a position 180 degrees to him and for the first time was no longer in a purely defensive position. Now the odds were even and I had time to think about my next move. There were two options: first I could continue in the Lufbery to a position where I could possibly destroy my attacker, or I could make a run for it. The first was not at all appealing in view of my fuel supply. Furthermore, I wasn't sure that I could secure a position to effect a kill, not could I be sure other German fighters wouldn't join the scrap. To make a run for it was my best bet. Besides, I'd had enough combat experience for one day. Having made my decision and while the nose of my aircraft was passing through a northerly heading, I saw my opponent roll his 109 over in a dive heading east and I assume home. Needless to say, this was the most gratifying manoeuvre I had witnessed during the past twelve minutes. It was over. Fuel low, I reduced power and leaned back the mixture control, setting course for England. As I began to relax a bit, I recall taking off my oxygen mask, leaning over and pressing my lips to the canopy, kissing the old girl for bringing me through."

The weather, which was starting to deteriorate, kept the bombers grounded next day, but improvement on the 24th allowed missions to Schweinfurt and Gotha which were hotly contested by the Luftwaffe. The 56th took another eight Luftwaffe aircraft out of the sky, from the 38 credited to US fighters flying escort and support that day. The last major Big Week mission was flown on the 25th when almost 900 fighters went out to aid bombers sent to Regensburg, Augsburg, Stuttgart and Fürth. The 56th had three victories. Of the 26 shot down by US fighters, nine were by the new P-51 Mustangs, which were taking an increasing percentage of the claims. One of the 56th's victims fell to the guns of Captain Mike Quirk, leading the 62nd, who took his flight of yellow-nosed P-47s down to surprise two low flying yellow-nosed FW190s. The Luftwaffe pilot baled out and passed close to 2nd Lieutenant Buszko's P-47. Buszko gave him a wave and was surprised to see the German wave back. This was Quirk's tenth victory, although one had been shared. Quirk, a smallish man of Irish descent with dark curly hair, was a humourist, never lost for a funny story to tell. Lieutenant Robert Cherry, flying as his wingman had a disturbing experience:

"The first time I fired at an enemy aircraft was also the day I was first hit by enemy fire. Flying wing to one of my favourite leaders, Mike Quirk, he engaged an FW190 on the deck. As he hit it quite well and broke off due to high closure rate, the enemy aircraft pulled up into the sun directly in front of me. I followed, firing, until he rolled left and went into the ground. I made no claim since Mike had really hit the aircraft effectively and I am certain the German pilot only pulled up to bale out. While returning over France I was tagged by a single burst of 88 flak which took out two top cylinders of my engine. I called Mike and told him my bird was losing speed and I could only see out of a small area on the left side of my canopy. He acknowledged and that was the last I saw or heard of him. When I realised I was alone I switched to emergency channel and contacted the RAF lifesavers for vectors to the nearest field on the coast of England. They responded immediately and got me down just in time because when I retarded the throttle to land the engine froze. I put down on a B-26 Marauder base. The unit had been badly mauled that day after its escort of Spitfires departed. It was reasonably late when I landed and Halesworth told me to stay for the night and they would send a plane in the morning. When I entered the Nissen of my host squadron for the night, one of the B-26 pilots said, 'You can bunk here. You should feel right at home. We lost Captain Cherry today and this was his bed.'

Inclement winter weather blighted the rest of February and two more missions were relatively uneventful. In fact, on the 29th the only claim by the Eighth Air Force was a Ju52 transport that Gerry Johnson despatched. Overall during the month, however, the 56th had been remarkably successful. Not only had its pilots been credited with shooting down a total of 72 enemy aircraft, but only two of the group's Thunderbolts were lost and only one of those in air combat. This was John Patton's, a 63rd Squadron combat original who fell during a bounce by FW190s on 5 February. The story told, apocryphal or not, was that a week earlier Patton had attempted to make a pet of an ailing seagull found perched on the tail of his Thunderbolt. Three days later the bird died and three days after that Patton was killed. The other loss was Lieutenant Wilbur Kelley who has the unfortunate distinction of being the first member of the group brought down while strafing. If conditions and circumstances were right, after bomber escort commitments fighters were permitted to drop down to low altitude and shoot up any aircraft seen on enemy airfields. After breaking off escort on the 24th, Lieutenant Fred Christensen, with Kelley as his wingman, spotted aircraft on an airfield near Quakenbruck. Evidently their attack was anticipated as they were greeted by machine-gun and cannon fire. Kelley's P-47 was hit and he was killed. As a result, some sober consideration of the dangers of strafing heavily defended airfields led to a review of tactics to employ.

Even if the group's 72 air victories for the month was not completely accurate through misinterpretation of gun camera film and pilots' reports, the figure was still substantial weighed against a single loss in combat. While the Luftwaffe may have been facing an overwhelming number of Allied fighters these were not present in overwhelming numbers along the line of the bombers' route. Rather, the situation reflected poor tactics and an earlier failure of the Luftwaffe hierarchy to appreciate the threat. Further, attrition was thinning the ranks of experienced Luftwaffe fighter pilots and replacements were generally not of the same calibre. Such was spirit and confidence in the 56th that its pilots had now come to think of themselves as hunters of enemy fighters rather than defenders of the bombers. Someone suggested they were like a wolf pack; Zemke liked that and public relations did too. Inevitably the *Stars and Stripes* journalists took to it and coined 'Zemke's Wolfpack'. This lauding of the most successful American fighter unit had stimulated others to achieve. That single-engine fighters of equal performance to the Luftwaffe's were flying deep into the enemy airspace and besting the opposition was a development that high command had not thought possible even a year previous; and the 56th had led the way. Technical means such as pressurised drop tanks played a major part, but the winning streak for the 56th was leadership and air discipline, here neatly summed up by Frank Klibbe, successful 61st Squadron pilot:

> "The demand to fly to the standards and tactics established within the group without deviation set our group apart from many. Every pilot knew what to do and how to react as a flight of four or a squadron of 12 or 16. Each wingman to his leader knew exactly his role as a defender and observer to his flight leader. You were married to your leader and never left his side without approval or direction. Team work and unit were the key to and effectiveness of flight, squadron and group. Communications discipline was equally important. Only talk on the radio when absolutely essential to important matters of combat to emergencies. Know the capabilities and limitations of the aircraft and equipment, and employ the strengths fully and avoid weakness at all cost."

17 Keeping 'em Flying

Organisation and efficiency on the ground were as important as in the air. As weather was a frequent hazard for pilots, particularly if separated and alone, the weather officer was somewhat revered. In the autumn of 1943 the group acquired a new weather officer, Captain Alexander Sadowski, who became known as 'Stormy'. Sadowski was a weather enthusiast. Before each mission three men spoke to the assembled pilots at briefing: the CO, Intelligence Officer and the Staff Weather Officer in that order. The CO or his deputy outlined the mission: for example, an escort of heavy bombers to a target, giving the altitude at which the group would fly to protect the big friends. The Intelligence Officer pointed out the locations of anti-aircraft batteries along the route that were to be avoided, suggested where enemy fighters might be encountered and gave information relative to the enemy's defences. Then Stormy told of the weather along the mission route, recommending ways of avoiding dangerous conditions like heavy icing, which could occur as low as 2,000 feet over the North Sea even in summer. Stormy commenced his presentation by pointing out the board scale features like highs, lows, cold and warm fronts, on the latest weather chart of Europe and adjacent waters. Then he would present the detail with the aid of a blackboard, actually a sheet of plywood painted black with altitude lines at every 5,000 feet. On the blackboard he outlined the clouds as individual forms like cumulus or stratocumulus, which had openings between them, or as sheets and layers like stratus with no openings. The clouds were drawn at the proper altitudes with notations of their bases and tops and expected amounts in tenths of coverage. If turbulence was expected in the clouds, the degree (moderate or severe) was written across the clouds at the expected altitudes. The freezing level was drawn to show the region of icing. At the top of the blackboard was written the zone in which condensation trails could be formed by aircraft. This was important to avoid giving the group's position away to enemy aircraft. Along the left edge of the blackboard was entered the wind direction and speed at the designated altitudes up to 30,000 feet. Using the portrayal on the blackboard, Stormy described the expected weather on take-off and during ascent over the airfield to about 15,000 ft, before the group headed to the continent, then along the route of the mission to the target and return. He concluded his presentation by showing the best alternate airfield in case fog should roll in from the North Sea and 'sock in' Halesworth. When this happened, which was rare, Sadowski would use the radio microphone in the control tower and announce on the fighter frequency, 'Yardstick, this is Stormy. Oranges are sour at Sturdy. Proceed to alternate.'

Because Stormy was the last person to talk at briefings he concluded with a joke or some kind of levity. When the pilots landed from a mission, Stormy would be there to greet them and ask what sort of weather they encountered over the continent to aid the RAF if they were preparing a night mission. Stormy's day started three hours before briefing, usually around 3 am. Woken, he would then go by jeep to the Operations Room. One of the officers pointed out the target on the wall map and traced the route to follow. With the location by latitude and longitude of the target and a mental picture of the route, Stormy hastened to the weather station in the control tower to determine the weather. His first duty was to provide the upper winds and temperatures to Operations personnel so that a heading could be computed for the group to fly. Next he contacted Flying Control in the tower and gave the best two runways for take-off based on expected surface winds. Then he got down to preparing his weather briefing for the pilots.

The control tower was the nerve centre of flight operations. Tower operative Sergeant Albert White described its function:

"There were always one officer and two enlisted men on duty during the daytime and one of each through the night. Normal non-combat duties were to give runway information by telephone or in person to any pilot leaving the airfield, notify the destination of his name, aircraft type, time and leaving and estimated time of arrival. Give landing instructions to own and visiting aircraft. When a combat mission was to be launched we would first be advised on the force to be dispatched, together with a listing of pilot call-signs and aircraft letters. Operations would give us take-off times and time of return, and some of these details were passed to the operators of the chequered vehicle at the runway head. As each aircraft took off its letters were recorded; there was no radio communication at this time unless of an emergency. Aircraft were ticked off as they landed. A returning pilot often called for a homing bearing over the radio. He was told to give a sound count (6-5-4-3-2-1) which was picked up by our direction-finding station situated off the field. The DF [Direction Finding] station gave us a bearing which was passed on to the pilot. If a pilot was in trouble there was plenty of radio chatter. It was the tower duty staff's responsibility to alert the crash trucks and the men in the chequered vehicle. It was also their job to check that landing gear was down when aircraft made a runway approach.

"I don't think that anyone ever faced me and said there's going to be a mission. One just knew it. The tower was within the perimeter on the airfield. When you came on duty on your bike, you could tell the way the crew chiefs and mechanics and armament men were acting. Or, maybe you'd see the Catholic chaplain silently climb in his jeep with one hand tucked in his jacket holding onto a packet of hosts (consecrated bread or wafer) to be distributed to his pilots after a briefing. There were no baseball games, men gobbled down their meals, coffee was spilled. That's how we knew without being told."

Briefing for a mission always concluded with a time check; every pilot present set his watch to the same second when the senior officer on the podium called 'Hack'. Thereafter pilots would be driven to their respective squadron ready rooms to collect flight equipment. Pilots' clothing was very individualistic and amounted to personal preference although mostly topped off with the standard olive coverall. RAF helmets, goggles and boots were preferred by many, the leg part of the boots being detachable to leave a pair of shoes if the wearer found himself down in enemy territory. The equipment store was off the ready room and held the individual's parachute, harness, Mae West water lifesaver, in addition to gloves, helmet and goggles. Three pairs of gloves were available, long white silk, short chamois and long leather over gloves and combinations of these were a matter of choice. Squadron operations personnel issued escape kits which were placed in the parachute pack pouch and they also took into safe-keeping pilot's pocket material which was not to be taken on operations, lest if captured it might give the enemy information. The time spent waiting in the ready room prior to a mission until taken to the aircraft was reckoned by many to be the hardest on pilots' nerves.

Bad weather often meant several days without operations and restricted local flight training. Such periods brought classes and lectures for the pilots, aircraft recognition and continental geography being regular subjects. The opportunity was also taken to hold critiques on recent 'shows'. VIII Fighter Command arranged visits from experts on factors affecting fighter operations and new equipment while squadron commanders, successful pilots and other senior airmen of the group were often selected to go and talk to the men at the recently arrived fighter groups elsewhere in the area.

Award ceremonies, when lesser decorations were dispensed on the station, usually took place during inclement weather. VIII Fighter Command operated a points system whereby the completion of ten operational sorties or alternatively the destruction of one enemy aircraft or an incident involving difficulty in bringing an aircraft back amounted to one unit. An Air Medal was given for each unit. If a pilot collected five units he was awarded the Distinguished Flying Cross. The awards system came in for ridicule, not least among some recipients who considered it mixed achievement with valour to the extent that there was no distinction between an undoubted act of bravery and the execution of normal operational duty. "We reckoned they were just something for the folk back home; and writing out citations something for the guys at Saffron Walden [65th Fighter Wing HQ] to do," was one pilot's comment.

The situation regarding awards was gently mocked by some of the ground staff. Captain William 'Pop' Huger and some of the men in the headquarters intelligence section drew up several citations, one with kind sarcasm of the quality of the fuel ration received:

> 'The Distinguished Coal Medal to Lawrence Van B. Nichols, 1/Lt. QMC, US Army, for exceptionally meritorious conduct during the winter of 1943-44, by developing and applying a new method of distributing coal. In order to effect an equitable distribution and increase the weight without increasing the combustibility, Lt Nichols, through his own initiative, and after months of research, devised a method whereby rocks, stones, bricks, and other non-inflammable substances were added to the coal deliveries. His mixture has become standard in the ETO.'

Such humour could also be found amongst the enlisted men. Above the cots in a Nissen hut bearing the sign 'Ye Olde Buddie Hutte' on 41st Service Squadron's domestic site was a mock citation that awarded the Distinguished Snoring Cross to Mike Harak and Bob 'Horizontal'Harvey on 'successfully completing 5,475 ETO sack hours'. It was pointed out in the citation that this was '475 sack hours above, beyond and during the call of duty'.

The 41st Service Squadron handled work in the two hangars although fighter squadron mechanics also worked there as required. Inclement weather meant that engine changes and work which could have been performed on the hardstandings was performed under cover, each hangar holding a dozen P-47s if carefully parked. One of the characters in the 41st was Raymond Corbett, a giant of a man nicknamed Mike. Sergeant John Sipek:

> "Mike was one of my crew, a hard working rugged fellow from Oregon. He was as strong as a bull and many time used his strength to assist us in our repairs. Whenever it was necessary for us to lift the tail of a P-47 it would usually be time consuming work using two hydraulic jacks. With Mike around it was a simple task. He would say, 'Let me put my back to it.' Mike would place his back under the tail and lift it up so we could put a round steel bar through a hole in the tail section of the aircraft and let the ends of the bar rest on two stands. Mike was our human derrick."

The so-called technical site close to Holton Hall had a number of Romney buildings, like over-sized Nissens, where there was always much industry in repair and manufacture. Dave Schilling, who had a bent for things mechanical, was sometimes to be found in this area. With the help of Staff Sergeant John Brennan, prior to coming overseas he had devised an A-frame fitted to a Cletrac for the replacement of wings and engines. This was made up in the repair shops and proved most successful. At Halesworth Schilling had a machine shop set up in one of the buildings at Schilling's Acres where he spent many hours. Captain Eugene O'Neill:

> "Schilling loved to work with the airmen in the shops. He liked to mess

around with lathes and stuff like that. The enlisted men loved him because he spent more time with them than with us. Everybody respected him for it. He spent a lot of time making hunting knives out of files. Beautiful knives and he put leather handles on them. He took an officer's 45 pistol and changed the firing mechanism to make it fire rapid with a big ammunition clip. He dreamed up modifications for his P-47; got the ground crew to fit electrically operated trim tabs and he had some perspex bubbles that the British made fitted in the side windows so it was easier to look behind the plane."

While Schilling was generally popular with the ground men, particularly those of the 62nd Squadron where he still kept his personal aircraft for maintenance, this was largely due to his reputation of cheating authority if he so chose, such as the whisky appropriation episode back at King's Cliffe. There was also his easy man-to-man manner that he could show with enlisted men. Zemke, on the other hand, was viewed as typically military, an officer whom it was difficult to size up. There was respect for his leadership and combat prowess and while it was plain that he turned a blind eye to much that went on at Halesworth he could be severe in dealing with some matters. During the first few weeks after his return from the US tour Zemke flew any available P-47 in leading a mission. Meanwhile a new P-47D with the latest modifications was being prepared for him. The 41st Service Squadron's Technical Sergeant James Mindeck, responsible for a cursory inspection, passed it as okay. When the assigned crew chief started the engine it ran perfectly for a minute or two then flames burst out from behind the cockpit in the lower turbo tunnel. The crew chief, busy in the cockpit, did not notice this and not until he saw panic stricken men frantically waving did he shut the engine off. By this time the aircraft was well alight, the crew chief hastily extracted himself from the cockpit and jumped down off the front of the wing. The aircraft was a total loss.

It was found that one of the fuel connections was loose. Mindeck was reduced to private as a result and remained somewhat bitter in what he viewed as an accident not of his making. In bestowing this demotion Zemke was as much concerned with providing a warning to others as punishing Mindeck. There is no doubting Zemke's endeavours to show his concern for the welfare of the enlisted men in his frequent visits to various parts of his station. Dave Hubler:

"The mess halls at Halesworth were pretty lousy. The cooks didn't know how to operate the big steam vats. One day Zemke came to visit our mess hall. We had a cross-eyed cook who was up there dishing out chili, just slopping it on trays when you went through. Zemke's arm went out and this cook was going to fix him a special meal but Zemke said no and went on down the line. Then he came over to where Sgt Andy Remeta, Jack Holleman and myself were sitting at a table. He said, do you mind if I join you? We all stood up and he said sit down. Then he looked at his food and said 'How long have you been eating this slop?' Then he chewed us out for not saying anything about it. Next thing we knew they'd shut the mess-hall down, and we had cold rations. They sent down a big fat RAF cook who taught 'em how to cook in there before they reopened the thing."

18 The Happy Hunting Ground

If February had endorsed the 56th Fighter Group's prowess, March 1944 was to show it as never before.

The month did not start well with the loss of two pilots by other cause than enemy action. After a largely abortive attempt by the bombers to make their first assault on the enemy capital, two day later, 6 March, they succeeded and produced the largest and fiercest air battle of the war between the Luftwaffe and the Eighth Air Force. It brought the Eighth its highest loss for one mission when 69 bombers and 11 fighters failed to return, plus many badly damaged, but the American fighters alone were credited with shooting down 81 of the enemy. Notably 41 of these fell to the three P-51 Mustang groups then operational, again an indication of the range advantage of this type. The 56th's contribution to the total was 10 for the loss of one in combat. At this date the group could boast 23 aces. Marhurin and Bob Johnson both had 17 victories, one less than the total of 353rd Group's Walter Beckham who had been shot down and made prisoner late in February. Next in line was Gerry Johnson with 15, Gabreski with 14, Zemke had 11, Schilling, Schreiber and Quirk 10 each.

If the 56th pilots were becoming a little too confident, the battles of 8 March, when the bombers again made for Berlin, brought a sobering result. Although the group was credited with 28 of the 30 victories it claimed and passed the 300 destroyed mark, five of its aircraft were missing, four through air combat. The A group led by Schilling had only reached 24,000 feet when the bombers it was to protect were sighted. Robert Cherry, 62nd Squadron:

"We had just made rendezvous with the B-17s but were still slightly below them when they were hit by a large force of fighters. We were flying a split group that day and Colonel Schilling was leading A group with me on his wing, Joe Icard leading the element and Fred Roy flying on Icard. As the enemy aircraft came through the bombers we were next in line and they took advantage of the situation. My estimate was 50 plus against 12 and Schilling estimated 200. I will stick with the 50 plus figure since it got very busy about then and an accurate estimate was not possible. I last saw Icard and Roy in a turn to the left away from the flight. I was able to turn into the first 190 that attacked Schilling and he broke off. Another tried and I hit him quite effectively, saw fire but could not follow since another was attacking my leader. I fired on him and saw a few hits, and he too broke off. During the last short engagement I lost sight of Schilling and in fact the sky was empty of all fighters.

"The radio was jammed by unnecessary calls of 'Where is the fight?' etcetera, making it impossible for those of us in the fight to communicate. B group was the one causing problems with that which angered me. I had seen several bombers go down, assumed my aircraft was the only one still flying out of my flight and lost my cool a bit. When I saw a lone FW190 on the deck heading east I started a high speed dive to intercept, caught him and eliminated him from further combat. As I pulled off my squadron commander's voice (Schreiber) came through the headset: 'P-47 that just got one on the deck, you've cover at 9 o'clock.' Oh happy day. I had been feeling quite lonesome and vulnerable but was now reasonably safe. The flight home was uneventful. I expected two confirmed victories but my camera was iced over resulting in a probable for the first and visual confirmation for the second. Schilling made it back safely also but Icard and Roy were lost. During the critique the B group leader, Lt Col Gabreski, said I should be grounded for leaving my leader and I was really upset: being a new 2nd Lieutenant I said nothing. My squadron commander, Leroy Schreiber, immediately called a pilot meeting for the 62nd and stated no one would be grounded for shooting an enemy off another's tail. Col. Schilling, who may have known about the radio problem and how it was exacerbated by Gabby, himself came by to thank me and I heard no more from Gabreski."

Tony Carcione was one of the pilots shot down and killed. A popular character, this photography enthusiast had a reputation for shouting over the radio when excited or scared and this day was no exception. When under attack he kept his finger on the transmit button and no one else in A group could ask where he was and come to his aid. Icard and Roy were also both killed but the other two pilots lost baled out to became prisoners. Captain Joe Bennett had three victories and gained acehood. He had come from the 356th Fighter Group in exchange for Gerry Johnson back in November but had remained with the 56th. These, however were his last with the Wolfpack as at the end of the month he was transferred to the 4th Group to fly Mustangs. Both the group's top aces had successes this day and Mahurin's triple elevated him to the position of leading VIII Fighter Command ace with 20 victories, the first to reach this mark. Later reassessment reduced this to 19 and two shared, but few if any pilot's score could be truly proven. Dark-eyed and handsome, Bud Mahurin was modest about his success despite being subjected to press interviews and local adulation. He said he was "scared to death" on every mission. "I think a lot of us are." He described his recipe for success: "Keep cool and take it easy. Watch for an opening and then take it. A boxer who wades in swinging wildly gets hurt. That's the way it is in this business." Fellow pilots said he had X-ray eyes and Mahurin had certainly exhibited the ability to see a far-off aircraft before others. He was not superstitious and unlike some pilots carried no charms or items for luck: "I used to think it was unlucky to fly without my big flying boots, but the first time I did I shot down two machines." Neither married nor engaged he professed: "My job is just a little too risky just now."

Another star on 8 March was Flight Lieutenant Michael Gladych, late of the RAF Polish element, who was forced to bale out of a battle-damaged Thunderbolt over England. The lean, serious Pole told of shooting one enemy fighter in the air and others on an airfield, following separation from his flight during the battle. Gladych looked older than most, probably to do with his hectic experiences. About 5 ft 11 in tall, he had long hair through which he would often run his hand. His regular garb was an RAF officer's cap, American trousers and a French pilot's jacket. Gabreski, who had recruited him for the 56th, had some reservations: "Gladych was a man it was hard to figure out. A little extrovert, he had an imagination and I always thought his imagination carried him way off. I couldn't always believe everything that he said. I'd listen but I didn't disagree. He was an aggressive pilot and did a lot of daring things, but it only happened when he was alone. Very much an individual."

Mike Gladych's hatred of Germans and his actions soon had him labelled as 'Killer'. He carried an unusual mascot, a small ceramic penguin, of which he said: "See this little beast? That's the best charm in the world. Thousands of bullets have missed it and generally missed me." To have survived the experiences he related there was seemingly a need of some protecting charm. A Polish air force pilot, he flew to Rumania when Poland collapsed, surrendered and was interned, owing to German insistence. Escaping, he and other Poles were followed by German agents but reached France. In a dark ally in Lyon Mike fought and killed a German agent only to be rendered unconscious in the fight. When he came to he found himself blinded and bound head and foot in an asylum. For five days he heard the inmates shouting and singing, and felt that he too was psychotic. A French doctor came and said that it was a mistake that Mike had been committed, and Mike became angry, feeling pain in his eyes. The doctor told him to open them, the blinds were drawn and Mike could see. The doctor diagnosed his case as acute strain on the optic nerves, which had been overcome by the shocks he had suffered. Taken into French air force service, he was not long in getting into action, and shot down two of the enemy, ramming another at 14,000 feet when running out of ammunition. Mike was struck by two pieces of the enemy aircraft slashing across his eyes. He managed to get his aircraft on the ground in a crash landing, ending up only 200 yards from a British-manned hospital. Unconscious, he did not wake up in hospital for two days. After escaping to England he flew with the Polish manned fighter squadrons and had 180 operational flights to his credit by the time he came to the 56th.

The success of the 56th brought special recognition six days later when the 'top brass' arrived at Halesworth. Lieutenant General Carl Spaatz, over-all commander of the USAAF in Europe, Major General Doolittle, head of the Eighth Air Force, Major General Kepner of VIII

Fighter Command, and accompanying entourage were shown around selected areas of the base by Zemke and Schilling on this bleak March day and then entertained in the officers' lounge. This was a large Nissen building well fitted out with second-hand carpets, easy chairs, numerous practice bomb cases positioned as ash trays and a row of slot machines. The walls were decorated with unit insignia and photographic enlargements of group celebrities and aircraft, plus a Messerschmitt wingtip trophy above the main entrance door. Spaatz took the opportunity to present Zemke – who was 30 this day – with a Distinguished Service Cross, the second highest rated award for bravery. Not withstanding that all combat involved individual bravery the DSC was usually given to fighter pilots for shooting down multiples of enemy aircraft. Zemke's award was based on his performance on the 6 March Berlin raid when he had two victories and his initiation of ground strafing on 20 February. Several other DSCs had been awarded to 56th pilots for their exploits although this decoration came to be looked on more as one of acknowledging achievement rather than any unusual bravery. In fact, it is apparent that the unofficial accolade of ace was a far more valued achievement among pilots than medals, judging by the group records and public relations output of the time. In the opinion of some officers Zemke, because of his pioneering endeavours, was probably more popular with the generals at this time than with members of his own group. He continued to forego the pleasures of close camaraderie in the interests of a well-disciplined, smooth functioning organisation; but in truth Hub was something of a loner.

The following day his group once again showed its prowess with claims of 24 for the loss of one in combat. Most of this action took place in the area near Drummer Lake which the Wolfpack now called the 'Happy Hunting Ground'. The personable CO of the 63rd, Major Gerry Johnson, lifted his score to 15 while his namesake Bob Johnson brought down three, elevating his total to 22 and replacing Bud Mahurin as the Eighth's leading active ace. Back at Halesworth Bob Johnson learned that he had been promoted captain. Faced with a reporter's question as to what he attributed this pilot's success, Zemke commented:

> "There is a coming of age for a fighter pilot. Captain Johnson and anyone who has studied his record or that of any of the others, knows it. A man goes along, then someday, like jumping into a cold shower, he goes into combat to get the other guy. After he has done that once and really meant it, he is a combat pilot, if he's had the proper training and gets the proper leadership. But you can't make aces out of the carefree racetrack type."

Bob Johnson, recently turned 24, was coming up to his 200 combat hours and decided to take a 25-hour extension: "Five more planes would suit me fine but after 25 more flying hours, whether I get them or not, I'd like to go back to the States for a visit to my wife, whom I haven't seen for a year and a half."

The group put in another good showing next day with 11 claims for no loss. The Thunderbolts of all three squadrons were now displaying a bright red band on the front of engine cowlings. Following the 56th's lead other fighter units in VIII Fighter Command had started to decorate their aircraft with bright colours. To bring some order to the scene Ajax decided that each group would have distinguishing nose colours as an identity feature. The 56th, however, maintained its individualism by transferring the squadron colours from noses to rudders, with the exception of the 63rd which was distinguished by having normal finish rudders.

The following eight missions undertaken during the remainder of the month would yield only another 10 air victories for the loss of eight pilots. On 22 March in an effort to increase the chances of meeting enemy aircraft the group despatched three different formations to support bombers going to Berlin, A, B and C groups, the last consisting of just two flights. The 61st Squadron element of B group lost four aircraft, one to ground fire while strafing, the pilot becoming a prisoner, the other three disappearing without trace. Fifteen minutes after take-off the flights entered the overcast at 5,500 feet, the 61st CO leading. When Jim Stewart broke out in the clear the three other aircraft of his White flight were nowhere to be seen. The cause of loss was unknown, possibly a mass collision, but it is assumed that Don Funcheon, Claude Mussey and Dale Stream crashed into the sea. No radio calls were reported and their loss remains a mystery. Stream, who had only been with the squadron a few weeks, was flying Bob Johnson's personal Thunderbolt named Lucky with which the ace had achieved 20 of his victories. This mystery loss cast some gloom upon the 61st; five days later the whole group was in low spirits through another four losses which included two of the top aces, Majors Walker (Bud) Mahurin and Gerald Johnson, although his fellow pilots believed both had survived.

The group had provided an A and B formation for escort to and from targets in France and having completed their duty in this respect the Thunderbolts descended to lower altitude to look for targets to strafe, then a frequent feature of missions. Bud Mahurin:

"Our group leader spotted an enemy aircraft on a grass field below, and, while making a strafing attack, directed me to provide cover above. From a height of approximately 15,000 feet, I discovered another enemy machine flying down a railroad at very low level in the direction of Paris. With the rest of my flight I headed for the enemy to make an attack. I reached him rapidly, firing well out of range in hopes that the crew would abandon the machine in view of the odds of destruction. I could see the enemy tail gunner firing at me as I closed range and rapidly broke off to re-establish the attack. I settled in behind the Dornier on a second firing run and watched both engines catch on fire and the crew bale out of the bottom hatch almost at deck level. The aircraft then hit the ground and exploded. When I had broken off attack to begin my climb back to

altitude, I saw the shadow of my aircraft on the ground and noticed a long
stream of black smoke billowing from the tail. This is a cause for panic.
I called my leader to advise that I had been hit, but was climbing up to
rejoin just as I heard an explosion and noticed fire coming from beneath
the engine cowling of the P-47.... The last words I heard on the radio
came from Dave Schilling: 'Watch it boy! Your ship is on fire!'"

Bud baled out at under a thousand feet, his parachute only just having
time to open fully before he hit the ground. Uninjured he quickly made
off into nearby woodland and was able to avoid capture. Ironically, some
weeks before Mahurin had been sitting on the edge of Stormy Sadowski's
bed in the Nissen hut they shared with other 63rd officers, discussing how
he planned to approach twin-engine fighters in the blind spot of the rear
gunner's cone of fire in order to use fewer bullets in shooting the aircraft
down.

Gerry Johnson, leading his squadron in the A group also engaged in
strafing with his White flight. What happened was narrated by 1st
Lieutenant Archie Robey, the element leader:

"After we had dropped down to find an airport or some other target to
strafe, I fired at some high tension wires in the vicinity of Lassey and saw
one pole and wires fall to the ground. At approximately 1545 hours we
sighted some trucks with soldiers in them, and Major Johnson, Lt Everett
and myself went down to attack. My wingman, 2/Lt Lovett had
supercharger trouble and had to abort. We then strafed and severely
damaged some of the trucks. After we had made a couple of passes on
different trucks, we headed out to the coast. At that time someone called
in a line of trucks on our right just entering a small town. We then flew
over the town of Condé to see if we could sight them. As we passed over
Condé at about a thousand feet, my plane was hit by .303 and 20 mm fire.
I caught up with Major Johnson and after we had gone approximately
five miles east he called to say that he was hit and was crash-landing. Lt
Everett and myself circled and saw him belly in an open field. Major
Johnson got out of his plane and apparently opened the parachute in the
cockpit and set it on fire, as smoke was coming from the cockpit. I called
Yardstick (Gabreski) and said, 'Postgate White 1 has landed on his belly.
I think I can land. Shall I go down and pick him up?' To this Yardstick
answered 'Roger, Roger.' I then lowered my wheels but my flaps would
not come down because of the battle damage my plane had received. Not
being able to cut my speed, I was unable to land in such a small field.
However, as I was circling around, I saw Major Johnson surrounded by
a group of civilians, all of whom were shaking his hand and with his free
hand he waved me on. He then started to run towards adjoining woods
accompanied by civilians."

Lieutenant Everett, having overheard Robey's predicament, then
attempted a landing but had to abandon his approach when a wing hit a

tree and was damaged. Heading home at low altitude they encountered small arms fire. Whether it was due to this or earlier damage, some five miles out from France Everett called Robey and said he would have to turn back and attempt to ditch. Robey told him to bale out and notified air/sea rescue. Everett was never heard from again. Johnson was taken prisoner and did not know about Everett's attempt until his release. The fourth pilot downed was also a victim of fire from small arms.

With the 63rd Squadron's commander and deputy lost, Zemke moved Captain Robert Lamb from the 61st to be the new CO. With many of the 'originals' finishing their tours Zemke was hard-placed to find experienced men who were not near time expired to fill command posts. One of those reaching the 200-hour mark was the 62nd Squadron's Johnson, Ralph. Pilots would empathise with his reflective sentiments:

"After the first two or three missions, I realised that this was a serious business. When my friends failed to return it really made me very sad. Not knowing whether they were dead or alive had further impact. Most of us had trained, lived and flown together for about two years. It got to the point where I did not want to know the replacement pilots too personally. It really hurt if they failed to return. In fact, after a mission when someone would say that so-and-so had failed to return, I would ask which one was so-and-so and the answer usually was he had been here only a couple of weeks. When I was ready to return to the States, out of the 27 pilots in my squadron that had gone over together there were only six in the free world. Of the others we knew that 14 had been lost on missions and three had been killed in accidents. I count these latter as combat losses because they were over here to fly against our enemy. Some were POWs but we had not received notices on all of them. Finding that one of them was a POW caused mixed emotions in that I was glad he was alive but sad he was a prisoner with an uncertain future. We had a great bunch of people and I wanted so much for them to live out their lives."

Feelings about the mortality of their opponents were less charitable if understandable. As Robert Rankin stated, "We did not really think about the enemy pilots, only of shooting down aircraft." It would not have helped personal morale for a pilot to dwell on the fate of the enemy he had despatched. No doubt some did but with the majority any such concern was subjugated by disdain and the desire to vanquish. Frank Klibbe: "My motivation was a mixture of hatred and knowing it was a serious game of kill or be killed. The latter represented the stronger feelings for there are no stakes higher than to challenge an opponent in combat with your or his life. It mattered not if or how my opponent died, it was victory that counted." If humanity was suspended there was no lack of respect for the expertise and aggressiveness of Luftwaffe pilots met in battle, even if Allied propaganda suggested otherwise.

Accidents have always been an unfortunate feature of warfare, none so disturbing as those that involve a life-saving service, as happened on 23 March. Bunny Comstock:

"My wingman Warren 'Gene' Kerr and I were on our way home over the North Sea at about a comfortable 100 feet. I was smoking a cigarette with the canopy cracked and Gene was off my right in a very loose formation. Dead ahead I spotted two aircraft making diving passes at a column of smoke. Throwing the cigarette out, I closed the canopy, jumped up to about 1,500 feet and called Gene to turn on his gun switch and be alert. My first reaction was that they must be FW190s but as we got closer, I could see they were a pair of P-47s and that they had what appeared to be a torpedo boat under attack. It was burning and as we got closer I could make out that it was an RAF rescue boat with a chequered foredeck, roundels on the nose, RAF blue ensign on the mast and the British flag on the stern. My mind shifted gears and I figured that the P-47s were captured and that the Luftwaffe were having a little revenge, even though both aircraft had US markings. I put Gene up above and I flew alongside the leader and fired a short burst in front of him and he discontinued the attack. I pointed toward England and indicated for him to head that way. He and his wingman complied. I still was not convinced as to who they were so I told Gene to stay behind the wingman and if the wingman made any move to turn around he was to be killed immediately. I did the same with the leader and we proceeded towards England. I still was not sure if they were a pair of gutsy Germans who were going to play the game to the end and then take off again. We landed at Martlesham Heath and we followed them all the way to the handstands where we blocked the entrance so they couldn't get out. When they shut the engines off we did the same. Got out, flagged down a jeep and we told the driver to take us to the group CO, and lo and behold it turned out to be Phil Tukey, once my squadron CO in the 63rd. When I told him about the incident, he said I must be mistaken. The two pilots were sent for and when they arrived the leader insisted that the vessel was a German torpedo boat and that he had once worked in the factory that built torpedo boats and thus knew all about them. About this time the phone rang for Tukey and it was the RAF rescue people at Martlesham and they were most unhappy. They had a Walrus at the boat and reported all the boats' crew killed except the gunner who had both legs shot off. Phil allowed that I was right and he would take care of it. Gene and I went home to Halesworth and reported the incident during debriefing. Those guys should have been court-martialed, but I believe all that happened is they were sent back to the States – and that wasn't punishment!"

The vessel was rescue launch HSL 2706, whose crew had rescued a complete B-17 crew the previous day.

Halesworth personnel were involved in a major accident a few days later, in which one of those killed was Captain Stanley Morrill, an ace who had come to the group three months before his namesake, Byron

Morrill, had been lost. Stan Morrill, who had notched up ten victories, was not scheduled to fly in the mission that was being set up on the morning of 29 March when two Liberators collided near the base and fell about four miles away. Morrill took a jeep and went to see if he could help. While rescuers and fire fighters were working on one of the wrecks in Henham Park part of its 8,000-lb bomb load exploded and Stan Morrill was one of the 36 fatal out of the 89 casualties. Nineteen of the dead and 38 of the injured were from Halesworth. The fire crews were decimated. Fate played a strong hand that day. Private First Class Anthony Bolles:

"At 19 I was the youngest man in the 56th Fighter Group when it came overseas. A Fire Engineer, on the morning of March 29th I was on station near the tower as we had a big mission going out and two fire trucks and two ambulances were required to be manned and ready for any accidents. There were many bombers up in the clouds and around 10.45 am two collided and I saw them come down not far away. Lt Joyce, who was the fire officer in charge, said that only one fire truck and one ambulance could go to offer what assistance we could. I was a member of the fire crew that went. On arrival at the scene of one of the burning wrecks I took a hose off our fire truck and proceeded to lay layers of foam on the debris while men were trying to pick up the dead crew members of the B-24. After some time our fire truck ran out of foamite. I shut down my hose and started to look around for something to wipe my hands because they were sticky with foam. I spotted a piece of paper and bent down to pick it up. The next thing I remember was finding myself in a hospital bed. My nurse told me I had been in a coma for four days. They thought I was gone and the hospital chaplain had administered the Last Rites! Both eardrums were ruptured and I had lost the ring finger on my right hand. No one had told us that there were bombs in the wreck but when I had bent down they exploded. Blast goes up and then out, so I was below the full force of the explosion. My buddy Benny Cala was standing up at the time right next to me and took the full blast which killed him."

This day's tragedy vexed Zemke, as in addition to Morrill several of the casualties were not fire and ambulance men and had no right to be there, whatever their motives.

For the first time, on 5 April, fighters were sent out on a planned offensive mission to strafe enemy airfields in western Germany and adjacent occupied territory. It provided little success for the Wolfpack while the range advantage of the Mustang was again highlighted by their making over a hundred claims on distant Luftwaffe bases, albeit that many were disallowed. The particularly dangerous nature of strafing airfields caused VIII Fighter Command HQ to advise the groups that they would consider aircraft destroyed on the ground of equal status to those shot down in accessing individual pilot and unit scores. Even so, in the view of pilots strafing victories never rated as high as those obtained in air combat; the air ace was still the supreme accolade for the fighter pilot.

The comparative dearth of enemy fighter contacts for the 56th continued through April 1944, while much to the disappointment of its eager pilots the P-51-equipped units saw plenty of action. The best showing for the Wolfpack came during support for bombers on 9 April when eight of the enemy were claimed in the air and four by strafing. The star of the day was Dave Schilling leading A group. His combat report read:

"My wingman (Lt Wendell McClure) and I had become separated from the group when we sighted a gaggle of between 30 and 35 FW190s flying in tight formation and circling to the right at 21,000 feet about twenty miles north east of Schleswig. We immediately swung around to the rear of the formation and sneaked in range from underneath and the outside. I opened fire from about three hundred yards with about a ten-degree deflection from above and immediately saw strikes all over the aircraft. I continued firing until I had closed to 150 yards when I pulled up violently to avoid a collision with particles from the aircraft, which had exploded. Several pieces struck my aircraft, knocking two holes in the leading edge of my right wing and one in the blister of the canopy. Immediately after this several of the rear-end Charlies saw my wingman and I and flick-rolled to the deck. I picked another target at about 30-degree deflection at about 300 yards and opened fire. He saw me, turned right, rolled and went down. I saw several strikes and followed him to 15,000 feet, where I broke off and climbed back up. I then saw my wingman diving on the tail of an FW190 as I rejoined the rear end of the formation. By this time they had me spotted and split into two formations, half of them getting behind me. I flicked, hit the switch, and went down. At about 12,000 feet I overboosted my engine due to excessive rpm and blew a cylinder head, causing a lot of oil and smoke to come out of the left side of my engine. I had no sooner hit the deck with everything cut back trying to stop the smoke, when I saw two FW190s ahead, turning to the left. I was still indicating over 400 and lined him up from 380 yards with a ten-degree deflection. I noticed a large concentration of strikes on the wing roots, cockpit and canopy. As I passed him, he pulled up steeply to the left, winged over, and went straight in and exploded, leaving a large column of smoke.

"I continued on course and happened across a lake several miles south east of Schleswig, saw an Arado 196 on floats ahead and fired at it from about 900 yards. I undershot but raised my sights and hit it squarely with a heavy concentration of strikes all over it. It began to smoke just as I passed over it. After I crossed the lake, I saw a Ju34W ahead and slightly to the right preparing to land at Schleswig airdrome. I was over-eager and fired too soon, and only got about five to seven hits before I ran out of ammunition. I then proceeded out on course and saw an FW190 firing at me from about 500 yards. I figured that excessive pressure would set the accessory section on fire but took a chance. As I did so smoke and oil again poured from the cowling, and the FW190 pulled up to my right and turned back. I waited until he was out of sight and then cut back to 1,800 and 29 inches. The fire stopped and I figured I might make it. Shortly after I had crossed out I saw Heligoland out ahead and to my right and turned left, but due to the haze almost flew over a large convoy led by three destroyers. I turned right and figured I could get between them. They must have been asleep because I was past the two of them before they opened up, and then they shot everything from both places. After getting out of range I called the boys and told them my predicament, speed, course, and time I passed out (from the enemy coast). The trip home was uneventful."

This was not an isolated instance of a leader and his wingman choosing to attack a larger number of enemy fighters and illustrates the general confidence among these American pilots in their ability to win. Schilling later received a DSC for this action. Other aircraft received damage but the only loss was a case of misfortune. B group, led by Gabreski, had also seen combat and was low on fuel on leaving enemy airspace. A recent 62nd Squadron replacement, 2nd Lieutenant Ward Canizaries, who had already shown promise, was a wingman and had taxed his fuel so severely that he was forced to bale out over the sea. Major Schreiber called air/sea rescue and circled the downed pilot even though his own fuel supply was critical. Schreiber radioed a message for his thanks to be conveyed to air/sea rescue for responding so quickly "in case I don't make it back." He did make it back but the incident illustrates his popularity in that disregarding his own predicament he wanted his appreciation conveyed to Canizaries' rescuers. RAF air/sea rescue reached Canizaries within a few minutes only to discover he was dead. In exiting his aircraft he had apparently struck the tail. The delicate-looking Canizaries with aquiline nose, translucent skin and slightly bulging eyes was said to have the looks of the Spanish nobility, as his forbears had sailed with the Conquistadors to Cuba. He was the last of the male line in his family.

Bob Johnson shot down an FW190 to make his total 23, levelling with the 4th Group's Don Gentile, but Gentile's score included ground strafing credits. The competitive Zemke was troubled by the rising total of the 4th Group's Mustangs, which the previous day had broken the 56th's record for one mission by shooting down 31 of the enemy. The 4th's combined air and ground total for March was 156 enemy aircraft destroyed as against the Wolfpack's 88. Bob Johnson further advanced his position as the Eighth's leading air ace by adding two more victories on 13 April.

A second planned strafing mission of airfields was set up by Ajax on 15 April and, as on the previous occasion, was conducted on a cloud-shrouded day. The weather was particularly poor but the Wolfpack acquitted itself well with five air victories and at least 12 Luftwaffe aircraft destroyed on the ground. The cost was dear: two original combat pilots with but a few hours to complete their tours, Charlie Harrison and Dick Mudge, plus the popular commander of the 62nd, Leroy Schreiber. Harrison was shot down and killed in a fight with FW190s and Mudge

baled out after his P-47 took flak hits. It was during the attack on the
heavily defended airfield at Flensburg that Schreiber's Thunderbolt was
seen to climb to about 700 feet, roll over and dive into the ground. There
was an unusual air of gloom in the Officers' Club that evening.
Schreiber's loss was felt particularly strongly by the 62nd, not only by the
pilots, as the sadness affected ground personnel as well. Captain Virgil
Durrance, the squadron's adjutant, considered Schreiber the most
outstanding of all its commanders, "intelligent, competent and a nice
man". This was echoed by Line Chief Dave Hubler: "One of the best
squadron commanders we had was Leroy Schreiber who was pretty much
a carbon copy of Zemke. He didn't have Schilling's personality but
everybody respected him. He was an older pilot, smart. He wasn't as
harsh as Zemke. I don't fault Zemke for that, he had to be." It appears that
Schreiber had attacked a decoy site some two miles distant from the real
airfield and was met with intense 20-mm fire.

During March and April several surviving 'originals' reached the end
of their tours. Some took a 25-hour extension, others decided they had
had enough and let VIII Fighter Command decide their future, which
normally meant a period instructing at Atcham before being returned to
the US. The enthusiasts were those taking the option of a month's leave
in the States with a return to the 56th and included Comstock, Conger,
Egan, Hall, Quirk, Schilling, Don and Les Smith. George Hall intended
to get married while back home and Egan and Schilling talked him into
getting circumcised before the event. "George was a little naive along
those lines. Joe had lots of experience with women, much more than most
of us."

Schilling undoubtedly savoured his exalted status with the 56th. Even
Zemke, who once had misgivings, now appreciated his air executive's
capabilities and was loath to lose him. Although very different
personalities their association was reasonably amicable, Hub still
indulged Dave's oft outlandish opinions and suggestions, dismissing
them with a chuckle, although ready to take up anything of promise. The
Flying Executive would be particularly missed by many of the 62nd
ground men; the following being a good example of why he was held in
such esteem. Dave Hubler:

"I happened to be out there at lunch time by myself. Schilling drives up
in a jeep – he drove like a mad ass Indian. Crazy talking. Then he said,
'D'you know I'm going back to the States?' I said yes. 'Well I'm leavin'
tomorrow morning.' And with that he reaches down and pulls up a box of
cigars. He said 'Look these won't keep until I come back so you better
have 'em.' It was his way of saying I appreciate what you've done. When
we had beer parties he was back of the bar handing out the beer and
threatening to whip anybody who didn't like that. He got lots of things
done the way he operated. Everyone kind of protected him in a lot of
ways because he was so popular."

Apart from the difficulty of filling the positions when his time-expired pilots left, Zemke had the unwanted business of moving base. Alerted early in the month that a B-24 bomb group would be arriving from the States to move into Halesworth, he was informed that the 56th's new airfield would be Boxted on the northern outskirts of the town of Colchester, some 40 miles to the south. Hub's reasoned protest that the B-24 group could go to Boxted as this was built as a bomber base, was countered by command's statement that Halesworth had only been on loan from the B-24 equipped division which wanted all its groups in the same area. The move to Boxted took place without a hitch 17 to 19 April. The station was found to be complete and in good order, having just been vacated by a Ninth Air Force Mustang group. And there was no sticky mud!

19 Lead up to D-Day

The Easter weekend move to Boxted, Station 150, was made in fine weather. Everyone without a specified task at Halesworth was recruited to help. It did not matter much who you were or what you did. Men who handled food found themselves loading small bombs onto trucks. Although few wanted to move from Halesworth for no other reason than they were nicely settled in and had got to know the neighbourhood, most found Boxted a more favourable location being close to a sizeable town with good communications to London. Like Halesworth the domestic sites were spread in the countryside adjoining the airfield if not quite so isolated. The Seco-hutted prime site, close to the main London road, a pub and the base communal facilities, was occupied by the 61st Fighter Squadron. The 41st Service Squadron also had a main roadside site but with the familiar Nissen huts accommodation. The 62nd and 63rd Fighter Squadron personnel were housed in Nissens beyond a little valley in and on the borough boundary of Colchester, the centre of which was a two mile cycle ride. As at Halesworth, Zemke had his quarters and those of his air executives and squadron commanders together in one location, and at Boxted this was in a substantial farmhouse vacated when the station was built. This also became known as the Wheelhouse. Ready rooms for the squadrons were large Nissen structures, those of the 62nd and 63rd by the technical site and the 61st on the airfield's western side near No. 2 hangar. From an operational standpoint Boxted was good, only some twelve miles from the coast and three from a prominent estuary which made it relatively easy to locate in poor weather. Being further south and closer to the continent a longer range was provided. With the new venue, group and squadron call signs were changed, Yardstick being replaced by Fairbank.

The move was also in conjunction with an improved flight communication system. John Brady:

"I was Master Sergeant, Communications Chief, HQ 56th FG. My prime responsibility was the installation, maintenance and functioning of the fighter control system necessary for communication with the aircraft of our group. The system consisted of receiver, transmitter, and Direction Finding/Homing sites operating on the various radio frequencies used between aircraft and the ground. All these sites were interconnected to be controlled from the control tower. The DF site was able to control the transmitters. I had no assigned personnel directly under my control so the total responsibility for operation and maintenance was mine. Some days prior to the 56th's move from Halesworth I was detailed to proceed to Boxted to determine satisfactory site locations for radio installations. New aircraft control and communication equipment were to be received and would require specific locations, assembly and placing into operation. A location for the receiver site was selected in a field near the south boundary of the station. This equipment would be a mobile unit as no building was available, with the antennas on a 50-foot mast. The transmitter site was an existing building on the south side of Severalls Lane, which though vacant must have been previously used for radio communications as a tall tower was already adjacent and convenient to mount the antennas as high as possible. Additionally there was already an emergency power unit at the location. I thought this to be quite peculiar as the generator was driven by a Ford automobile V8 motor. It required hand cranking and was contrary in that it could kick backwards and break your arm. The DF/Homing site was also off the base to the east in a field near Wick Farm. The DF equipment had its own specially designed building, so designed and located to lessen general interference. These sites were all interconnected to each other and the control tower through telephone lines. The tower and DF facility had control of the transmitters as necessary. The equipment turned out to be newly developed so as to operate more effectively with equally new equipment installed in the P-47 aircraft, and was more powerful to permit communication on VHF radio frequencies well into the continent."

Part of Brady's installation had a short working life for in the early hours of 25 April an RAF Lancaster returning from a raid, was shot down by an enemy intruder and crashed close to the domestic site of the 63rd Fighter Squadron, destroying the mobile radio receiver installation. A replacement set-up, obtained from Burtonwood, was not forthcoming for two weeks. One airman had fallen or jumped from the aircraft. Where his body hit the ground it left a clearly defined imprint, the force was such that in a few days the grass within this depression turned yellow. Part of one of the engines, believed to have been a generator, was hurled through a Nissen hut roof and buried itself in the floor between the bunks of two sleeping men.

There was no break in operations occasioned by the move. The last missions from Halesworth were flown on 18 April landing at Boxted on return, and the first from the new station the next day. The first enemy aircraft claim was made on the 20th when Captain Felix Williamson and Lieutenant Wendell McClure happened upon a Ju88 flying north of Paris. If any reminder was needed of the hazards of flying single-engine fighters of the time, 22 April was it. Three aircraft were wrecked and two pilots killed in unrelated training accidents. Dive-bombing practice was undertaken on a sea marker some 20 miles off Orfordness. For some reason the P-47 flown by Lieutenant Archie Robey did not pull out of its dive from 10,000 feet, as it was never seen again. George Bracken, a recently arrived replacement, lost his life when his aircraft got into difficulties and crashed near Lindsey village. The third P-47, suffering engine failure, bellied in near the base, ending up in the garden of a cottage. It is said that the lady occupier on coming out to see if the pilot (Sam Lowman) was injured remarked: "I've often wondered what a Thunderbolt was like as my son is flying one these in Burma. But I never thought I'd see one this close."

The dive-bombing practice was to develop the best method of carrying out this form of attack. The group put it to a combat test on the afternoon of the 28th when 24 P-47s departed Boxted with two clusters of 20-lb fragmentation bombs on each wing rack. The briefed target, Orléans/Bricy airfield, was obscured by cloud so the attack was carried out on another airfield north-east of Paris. Led by Zemke, 45-degree angle dives were made from between 11,000 and 13,000 feet with releases between 7,000 and 10,000 feet. Few bombs were believed to have landed on the target and release of this type of ordnance from these altitudes was adjudged unsatisfactory. Moreover some bombs hung up on the racks and two aircraft had to bring them back to Boxted, whose pilots were understandably relieved that the clusters did not fall off on landing impact.

The shortage of pilots was still acute and at times during April there were 20 more aircraft than pilots at Boxted. This situation also troubled the other Eighth Air Force fighter groups that had been on operations since the previous spring. After Gabsezewicz returned to RAF service, Flight Lieutenant Anderz joined Gladych, and with Gabreski's encouragement other 'resting' Poles came to fly with the Wolfpack, forming an all-Polish flight in the 61st Squadron. Also at this time Brigadier General Curtis LeMay, head of the 3rd Bomb Division, contacted Zemke and asked if he could use a pilot who no longer felt able to fly bombers. Lt Colonel Preston Piper had lost crew members in a North Sea B-17 ditching, so upsetting him that he no longer wanted the responsibility of other men's lives although perfectly willing to fly missions on his own. Hub's response was in the affirmative; he could use any combat-experienced pilot. This led to Zemke exploring the possibility of obtaining tour-expired bomber pilots who might want to fly fighters. With approval from Ajax word went out to the B-17 and B-24 bases and soon six volunteers were on their way to Boxted. With so many 'old hands' finishing tours it was necessary to transfer the remaining experienced pilots to fill flight leader positions in other squadrons. The 62nd was particularly short on experience by late April and Zemke transferred Bob Johnson and Joe Powers from the 61st easing the situation. To add to the 56th's load the controlling 65th Fighter Wing decided to organise an air/sea rescue spotter squadron at Boxted early in May. Equipped with well used P-47s that carried dinghy packs and rescue equipment, aircraft and personnel were drawn from several groups although around a third had to come from the 56th.

For Zemke and his aggressive cohorts the now limited contact with the enemy in the air was an irritating situation. There was no doubting that the losses sustained by the Luftwaffe during the battles of the last six months had been crippling. Overwhelmed by the combined Allied fighter forces in the west the Luftwaffe had withdrawn a large number of its day interceptor units to within the borders of the Reich, continuing to direct most effort against the bombers, where possible avoiding the fighters. To this end the Luftwaffe raid reporting organisation had improved and afforded much better direction to its fighters during Eighth Air Force intrusions. Zemke, who tended to bypass wing headquarters and take his requests and ideas straight to VIII Fighter Command, had long suggested that a fighter sweep some minutes ahead of a mission stood a good chance of catching enemy fighters assembling for an onslaught on the bombers. He was finally given permission to send part of the group out to sweep the 'Happy Hunting Ground' ahead of a major mission to Berlin on 8 May.

The plan was certainly valid as near Celle the 61st and 62nd Squadrons became involved in a series of interceptions with two types of enemy interceptors. The result was six destroyed claims for the loss of two.

Lieutenant Robert Cherry:

"I watched Lewis's plane go in but saw no chute since I was below the clouds where I had surrounded a bunch of 109s, and, although he was my wingman, I did not know he had baled out. Bob Johnson was leading the squadron that day which proved to be his last mission. The flight consisted of Bob, Hartney on his wing, and I had the element with Lewis on my wing. Hartney was very new and Lewis had limited experience. I had spotted a large gaggle of enemy aircraft ahead and above us and called them in to Johnson. With all eyes looking ahead trying to see those aircraft a single 109 jumped me and a 20 mm exploded on my prop. I broke hard left, then reversed to stay in position and saw a 190 headed for the clouds. I called Bob that I was after him and started the chase. Bob called and I thought he said 'Chase him under the clouds.' He had actually said, ' Don't....' At the clouds Lewis broke off leaving me alone underneath with what looked like the entire Luftwaffe. Bob got his last two that day and, after we landed, explained what he had actually said. He was great to fly with. Prior to the launch he briefed us that we were out to get Germans and if we saw a good target to call and go after it; he would fly cover. I wish more leaders had had that attitude."

Cherry had been mistaken for it was an errant 352nd Group P-51 pilot who had shot down Gordon Lewis and holed Cherry's propeller with .50 ammunition. Another example of the poor standard of aircraft recognition by some airmen had occurred a few days earlier when Sam Lowman and Tony Cavello of the 63rd were shot up by a B-17 gunner; Cavello's aircraft received 10 hits in the right wing and three in the tail.

Surprisingly this happened over Dunkirk as the Thunderbolts were penetrating enemy airspace and the B-17 was the lead of a formation coming out. Both P-47 pilots had to turn back and made Boxted safely.

For Bob Johnson the 8 May flight would be his 89th and final combat mission. Higher authority saw the morale-building potential of sending him back to the US for tours and lectures, particularly as he had passed the 26 air victories of First World War American ace Eddie Rickenbacker. By coincidence 62nd's Lieutenant Harold Evans who was on this mission was the son of Rickenbacker's CO in 1918. Bob's description of the action that reinforced his position as the top American ace in Britain began with intercepting an Me109 shooting at a troubled B-17:

> "I went down, followed him a few minutes and shot him down. He just went all to hell. Then we were climbing back up, one of my flight saw two FW190s in a dive. We went after them. One of the flight chased two of them under a cloud. I said over the radio I would pick up the Germans as they came out the other side. As they came out, there were not two but four, and they were on the tail of Hartney's plane. He was circling with them. I yelled that I was on my way to help him. I couldn't get on them, however, as I was turning in the opposite direction, so I made several head-on passes at them and was chasing them off one or two at a time. I sailed into one of the Jerries head-on and shot him down. The German went into a burning spin and blew up. We started climbing for altitude and came home."

The 145-pound, 5 feet 9 inches tall, brown-haired pilot who spoke with a mixture of Oklahoma drawl and clipped British expressions, exuded self-confidence. Even so, the almost casual description of the action belies his true understanding of the dangerous business in which he had been involved. Bob was basically a serious individual, determined to succeed. Some of his fellow pilots thought him too determined and intent on shooting down enemy aircraft at the expense of air discipline, which was being based on the number of times he was said to have gone after the enemy without his squadron leader's direction.

Bob Johnson was promoted to major prior to returning to the US to be decorated by President Roosevelt. Before leaving Boxted he gave his captain's silver shoulder bars to Stormy Shadowski, who had Bob's name engraved on them to wear on his shirt collar as a souvenir. Johnson, on the other hand, took home an unusual keepsake. When Walker Mahurin arrived at Boxted after successfully evading capture he went looking for Bob in the 62nd Squadron area. Told that Johnson was away, Mahurin took the Form 1 block, the pilot's aircraft acceptance form, and wrote a jocular if crude salutation across the top of the sheet and signed his name. When Johnson returned and saw the vulgar greeting from his friend he decided to keep the form.

The 8 May sweep had been fruitful but Zemke had another idea in his quest for air action: a group formation to fly out well ahead of a bomber mission to a planned point deep in enemy airspace. At this point each flight would separate and fan out in a 180-degree arc. If the enemy was engaged other units of the Wolfpack could be called in by radio to assist. Not only would this give a much greater chance of making contact with Luftwaffe fighters, it would also confuse enemy ground controllers. Zemke went down to Bushey Hall to discuss this with the VIII Fighter Command operations officer and received permission to try this tactic, which became known at Ajax as the Zemke Fan.

On 12 May A and B group formations left Boxted ten minutes apart, the first led by Zemke, the second by Gabreski. It proved quite a day, particularly for the instigator. A distinctive bend in the Rhine was the separation point with squadrons and flights fanning out. Zemke had only two other aircraft in his flight, owing to one having turned back with mechanical difficulties. Zemke's description of what occurred follows:

"After some 40 miles I turned to begin a north-south patrol. All three of us scanned the hazy horizons of the blue void, periodically dropping a wing to get a better view below where we hoped to spot enemy aircraft forming up. No moving specks observed, I flipped the radio switch to the Bomber-Fighter channel for word of action elsewhere. Nothing. Flipping the switch back I just caught the electrifying alarm: 'Fairbank, break left!' The instinctive reaction was violent movement of stick and rudder pedals. As the Thunderbolt skidded round I was conscious of the all-too familiar white puffs – time fused cannon shells exploding. 'Fairbank to Daily White Flight. Turn in trail, make a Lufbery.' Obviously outnumbered, until I had time to size up the situation the protective turning circle with each of us covering the man ahead's rear was my reaction. It was a mistake; we were picking up speed too slowly and I could now see there were seven Me109s about 5,000 feet above waiting to pick us off. They had the advantages of altitude and speed and periodically launched an element of two to come down, shoot at us and then recover; the same tactics as we so often pulled on some unsuspecting Luftwaffe outfit.

"As we turned I made repeated calls for assistance hoping another of our flights was near. Suddenly a single Me109 cut across our circle and took a shot at Willard Johnson's plane [Zemke's wingman]. Flames enveloped the fuselage and the Thunderbolt turned over and disappeared from view. Where was help? I called again. Piper [Preston Piper the ex-B-17 pilot] and I tightened our circle. Desperation rather than fear gripped me as I looked for an opening to escape. If we attempted to dive our initial acceleration would be sluggish and they could nail us before we built up sufficient speed. The lone Me109 repeated its previous act: diving down across our circle he opened up with a deflection shot on Piper. Again, out of the corner of my eye, I saw smoke and flame erupt. Two down, one to go. Fear took hold, in that racing jumble of thought the prospect of death spun by. Is this the exit of Mrs Zemke's little 'Hobart'? Perhaps my dread would have been all the greater had I known that the pilot I had just seen despatch Johnson and Piper was the third ranking ace of the Luftwaffe, Major Günther Rall, commanding II/JG 11, with more than 200 victories to his credit. The fact is there is no time for such conjecture when one instinctively knows termination of life is possibly only seconds away. And it was only a matter of time before an enemy slipped in behind my violently turning Thunderbolt to claim the final scalp. With a shouted oath to spur myself into action, I took the only possible course of escape. With violent movement of the controls I rolled UN-Z over with a fast aileron flip and headed vertically for the ground, barrel rolling as I went to make a difficult target for my pursuers. Down, full power, into the realms of compressibility. By the time the altimeter had unwound a couple of times and the airspeed indicator had hit the peg, the Thunderbolt was rumbling and vibrating so much I expected it to fly apart. It was time to start recovery; cutting power, centralising the stick to stop the barrel roll, and starting a long and gentle pull back to bottom out at around 5,000 feet. A quick glance over each shoulder and a buck to clear my tail. To my relief, no frontal view of a Messerschmitt in hot pursuit or blinking cannon. Perhaps they couldn't catch me; perhaps they thought I was out of control."

Making for home Zemke had to avoid another interception, and recruiting two other Wolfpack aircraft he engaged a large formation of enemy fighters caught assembling and shot one down.

The day's fighting resulted in 19 destroyed and one probable claim for the 56th for three losses. One of the pilots who joined Zemke, Lieutenant Robert Rankin, shot down five enemy fighters, the first time a 56th Group pilot had achieved this on one mission. Popular and of pleasant disposition, Rankin was known as Shorty, being just over 5 feet 4 inches tall, and suffered leg-pulling as 'the walking parachute' as this bulky item dominated his physique when carried. "Short, solid with a uniform to match in that it accentuated his build. Almost knee length blouse and pegged trousers," was a newsman's description. In civilian life Rankin had played cello for two years with the Washington Symphony Orchestra. A replacement pilot who joined the 61st Squadron the previous September, he had already proved himself as an excellent fighter pilot having four confirmed victories. The critique held for this operation found that while the Zemke Fan had proven merit, its weakness lay in that individual flights dispersed over a wide area were too vulnerable if encountering a superior number of the enemy. Unbeknown at that time, an Me109 pursued at low level and shot down by Captain Joe Powers and his wingman Joe Vitale was flown by Günther Rall, the Luftwaffe Experte who had caught Zemke's flight. Rall lost a thumb, but survived a hasty bale-out. All three Wolfpack pilots missing that day survived as prisoners.

During the following day's mission the group suffered a single loss when Lieutenant Harold Hartney's aircraft was bounced and shot down. Hartney, whose father had commanded the 1st Fighter Group in France during the First World War, was killed. A few weeks earlier he had been surprised to meet his sister June who arrived on the airfield with a Red Crossmobile to dispense coffee and doughnuts. She was married and her husband a prisoner of war of the Japanese.

Soon after moving to Boxted Zemke heard that a new model Thunderbolt with major changes had arrived in the UK. Shortly after the first use of the Zemke Fan three of these aircraft were received. Their prominent feature was the reduction of rear fuselage height to allow an all-round vision 'bubble' cockpit canopy. More important was enlarged internal fuel tankage, which provided an additional 65 US gallons; this allowed up to an extra fifteen minutes over enemy territory after drop tank release. The new model, identified as the P-47D-25, became known in the 56th as the Superbolt. Zemke took the first and Gabreski and Pete Dade the other two as personal mounts. Performance and handling were little different from preceding models except that the loss of the rear fuselage spine had a slight adverse affect on directional stability. The Thunderbolt had undergone continual improvement since the early days of combat.

Pilot Bill Gordon, who had previously flown with the 78th Fighter Group, expressed his views on its development as follows:

"The P-47 was heavier than any other fighter in the theatre. It was also the most powerful and had the highest Mach number – about 0.90. With the disadvantage of a slow climb because of its weight came a great advantage in diving speed with a terminal velocity few other aircraft could match. This meant that you didn't try to climb while under attack but rather cut the throttle, horsed it into a skidding steep turn, added throttle up to full power and turned, literally hanging on the prop. The fact that firing your guns would stall you out never seemed to register with the enemy. As he saw the lead of your guns creeping past his nose he'd leave. The smart ones, and there were many, would do a half snap roll and pull straight through – a manoeuvre the P-47 couldn't handle with any grace at all. Because of its weight the P-47 suffered one disadvantage for which there was no cure – range. It burned 270 gallons per hour at full military power. With an internal fuel capacity of 305 gallons in early models even additional fuel in drop tanks wouldn't get you more than halfway to the bombers' targets. During the fall and winter of 1943-44 the P-47s of the 56th Group were being constantly modified. We were the pride and joy of Republic Aviation and they couldn't do enough for us. At times it seemed we had as many Republic Tech Reps on the field as we had crew chiefs. Any promising development to increase performance was retrofitted on some or all of our aircraft and we evaluated in combat. For that reason Tech Orders, specifications and pilot manual descriptions did just not apply to that fleet of bastard birds. My aircraft LM:<u>G</u> was a D-7RE, one of the newer aircraft in the group when I transferred in January 1944. Before I finished my first tour in late May it had been equipped with water injection and a fat paddle blade prop' which increased maximum available power by a whopping 20 per cent and performance in speed and climb by God knows how much. I never believed the airspeed indicator worked properly at low altitude, especially at high speeds. I never saw over 400 mph in sustained level flight on the deck but I caught an FW190D in a 50-odd mile chase at tree top level and his top speed was supposed to be 425 mph. Much of the credit for the way old G bar [individual letter G with an underlining bar to distinguish it from aircraft with plain G] performed had to go to her crew chief, T/Sgt Albert Holliday. A full blood Cherokee (non reservation since high school) he was not only a genius in airframe and engine maintenance, he was indefatigable in his loyalty to me and his charge. LM:G bar was not far from the last P-47s with camouflage paint. Holliday rubbed it down with two coats of Simonize and it was slicker than the bare skin models that followed. It was always off for maintenance when I wasn't scheduled to fly and almost always on the line when I was up for a mission. There was not one air leak in the cabin because all sources of outside air had been identified in flight by holding a lighted cigarette around the cockpit and marking spots where the smoke wavered, with chalk. These spots were drilled, tapped and screws installed. At minus 67 degrees F outside temperature a jacket and wool shirt were comfortable because he invented a heat diverter from the windshield heater to a T-bar outlet on the floor."

In the previous summer there had been attempts to lessen Thunderbolt weight by removing equipment viewed as non-essential – such as the windshield's bullet proof glass backing panel – and reducing armament from eight to six guns. This was not pursued as the advantages were marginal and it was found more profitable to retain full armament and most of the items at first thought questionable. However, in the spring of 1944, there were occasions when Me109s had bounced the group from altitudes estimated in excess of 35,000 feet. Schilling is said to have promoted the idea of having a few aircraft on which a severe weight reduction scheme had been carried out so that these could operate as a special top cover to counter these high altitude Messerschmitts. With an intelligence warning that Me109s with nitra-oxide boost might be encountered permission was obtained to use four war-weary P-47Ds for experimental weight reduction. The armour plate, some of the hydraulic equipment and four guns plus other items were removed saving approximately a ton. Two drop tanks carried 110/120 octane gasoline and the internal tanks were filled with 140/150 nicknamed 'Blue gas'. Painted sky blue on their undersides, these aircraft were used as an occasional Purple flight which cruised at 38,000 feet to provide extreme top cover although they never encountered any opposition.

Zemke, giving his Superbolt its first outing in hostile airspace on 19

May, was favourably impressed. The inscription Oregon's Britannia was carried on the fuselage, indicating that the state of Oregon had 'bought' the aircraft with saving bonds. He used it again three days later for another Zemke Fan tactic. This time the group flew to the 'Happy Hunting Ground' and each squadron of 16 aircraft took different directions. The 62nd and 63rd Squadrons met no aerial opposition but the 61st, led by Gabreski, ran into plenty over an airfield near Bremen, claiming 11 victories. Lieutenant Joel Popplewell was flying Gabby's wing with Richard Heineman the element leader and Cletus Nale his wingman. Seeing a flight of FW190s taking off, Gabreski radioed that they should fly on and let the enemy get airborne. After making a 180-degree turn he went down on the Focke-Wulfs which had by then climbed to about 3,000 feet. Gabreski shot two of the unsuspecting enemy down in quick succession, so intent on his quarries that he was unaware of other Focke-Wulfs making an interception from behind until Popplewell called a warning. Popplewell turned to try and attack an FW190 shooting at Nale. As he fired at the enemy his Thunderbolt was struck by 20-mm shells from another FW190. Popplewell gave his aircraft full right rudder in an effort to evade and ended up just above the tree tops. He made for home safely and after landing and taxying to his hardstand was so agitated that he forgot to undue his dinghy strap when getting out of the cockpit, the dinghy inflating. Such was his state that Flight Surgeon Doc Horning took him into his room for scotch and water before a debriefing. His agitation was chiefly due to having seen Nale's aircraft go down. 'CB' Nale was a school friend and on a recent visit to London with Popplewell had conjectured that one of them probably wouldn't make it. Richard Heineman was also shot down in this fight, and both he and Nale were killed.

Gabreski destroyed another enemy aircraft in this battle elevating him to leading Eighth Air Force ace with 22 victory credits. Major Bob Lamb, having reached his limit of operational hours, 200 plus a 50 and 25 extension, relinquished his command of the 63rd Squadron to Captain Donald Goodfleisch shortly after this mission. 'Goodie' was another original combat pilot but having been placed in Group HQ Operations for a few weeks still had not expended his operational flying time. The flamboyant Bob Lamb, a former vocalist with a dance band, went home to the States.

Having spent over three hours on this mission, the same day the tireless Zemke set out to lead another experimental bombing raid, the target for which was a rail bridge at Hassalt in the Netherlands. Each P-47 carried a 500-lb general purpose (GP) bomb on each wing rack, in order to find the best angle and altitude for releasing the bombs. Low level, glide angle and near vertical dives were made from various heights all without hitting the target. Several other fighter-bomber raids were carried out during the following few days as the 56th strove to find the best means of accurate delivery although results were variable and no firm conclusions were drawn. Zemke, appreciating that the fighter-bombing missions they were given probably heralded the cross-Channel invasion, for which preparations in southern England were all too obvious, wanted to try formation bombing again. The winter trial using a B-24 to guide and sight on target had been a fiasco. What was needed was a sighting aircraft with the speed of a fighter and this was now available in the form of modified P-38 Lightnings taking a bombardier and Norden sight in a special nose compartment. P-38 groups had been using these aircraft to lead formation bombing of enemy airfields with fair results so there seemed no reason why one leading a P-47 formation could not be used. The buccaneering Colonel took his idea to Ajax and was given the go ahead to borrow one of these P-38s known as Droop Snoots. On 30 May 16 P-47s each with two 1000-lb GP bombs left Boxted, led by Zemke flying the Droop Snoot. Flak was deemed too heavy at the briefed target so the formation was taken to drop on a rail bridge some five miles distant from 12,000 feet. The results were encouraging but the major problem was that two 1000-lb bombs were far too heavy a load for a P-47 to take to altitude, making control difficult. Zemke would like to have retained the Droop Snoot for another try but it had to be returned.

The current dearth of combat experienced pilots led Eighth Air Force to increase the length of a tour by another 15 missions: unfortunate for those pilots who were just about to finish up. One was Sam Aggers who would have completed and moved out before this introduction had it not been for the result of a bit of friendly rough and tumble. Frank Klibbe:

"Routinely at the end of the day pilots rushed to load into a waiting vehicle to be transported to our respective quarters. The last to load faced the challenge to survive the horseplay that usually took place. Those seated on the very end of the bench seats must be prepared for pushing and shoving that is hilariously designed to hasten your departure for a long walk home. This was a way for pilots to ease their tensions and let off a little steam after a day of combat. Unfortunately in one of these tussles Sam Agger got pushed off and sustained a sprained ankle. He was grounded for a period pending recovery and it was during this time that a tour was increased. Being one of those who had shoved Sam off the seat and out the back of the truck I felt more than a little guilty about his having to fly those extra missions."

Tomfoolery continued to be tolerated and understood as a release for pent-up feelings. The tensions engendered by lengthy confinement in a single-seat fighter cockpit and an alien sky could become overpowering for some individuals. Once back on the ground they had to break out, often with recklessness or devilment: plus the refuge of alcohol meant matters occasionally got out of hand. George Butler:

"Five pilots occupied my Nissen hut at Boxted: Jack Carwell was one of them. Jack insisted he could fly with a machine gun in the cockpit of his plane for self defence if he was shot down. I don't know where or how Carwell got the machine gun but he sure had one. One night when four of us were soundly sleeping, we were suddenly awakened by someone stumbling in our hut. We shinned our flashlights and there stood Carwell who had obviously had too much to drink. The first thing he did was pick up that darn machine gun and started practising his aim at the ceiling. Next, with his finger on the trigger, he fell over backwards. When the roar of a several seconds blast was over we could see a great many holes in the roof. Jack picked himself up and said, 'I didn't know the son of a bitch was loaded!' We all knew the MPs would arrive shortly, so we threw Carwell into bed and the machine gun into a footlocker. Sure enough the MPs burst through the door with guns in their hands. Being sharp fighter pilots we played innocent and asked the MPs why there was shooting coming from the hut next door. The MPs took off for a dead run to the hut next door!"

There was the rare occasion when an individual seemed unable to dissipate his tensions. Flight Surgeons continually monitored their charges, resting anyone who was extremely disturbed. One case not recognised until too late involved Lieutenant John McDonnell who had been flying with the 63rd for three months. One day early in June he went berserk, threatening fellow pilots with a firearm until forcibly over-powered. He was permanently grounded.

After strafing and fighter-bombing missions there was often some contention as to the results achieved. The photographic reconnaissance units of the Eighth were then too busy with other assignments to take in the attacks on ground targets made by fighters. The idea of the group taking its own target photographs was mooted. Although gun cameras could be kept running their scope was limited. Larger cameras of the type used for photographic reconnaissance were needed but installation was not practical. That is until the arrival of the Superbolt with its large, clear and spacious cockpit canopy. Zemke had the idea of having a camera attached to the armour plate behind the pilot to photograph obliquely through the Plexiglas. At the Bovingdon experimental station a K-25 reconnaissance camera, which took $3^1/_2$ x $4^1/_2$ inch negative, was installed in Zemke's Thunderbolt, operated by a control button on the joystick. To shoot photographs it required a 90-degree bank towards the target. The installation proved successful, and like other ideas generated in the 56th, was taken up by other groups.

The canopy on the Superbolt, electrically operated, was considered an improvement as manually closing the old type, barred canopy, was awkward. However, there was a need to be wary. David Hubler:

"Tom Bradshaw and Oswald Cottrell (a French Cajun) were running up a new P-47 with a bubble canopy. They were buddies up in A Flight and the Flight Chief was Jim Spears, who was always known as J.J.

Bradshaw was in the cockpit and Cottrell could see him sort of raised up looking out and he thought what's he looking at? And what the hell is he doing running that thing at high rpm. So he walked around the front of the aircraft to one side and then he could see what had happened. Bradshaw had evidently looked out one side and then the other to check intercooler operation, as we always did with the high back '47s. In so doing he accidentally hit the switch for the electrical operation of the canopy. Didn't realise he'd done it until it caught him just above the eye and peeled up his eyebrow and trapped him there. J.J. came down and he and Cottrell finally got the canopy back and the engine shut down. Blood everywhere. Bradshaw went off to the hospital. Well, Willy Hibma, the fat Dutch boy from Iowa who drove the truck: very naive, a 35-year-old virgin. When Bradshaw came back, a few days later Willy happened to ask how he was, looked at his eye and said, 'That's healed up nice. I heard it took a lot of the skin off.' Bradshaw said, 'Well it did.' Willy said, 'You got hair there. Where did they get the hair?' Bradshaw said 'Well, they didn't have any hair like mine, so they took it off a nurse's pussy. The only trouble is that when I walk into the latrine my eye keeps going like this.' And he blinked his eye fast."

The pattern of operations conducted over north-west France and the Low Countries continued during the first few days of June. There was much conjecture that the 'invasion' would be launched at anytime. At 4 pm on the afternoon of 5 June a teletype was received from Ajax notifying that no unauthorised persons were to enter the base and those already there were to be retained until further notice. No passes were to be issued and any outstanding ones cancelled. The ground crews received an unusual instruction. Frank Gydik:

"We were told our airplanes had to be taken to the hangar. The Cletrac came and dragged mine in and the hangar doors were closed. There on the floor were buckets of black and white paint and brushes. They told us to paint black and white stripes of certain widths on the wings and fuselage. We asked why and were told not to ask questions, just paint but we guessed it was something to do with the invasion. So we got that done and got the planes back and on the line. It was getting dark when we got back to the barracks area."

Station 150's occupants would remember that June evening and night for many reasons. Robert Carnachan:

"Raymond Doherty, the Squadron Adjutant, and I shared a picket hut as our quarters on the 63rd camp. On the night of June 5th we were in the hut playing a game of chess when suddenly we heard machine-gun fire! Now, for some time this airbase had been warned of the possibility of German paratroopers or saboteurs attempting to disrupt our air cover over the landing beaches when the invasion came, by damaging our planes on the ground and killing our officers. As a result we had armed patrols around the field at night and the officers wore side arms. So, when we heard the gunfire, the Major and I knew the Germans were out there and we were prepared to sell our lives dearly! We crept out (I making sure the Major was in the lead) with our 45s in hand and sticking close to the buildings while we looked in every direction for the enemy. As it turned out, a British Bren gun carrier had caught fire, setting off the ammunition it was carrying."

Don Trudell:

"Around mid-night, all of a sudden we heard a lot of shouting up on the A 12 Ipswich-Colchester road above our camp. A British Bren carrier had caught fire, so two of my buddies and I walked from our barracks up the slope towards the road. About halfway up this thing blew up and mortar shells were going off and stupidly I'm seeing pieces of the trees popping out. Then I realised shrapnel was flying around. A British NCO was standing talking to our Sergeant Yahnke, when a piece of shrapnel entered his throat came out the back and severed his spine. Was this the first casualty of D-Day?"

When the Bren gun carrier caught fire and exploded it badly damaged a house just south of the little Lion and Lamb pub as well as severing the cables from the station transmitter site in Severalls Lane to the DF and airfield control tower. Men of the small signal corps company attached to the base worked all night and much of the next day laying temporary land lines along the road sides to restore the control circuits.

There was little time for sleep for anyone at Boxted 'field that night. Ralph Safford, Gabreski's crew chief:

"We didn't get to bed until 11.30 and an hour later our line chief woke us up. As I sat in the cockpit warming the engine up, bombers were going over. Crew chiefs were told to do guard duty, four hours and then your assistant took over and you could get some sleep. We had to do this in the tent near our hardstand. There was no going back to the barracks and we were told we would have to do double duty for awhile."

With all the activity most guessed the invasion was being launched even if those who might know remained tight-lipped. At 11 am on the morning of the 5th, shortly after Zemke had returned from leading an uneventful patrol over French coastal regions, there had been a message for him to proceed to Ajax for a 4 pm meeting. Four hours later Zemke appeared in the Officers' Club and told his operations and intelligence officers to report to the briefing room. No one else had been admitted and the doors were locked and only the five men within heard what the Colonel had to say. Pilots were surprised to find themselves wakened soon after midnight but from the activity in the heavens they did not need telling what this unusually early call was all about. Briefing was ordered for 0130 hours and when they entered the briefing room any remaining sleepiness was banished. Chalked across the briefing blackboard by the podium in large letters was THIS IS IT!

20 Summer at Boxted

The sky over southern England in the morning dark hours of 6 June 1944 was filled with red, green and amber lights as never seen before or since. Literally thousands of aircraft were in the air, navigation lights and formation assembly flares aiding their passage in the gloom. Because of its experience the 56th Fighter Group was called on early, taking off in darkness with a mission to patrol an area from Boulogne to Dunkirk in case Luftwaffe bombers were brought down from Norway to attack the D-Day shipping. Gabreski led, starting his take-off run at Boxted at 0325 hours to be followed by 31 P-47s of the 61st and 63rd, for this, like most missions flown in support of the D-Day landings over the next few weeks would often be at one or two squadron strength. Seven separate missions were flown that day, a mixture of patrols and fighter-bombing commissions. The patrols, with each P-47 carrying up to 200 gallons of fuel in two drop tanks, lasted over four hours in some cases, a far cry from a year ago when missions were around one and a half hours'duration. The last of the D-Day missions was led by Zemke who, because of his knowledge of the actual landings, was not permitted to fly earlier in case he was shot down and captured. The aircraft from this last mission were back on Boxted by half eight that evening.

All sections at Boxted had been put on a 24-hour duty basis until further notice. Ground crews had to remain at their aircraft parking places and get what rest they could following the despatch of their charge. This had to be taken in the tents that served the men for shelter at each cluster of hardstands, as return to barracks for sleep was forbidden. Mess halls were open 24 hours. Intelligence and operations staff had to be on duty every day and one night in three. Pilots were also kept from their barracks with cots and food provided in the squadron ready rooms so that they were immediately available for operations. As the days passed the situation was gradually relaxed but the 24-hour status remained for three weeks.

The intensity of operations during this period was such that the group despatched 46 separate missions, the large majority fighter-bombing. Most pilots participated in at least half these missions of which Zemke led 16 and Gabreski 13. The cost was nine aircraft missing in action and another eight written off through battle damage and accidents. Three pilots of the missing aircraft evaded capture, and six were killed. Another pilot was killed in a collision over home base and one in a crash-landing. Allied acquisition of a bridgehead in Normandy opened up a new haven for pilots in distress: the first from the 56th to take advantage was 2nd Lieutenant Earl Hertel who, having fuel trouble on D+ 6, put down on a half completed landing ground; his aircraft ended up wrecked although he was uninjured. The majority of formations went out fighter-bombing in support of the invasion against tactical targets in north-west France. On D+1 alone five 56th P-47s were lost, four to ground fire and one to an exploding ammunition wagon in a rail yard at Gournay. The following day only three missions were flown as owing to low cloud and rain the group was not called upon to operate. Thereafter the Wolfpack was active on all but one day for the rest of June. There were several 'near thing' incidents. Lieutenant Richard Warboys:

"On my eighteenth mission I was assigned to fly wing for Colonel Zemke, who was leading the group on a dive-bombing mission, 10 June. This morning dawned very heavy with fog and about a 300-foot ceiling. My P-47 had 250-lb GP bombs on the wings and a 150-gallon belly tank. Our target was the Argentan marshalling yard. As we climbed through the soup to about 12,000 feet, very close to the Colonel's plane, I felt too close and applied right stick and rudder. I guess I had done it a bit too violently, as all my instruments began to tumble and the rudder pedals started kicking in and out. 'Oh, joy,' I thought. 'Now I'm in a spin in solid soup!' So I chopped the throttle and began the spin recovery process. The rudders stopped their kicking in and out as my instruments became stabilised. My air speed was increasing plus the altimeter was really unwinding. I began to level off after finally finding the English Channel. About now I found myself down to about 200 feet above the waves. As I began slowing down with the prop' windmilling, I applied throttle but nothing happened. Glancing at the fuel pressure gauge I saw it was reading zero! Remembering we were climbing on external tanks, I switched to my internal tanks. My engine finally caught: 'Thank you Lord.'

"I could now hear the group's R/T and they were breaking out at about 19,000 feet, so I tried to call them but received no answer. Evidently I could not transmit but was still capable of receiving. After taking a heading back to England the bombs were jettisoned in the Channel, but the belly tank would not drop. I turned on the IFF [electronic Identification Friend/Foe device] and found an RAF base near the coast. After getting the tower's attention they proceeded to give me landing instructions. As I threw the landing gear lever down there was a real crunching noise. After parking my aircraft RAF mechanics found the sway bars had become bent, obviously due to the pressures of the spin. This is why my belly tank would not jettison. The RAF gave me tea and called Boxted to let them know I was all right. When I returned to Boxted I got a good chewing out from my squadron CO, Don Goodfleisch, who immediately sent me on the next mission flown that day. When I returned Don said to me, 'You know what you got now? Five hours in the Link trainer.' Which I never did because I gave the corporal in charge a bottle

of Scotch and signed the log for the five days I was supposed to have
done these blind flying exercises."

Getting a pilot back in the air so soon as possible after some nerve
racking incident was to restore his confidence and a common practice.
Warboys was far from the first to fall out of formation and not a few
uncautioned pilots had this experience flying on the Colonel's wing.
Zemke had gained a reputation for being a hard man to follow through his
erratic changes in speed and climb to meet timing requirements, plus his
attention to map-reading. Considering the extensive overcasts that
frequently had to be penetrated and the risk of collisions while in cloud
this presented, the accident free record was remarkable. Collisions that
did occur happened in more relaxed or distracting circumstances.
Reaching Boxted after a fighter-bombing raid near midday on the 22nd,
Captain Charles Tucker pulled across into the path of a 63rd Squadron
aircraft. Lieutenant Walter Flagg survived a belly landing but Tucker was
killed, and his Thunderbolt, with its tail badly smashed, fell near the
Severalls Lane transmitter station. Tucker was the second former bomber
pilot to be killed in a collision; a month earlier James Elliott had hit a B-
26 Marauder over Debach. Zemke wondered if this had anything to do
with the difficulty in coming to terms with the responsiveness of a fighter
after the comparative sluggishness of a bomber's controls.

While all but three of the June missions were tactical or in support of
such operations over France, the group did encounter enemy aircraft and
again exhibited its prowess with claims of 34 shot down for only battle
damage to a half dozen of its Thunderbolts in these clashes. Gabreski
added five more to his total during the month, bringing down his 27th
enemy aircraft on 27 June and equalling Bob Johnson's total. Gabby had
been the Eighth's current top scoring ace for the past five weeks. Also
successful on 27 June was Captain Fred Christensen of the 62nd
Squadron who brought down an Me109, his fifteenth victory, advancing
his position as the current second highest scorer in the group. Chris, who
came to the group in August 1943, had shown himself to be a competent
and combative flyer. Unfortunately, his aggressive nature sometimes got
the better of him, and a most serious case occurred during this period
when he was arrested by Colchester police for an altercation with a local
mother and daughter. Zemke had to plead with the police that he was
essential to his operations. Chris was, as one of his comrades summed
him up: "Fiery. A diamond in the rough. But an outstanding pilot."

The continued good showing of the 56th's pilots in air combat was not
only through expertise and leadership, but the tools of their trade which
played a significant part. The Thunderbolt could and did sustain battle
damage that would have brought down less substantial airframes. Most
numerous causes of loss were adjudged pilot fatalities and fuel tank
ignitions. A 20-mm cannon shell had the potential of causing far greater
destruction than a .50-inch calibre bullet. However, the firepower of eight
.50 machine guns, with higher muzzle velocity and rate of fire than the

one or two cannon and rifle calibre weapons in Luftwaffe fighters afforded, if aim was good, a greater concentration of destruction. Moreover, the API (Armour Piercing Incendiary) ammunition of American guns might only punch comparatively small holes through a wing or tail surface but they could cause severe damage to engines and vital components. Me109 fuel tanks, situated behind the cockpit with only an aluminium matrix for protection, were highly vulnerable; in fact, it was the incendiary factor of 'point fifty' API fire that was the major cause of Messerschmitt 109 losses.

The 56th reached another milestone on Independence Day as it became the first fighter group flying in Europe to pass the 500 enemy aircraft destroyed in air combat mark when 17 claims were made for action over France. An extraordinary experience was that of 1st Lieutenant George Bostwick:

"On July 4th 1944 I was assigned element leader to Pete Dade, 62nd Squadron CO, on a routine mission in support of the Normandy landings: Hub Zemke was leading the group. Our squadron was to take off first, followed by Zemke flying with the 63rd and thence the 61st. Just as we were about to get the signal to roll, Pete had an aircraft malfunction and pulled off into the grass as did his wingman who was on his first mission. When we got tower go ahead, I started to roll but Zemke who got tired of all the confusion decided to take his squadron off first and also started to roll. Since our runways crossed this could have led to disaster. I stopped, he stopped and we pulled a real Alfonso Gaston [US comedian] act three times. Finally Hub got on the radio and said for God's sake go ahead and take off. I applied full power but noted we had already used about a 1,000 feet of runway. We were carrying two 250-lb bombs and a 1,400-pound belly tank; also, I was flying a new D model for the first time (D-25) which had 65 gallons more internal fuel. As we reached the end of one of the 4,200-foot runways at Boxted, I pulled my plane into the air with marginal air speed. My wingman followed and stayed airborne but my aircraft came back down. I bounced once off a British road and again in a wheatfield. At this point I caught the aircraft in a semi-stalled tail low altitude and began slowly to pick-up air speed and regain control. Just as I was about to retract the gear I flew through an English hedgerow and the aircraft began bouncing again. I again regained control only to hit a second and third hedgerow, the latter containing a rather large tree stump. My right wing collided with the stump and ripped the 250-pound bomb and pylon from the aircraft. I remember watching the bomb bounce end over end under the right wing. This time I had a little more room and was able to regain control and retract the landing gear.

"I proceeded to lead the 62nd until we formed up and Blue Leader took over. I then planned to return to Boxted, but thought I'd try the belly tank first and much to my surprise it fed. The 90-degree glass elbows which connect the belly tank fuel system to the aircraft, and which were externally fragile, had survived contact with three hedgerows. So I decided to proceed with the mission. The first part was uneventful, we dropped our bombs on a railroad marshalling yard and were heading for home when our controller called in 20 plus bandits in the Evreux area. We altered course in that direction and the bandits turned out to be Me109s which had taken off from Evreux airfield and were heading for the beachhead area. We attacked with a decided altitude and air speed advantage and destroyed about 17 of them. I got three and would have gotten a fourth if I had managed my ammunition better. Must brag a little – a review of my gun camera film showed that I had gotten many hits on the three I shot down at 45, 55 and 60-degree deflection which ain't bad with the old ring and bead gun sight. On the way home my aircraft began to vibrate violently, especially the instrument panel, and eventually disabled most of my indicators and instruments. It was a long but happy flight home. Upon approaching Boxted I put my gear down and asked my wingman to check the damage. He reported that the right wheel was smashed flat so I made my one and only two-wheel landing in a Thunderbolt. I was able to keep it straight until most of the airspeed bled off and then it ground-looped on the runway. Subsequent inspection revealed that all four propeller blades were bent back 12-14 inches and that the right wing had been twisted in excess of 10 degrees. In retrospect it had been a rather exciting mission – one I wouldn't want to repeat just every day."

Major Dade finally got airborne, joined his squadron and in the rout of the Me109s caught unawares he claimed two while still carrying two 250-lb bombs. Next day while leading the group over France to provide cover for B-17s returning to England, Gabreski shot down an Me109 to raise his total to 28 air victories, the highest yet achieved by any American pilot flying in Europe:

"Longest and best fight I ever had. There were three of them. Two tried to lure me down while the third stayed up to jump me. But I realised what they were trying to do, so I banked sharply and went after the top man. He saw me coming and we cut a dozen patterns all over the sky, each of us attempting to get the other. I banked out of the turn and gave him a 90-degree deflection shot, more or less to scare him, but the dope flew right off to come in again. I had to make about three turns and then he started to dive. At about 1,000 feet he straightened out. I overtook him fast and caught him in a steep turn and let him have it. His ship made a half roll to the left and lit up like a huge ball of fire."

An account that exudes self-confidence, a hallmark of Gabby in battle, no doubt buoyed by his deep religious commitment. Near the end of his tour he planned to take 30 days leave in the States to marry and hopefully return.

It was the Luftwaffe who sprung two interceptions of the group on 6

July. Zemke was leading a fighter-bomber mission when, west of Evreux, the 63rd was bounced by a Staffel of Me109s out of the sun. The Thunderbolts salvoed their bombs and broke right turning into the enemy attack but one Messerschmitt's fire hit Lieutenant Sam Lowman's P-47 in the turn. That morning when Lowman had arrived at his aircraft, adorned with a painting of a pretty girl and the slogan Target For Tonight on the cowling, he mentioned to his ground crew that he had a bottle of bourbon in his locker for them. When Lowman did not return and word came that he could not have survived, the ground crew, Billy Collins and Ed Lanham, went to his Nissen hut that evening, got the bottle and retired to a local pub to drink in sadness. Lowman, who had been with the group since February, always showed his appreciation of his ground crew's work and this was not lost on them.

In the same action 1st Lieutenant Joe Curtis found himself in a turning fight with two Me109s. It seemed his aircraft was being out-turned by his opponents when Curtis suddenly realised he had not released the steel drop tank from the fuselage shackles. Quickly remedying the situation, he was amazed to catch a glimpse in his rear view mirror of the released fuel tank striking and ripping off part of a following Messerschmitt's left wing. An unusual way to bring down the enemy. The remaining 109 continued to go round trying to close with Curtis's Thunderbolt until after a score of turns its pilot decided he had had enough and departed. Curtis had been an original combat pilot of the 61st where his operational failings led to transfer to a training unit. Even so he had been considered a great morale booster in the 61st through his cheerful disposition and regularly regaling other pilots with hilarious anecdotes. Curtis came back to the group in the spring of '44 and flew with the 63rd successfully completing his operational tour with three and one shared air victories to his credit.

Zemke, flying with the 62nd's White flight when the enemy attacked, took the squadron in a climb to engage. As his aircraft turned it received a cannon shell strike in the left wing gun bay. Fortunately, the element leader in White flight, George Bostwick, quickly dealt with Zemke's assailant while the Colonel struggled to maintain control of his aircraft on which the left aileron would no longer function. After losing a few thousand feet Zemke regained control and headed for home with Bostwick acting as guard. Zemke's wingman, 2nd Lieutenant Steven Murray, had disappeared and Hub suspected he had fallen during the battle. However, on landing at Boxted it was learned Murray had already returned safely but, when Bostwick revealed that Murray had been seen to flee as soon as the enemy attacked, Zemke's mood was grim. All wingmen had impressed upon them that their prime duty was to guard and warn their leader which Murray had clearly not. Zemke was all for having Murray, who had been with the group since April, transferred out. General Auton, the 65th Wing CO, said that Murray should be given another chance and in softer mood Hub relented but never had him as his wingman again. The de-briefing for that mission was not a happy affair for others were berated by the Colonel for their failure to identify river landmarks. While he "ranted and paced up and down" telling the assembled pilots they were going to get geography lessons to learn to identify French rivers, into the back of the briefing room came five returnees from leave in the ZI (Zone of the Interior, the USA) – Schilling, Don Smith, George Hall, Egan and Comstock. Zemke, seeing they were laughing at the proceedings, fixed them with his troubled gaze, named each one and threatened, "You too!" The laughter ceased.

Bomber missions to German oil installations and refineries usually brought fierce opposition and on 7 July, as so often the case then, it was the Mustangs who fought off the enemy interceptions while the Thunderbolts saw little such action. The 62nd Squadron did encounter enemy aircraft if not the usual combatant types. Lieutenant Michael Jackson:

"We were on an escort at about 25,000 feet. Everything looked serene, everything looked wide open. Kept looking around, didn't see anything unusual. Suddenly we started letting down, our flight of four. Fred Christensen was our leader and I was flying his wing. I thought to myself where the hell is this guy going and where is he taking us, because the bombers were over there and we're going down in this direction. When we got down to 5,000 feet looking ahead I could see Ju 52 transports over the airbase near Stendal. They were in a turn, one following the other, trying to get into the base to land. This is what Fred had seen. I was on his right, Billy Edens the element leader on his left. Fred shot down three of the Ju 52s in the initial run that I could see. One of the others trying to get away moved over right in front of me and I knocked him out of the sky. Now, of course, Billy Edens moved in and got three of the others. All together we shot down ten Ju 52s."

Christensen's six destroyed was a record for a US fighter pilot during one mission taking his personal total to 22. There was some whispering about easy targets but, as Zemke said, these Ju52s had probably done more for Hitler's war effort than any six fighter planes.

The old hands back from the States were a welcome relief in that they represented sorely needed leadership experience. A few days' re-orientation was required before missions were resumed by these men, however. Goodie Goodfleisch had completed his tour on 17 July and the tall Captain Joe Egan – so tall his head nearly touched the underside of the cockpit canopy – was to be given command of the 63rd Squadron. Two days later he was dead, supposedly a victim of ground fire, leaving his widow wife with a year-old son. Bunny Comstock:

"Charlie Rotzler, my wingman, and I got separated from the group down towards the German border. We ran across Joe Egan and George Hall. We teamed up with them for coming out and were between Nancy and Metz when we came across a little railroad station which had a control tower.

I was flying as Joe's second element. He decided we should shoot up this tower so we pounded it but did not set it on fire. Then we saw there was a big white goose down there and every time somebody would make a pass at the tower this goose would run across the station yard from one side to the other. Joe decided we ought to shoot the goose. When I came down I looked ahead and saw a lot of communication cable and wires on the other side of the yard and called them out. Joe came around and made another pass at the goose but went right into the wires. They looked like iron wires and there were several of them. Instead of the airplane cutting the wires they rotated round the engine and it went in upside down. George Hall called that he was going to land and pick him up. I called and said, 'George, don't be a damn fool. He's dead.' Joe was a Dartford graduate from a wealthy family. His father was president of Western Union."

After Egan was killed Comstock was made 63rd CO and George Hall his Operations Officer. A new commander had to be found for the 61st Squadron at this time as Gabreski was departing for 30 days' leave. The position was filled by Major Gordon E. Baker, a former instructor from the ZI, who wanted to see combat. He joined the 56th in June, and as with other high rank recruits, his presence tended to be resented by junior officers who saw a major as an obstacle to their own advancement. At first flying with the 62nd Squadron and looked on as something of a supernumerary, he proved an able leader leading to his transfer to the 61st command.

On the morning of 20 July Gabreski, bags packed, was due to be flown out on the first leg of an air journey back to the States with Jim Carter, who had also finished his tour. The group was being briefed for a deep penetration bomber escort where enemy air opposition was highly likely to be encountered, and this proved enticing for Gabby. He decided to forego his departure and fly one more mission, his 166th. The anticipated enemy air activity did not materialise and the squadrons sought strafing targets. Some Heinkel bombers were spotted on an airfield at Bassinheim which the 61st went down to strafe. As there appeared to be little defensive fire from the ground Gabby made a second pass in his immaculate HV:A. Other pilots saw a streak of dust going across the airfield, which at first was taken to be caused by strafing fire hitting the ground, until Gabby's Thunderbolt was seen to lift from the dust, cross over some trees and belly-in. His run across the airfield had been too low and in adjusting his aim to shoot up another Heinkel his propeller had struck the ground, buckling the blades. It is assumed that this was caused by the slight lateral instability noted in the P-47D-25 due to the extra internal fuel this model held. Gabby, uninjured, ran for concealment to some trees but he was taken prisoner. Other members of his squadron shot up HV:A to prevent the enemy gaining any intelligence on this new model.

As previously noted, Gabreski was not popular with all pilots. Some thought he lacked the finer qualities of compassionate leadership. Others considered him self-possessed and found his loquaciousness irritating. There were grumbles about his use of radio on missions. He may have had a personality that many did not warm to, yet he was cheerful and not known to have ever reprimanded his command by yelling at them, which both Zemke and Schilling were prone to do if really upset. Above all Gabby was an outstanding combat pilot and his 28 air victory credits would be unsurpassed by any other American pilot flying against the Luftwaffe.

Perhaps the most shocked men at Boxted when Gabreski did not return were his ground crew who had come to believe he was almost indestructible. Staff Sergeant Ralph Safford was his loyal crew chief:

"I was allocated a P-47 to crew at King's Cliffe and Gabreski picked that airplane. Then when I was taken off it he asked to have me back. He picked Felix Schacki as the assistant crew chief and the two of us stayed with him all through his tour. We did everything to his planes. We sanded them, waxed them till they shone. Gabby wanted this, he said it gave him more speed. He was very particular. He didn't want any buttons sticking up, no loose Zeus fasteners. Schacki fixed him up a special heater for his throttle hand. It was riding up there next to the canopy and it got pretty cold even though he wore gloves. He had another heater tube between the feet which he arranged with a tee over it to put warm air on both feet. It was manifold heat. One time we had radio trouble with static noise on the radio. I tried everything in the book to try to eliminate that, to ground that noise out. We just could not do it on that engine in this new airplane. Radio people tried; we tried; the ignition people tried. Finally we took the harness off an engine that had been taken out of another plane and put it on this engine and we had a quiet radio. Trouble was in the ignition harness but we just couldn't locate it. Static. Just like you could hear the ignition coming right through on the radio. Gabby was thorough and particular. Any little idiosyncrasies the airplane had he knew and studied them. He knew exactly what that airplane would do. One occasion Gabby got hit by a cannon shell in the side of the cockpit which cut the rudder pedals in half under his foot. Took the sole off his boot but didn't hurt his foot. On another mission Gabby came home with oil on his windshield and spinner. I said that oil didn't come from the engine. Gabby said that he blew up a German plane right in front of him and that was where the oil came from. Once I found a cannon slug sitting behind a push rod. He took it. Gabby would sometimes cross himself when we got him in the cockpit and hooked him up. But he was pretty much at peace with himself. Didn't say a lot when he came up to fly. Pretty serious. Gabby always saw his crew got credit in publicity. We had a good association with him."

Although 24-hour duty had been relaxed late in June ground personnel were still hard tasked as on most operational days two missions were being despatched. The ordnance men and armourers were still just as busy and ground fire encountered in low-level bombing and strafing trebled the amount of battle damage repair for the sheet metal men. Most took it in their stride without bitching, fully appreciating that they served men who put their lives on the line every time they flew a mission. But the pressure of work did get to the aircraft crew chiefs particularly. Dave Hubler, 62nd line chief:

"One day Father Durrance called me into the orderly room and said he wanted to talk to me about Sergeant Brennan. I said what about him? He said, 'Brennan asked to speak to me. It was a rather strange conversation. When I asked him what the problem was he said: 'I been over here eighteen months and I'd like to see my little boy; I've never seen him. I just reasoned it out that I'd like to declare a separate peace with the Germans. Surely you could find a German who's tired of the God damned war? We could sign papers. It seems a kinda logical way out.' Durrance was taken aback by this and said, 'We'll have to think about that, Brennan.' It was probably done with tongue in cheek but Brennan was trying to get a message across. Joe Brennan was the first guy drafted out of Pottstown, Pennsylvania. He was the head of the Young Republican League. The draft board were all Democrats so he went in early! One time he got gasoline in an eye which made it blind. I was feeling sorry for him and said so. He said, 'No, no: that's the greatest thing that ever happened. I'm going back to draw a pension. The bastards are going to pay me for comin' over here!'"

Virgil Durrance later became the group adjutant. He was one of the longest serving officers having first been assigned to the 56th in July 1941.

Aware of the extra work to which the various ground sections were subject Zemke advised a more generous attitude to passes. And as others had observed he could turn a blind eye to regulations in the cause of morale. Sylvester Walker:

"Sergeant B.G. Moore and I were in Colchester at a carnival one day. They were putting chances on a pig. We each bought one chance. I won the pig. I tried to give it back so they could raffle him off again but those Limeys wouldn't take him back. They put him in a small bag. We took him out to the base. That afternoon when Colonel Zemke came in from a mission I went to his office and asked permission to put the pig in a pen we were constructing out of bomb crates. After rolling it over in his head, he said, 'Walker. You are regular army. You know that's against all regulations. Do what you want with the pig but if the Inspector General finds that pig on this base, I won't know anything about it.' Well, we kept the pig, feeding it out of the mess hall. I finally butchered him and took him to a butcher shop in Colchester where we knew the proprietor. Cut the pig up, then passed it out to people in the town after a long argument about meat coupons."

Zemke probably had a soft spot for Walker, one of the few men from the 56th's activation cadre still with the group. Although an automobile mechanic Walker had acted as a crew chief on Zemke's aircraft back at Bridgeport.

"While at Boxted I was vehicle inspector. I got a three day pass and went to London, from there to Scotland. It was ten days before I made it back to base. After getting by the guard at the gate, I was informed I was to see Colonel Zemke about the refueling truck that had broken down. When his mission was over he came into his office to find me waiting. When he saw me he said, 'Walker, why are you here?' Before I could answer he said, 'Oh yes, about the refueling truck.' I assured him I had taken care of things but it would take some days to get the parts. While we waited for these he told me to be on the field every night helping the boys refuel the planes as it would take longer having to use tractors and two wheel trailers. When I was dismissed, as I left to go out the door, Zemke said, 'Walker, was it worth it?' I said, 'Yes Colonel. I enjoyed it lots'."

Walker should really have been in big trouble for his self-extended leave about which Zemke had obviously been informed.

Ground attack still occupied most of the group's effort, and Zemke was exploring better means of delivering ordnance. He had managed to acquire another Droop Snoot, the P-38 Lightning modified to carry a bombardier and sight in its nose. More thoughts of formation bombing were in mind but a lone sortie to test the accuracy of a 12,000 feet approach to a target resulted in near disaster. Heavy flak was encountered when he was intent on depositing two 250-lb bombs on Montdidier airfield near Paris. An 88-mm shell explosion wrecked the right engine to add yet another 'near thing' to Zemke's many as he fought to bring the crippled aircraft back to Boxted. Both troubled occupants survived the no-brakes landing but the Colonel decided there and then to terminate his interest in formation bombing. This sortie had been in conjunction with Dave Schilling leading 35 P-47s, each with a 150-gallon belly tank filled with an oil mixture, to see if it could be an effective incendiary weapon against three different types of target. Unfortunately, a warning that the formation was about to be bounced by enemy fighters, which proved false, caused all to jettison their loads all over the French countryside. The following day Zemke led a formation with each aircraft carrying two 108-gallon tanks filled with an oil/gasoline mix against a suspected wooded fuel dump area. There was no massive conflagration as desired from this delivery and the tanks caused damage to the retaining shackles during diving manoeuvres to release.

The low attitude fighter-bomber missions continued to predominate in operations and with the Allied breakout from Normandy in late July this activity increased. Even so, trading on the record established Zemke still looked upon air fighting as the 56th's major duty and this was conveyed to new replacement pilots. William Hartshorn was one of a batch of nine newcomers that arrived at Boxted on 1 August to be taken to Zemke's office for an introductory talk: "He welcomed us and said, 'There are two kinds of fighter pilots, the hunters and the hunted. The latter only think about surviving. You may have mixed feelings but this is the greatest sport in the world'." This was obviously an exercise in morale-building but Hub genuinely did find combat exhilarating, despite its dangers – which he certainly knew only too well. Five of that nine would not go home. Most of the new replacements were eager innocents who would learn the hard way what a deadly occupation they were involved in, and 2nd Lieutenant David Magel, who was assigned to the 63rd on 8 August, had this brought home to him brutally on arrival. He learned that his twin brother, Robert, who joined the 63rd in April, had been shot down by flak the day before, and was reported dead. With fate's irony Robert was later notified as a prisoner and it was David who would later lose his life. On the same mission that Robert Magel went down another collision had occurred. Pulling up from the dive to release bombs at 4,000 feet, Lieutenant Arthur Maul's wing caught and removed the left elevator and most of the rudder of Lieutenant Warren Patterson's aircraft. Patterson managed to nurse his crippled aircraft back to England. He was the third of the six bomber pilots who arrived in May to be involved in a collision. Maul never returned to base.

In July the 56th was notified that it had been awarded a Distinguished Unit Citation for the particularly successful period of action during the previous February and March. This award, for which each member of the group was entitled to wear a distinctive blue rectangular patch above the uniform breast pocket, was the first to a fighter organisation in Europe.

There was a general opinion that the publicity accorded the 56th was not popular with some at wing headquarters. Since the spring the group seemed to be given mission assignments that did not place it where enemy fighters were likely to be encountered, thus failing to take advantage of expertise built up over several months. The 65th Fighter Wing HQ at Saffron Walden had its staff aircraft at nearby Debden, the 4th Group's base, and rightly or wrongly there was a suspicion of favouritism. Zemke's habit of bypassing the wing and going straight to VIII Fighter Command on some matters did not endear him to the senior officers at Saffron Walden, although a fairly jaundiced view of that headquarters was common to most at Boxted. Major Dave Robinson, Group Intelligence Officer:

"The fighter wing was just an impediment to getting things done. Our difficulty with some of those at wing was they didn't understand the war. They'd call us up there for some important meeting but it was often information we didn't need or couldn't use. We got a message from them one night to send a special officer courier to get some information on German defences west of Normandy in an area where we rarely flew and yet they thought it important enough to get some officer up at midnight to drive up there."

Robinson, a lawyer by profession and in his late thirties, was known as The Silver Fox because of his hair.

Perhaps the 56th, having shown the way, did not want to accept the fact that the P-51 Mustang was a much better fighter for long-range escort. At this time ten of the Eighth Air Force's fifteen fighter groups were flying Mustangs and the rest were scheduled to convert before the end of the year. The 56th was last in line because Schilling had persuaded Landry back in January that they should not part with the Thunderbolt; this was the tool of trade the group had used to advantage and they should stick with it. Zemke had no such loyalty. In his view they were here to win an air war and should have the best fighter available, and if that was the P-51 so be it, even if the 56th was the pride of Republic Aviation. There had been little contact with the enemy in the air since early July and only two claims of aircraft shot down, yet some of the Mustang groups were involved in big air battles. This was frustrating to many of the eager Wolfpack pilots, particularly the innovative Zemke who felt particularly that his group was being sidelined. Then fate took a hand.

After leading a sweep over France on the morning of 11 August, Zemke was informed that General Griswold wanted to speak with him urgently. A call was made to VIII Fighter Command where Griswold had recently taken over the helm from Kepner. Griswold informed Zemke that he wanted David Schilling to take over command of the 479th at Wattisham. This, the youngest fighter group in the Eighth Air Force, had just had its CO shot down over France. Its showing had not been particularly favourable and Griswold wanted someone of experience to lead it. When the message was conveyed to him Schilling's reaction was one of disquiet if not horror. A group was the most prized combat command in the whole air force but Schilling did not want to take up this particular post. He was most unhappy, expressing his feelings with several expletives. The 479th was the last of the Eighth's four P-38 Lightning groups, shortly to convert to Mustangs, yet even this failed to attract. No one was more surprised than Schilling when Zemke announced, "Okay Dave, I'll tell you what we'll do. You take the 56th and I'll go to the 479th."

That their famed CO should choose to move on was something of a shock to many at Boxted, as the 56th was synonymous with Hub Zemke; wasn't it Zemke's Wolfpack? But Hub wanted a new challenge and purpose, believing the 56th would be increasingly sidelined as the war drew to a close, which at that time looked likely to be before the end of the year as Allied armies were sweeping across France. He also recognised that Schilling identified more with the 56th than he did and had always aspired to its full command. Indeed, although Schilling enjoyed a high degree of authority as the group Flying Executive he was a man who wanted to be the principal of any unit to which he was assigned. Receiving Griswold's approval of the arrangement, Zemke addressed a small assembly of men in No.1 hangar, packed his bags and left for Wattisham. His quest for challenge was certainly met, not only with the 479th where he led this group to success but, following the break-up of his Mustang over Germany, as the senior Allied officer in Stalag Luft I.

21 Schilling in Command

David Schilling's popularity, especially with the 62nd Squadron, helped the morale of the group after Zemke's sudden departure. If Schilling indulged in a merry social round he was none the less a competent and ambitious leader. In fact, on assuming command of the 56th there is a suggestion he appreciated that in following the chief architect of the group's success he should show similar intent to keep the leading position through achievement and innovation. Schilling had never been lost for ideas, indeed he had become known for them; many were wild and untenable, but now and again one was very worthy. Most were generated from his practical interest in engineering. Having learned on enquiry that bombs could be fused in the tail end, he had an 18-inches length of $2^1/_2$-inch diameter steel rod screwed into the nose. The idea of the so-called spike bomb was to cause the detonation to occur at ground level and thus obtain much more blast damage effect than resulted when a crater was made. Tried out in August, there did not appear to be any significant advantage and spike bomb use was discontinued. Another idea was even more innovative. Urban Sweeny, 41st Service Squadron:

> "I worked in the machine shop. One day Schilling came in and said that when he flew back from Germany he felt he was not doing enough. He said he'd like to get a great big anchor made and have a spool put in the bottom of the P-47 with a cable on it so when he came back he could drop it down and rip up telephone wires. We made it and found that we had to weight the hook otherwise it would trail out straight behind the aircraft. Schilling flew a trial and first time it was used it ripped the bottom out of the aircraft."

In fact, the assembly with a three-pronged anchor and 100 feet of reel cable was made to attach to the bomb or fuel tank shackles. In the trial the hook caught the ground and ripped the shackles and gear clean off the Thunderbolt. Donald Trudell, a 33rd Service Group clerk, was faced with one of Schilling's wilder ideas:

> "Colonel Schilling frequented the ordnance section on many occasions to get data on armament and explosives. He came in once and asked us if it was feasible to use hand grenades by throwing them from a P-47 at locomotives in low-level attacks. He loved to blow up rolling stock and especially locomotive boilers. We assured the Colonel that a 15-second

fuse on a hand grenade would likely blow up his plane first."

Popularity with the enlisted men stemmed mainly from his friendly manner. When in their presence on his own he would invariably tell an anecdote, often one with sexual connotations: the 'dirty story' was common ground for both officers and men. When in command of the 62nd Schilling had usually been referred to as Dave in his absence by the mechanics but never to his face. And as he continued to keep his personal aircraft in that squadron this hidden familiarity continued. If any enlisted man did step out of line in addressing Schilling other than as an officer they were quickly reprimanded. Among the pilots of lower rank a more open relationship existed with their ground crews with a good deal of friendly banter with those who had been around for sometime. Dave Hubler: "I was working on an airplane when Mike Quirk came driving up. Big smile, says, 'Hi.' Brennan says, 'What the hell you want?' Mike says, 'You're never gonna guess.' Brennan says, 'Get it over with, Mike, we're not here to play games.' Mike says 'I'm your new CO!' Brennan threw down his tools and says, 'Shit; the war is over!'" This reflects a long association with no disrespect for rank as both men had been in the original squadron complement that came to the UK. Quirk was made 62nd CO when Schilling assumed command of the group and moved Pete Dade to be his deputy. Dade had never been a generally popular CO with the 62nd. Apart from Schreiber being a hard act to follow, Dade was attuned to military position and conduct in a way that did not endear him to many of his command. Yet Dade was dependable and reliable in his posts, and having served for a long period in Group Operations was still only part way through his first tour.

The fluid position of the Allied armies in their advance across France led to a moratorium on ground strafing on 14 August. Planned fighter-bombing missions continued and on the 15th Dave Schilling tried out a new weapon, air-launched rockets. Basically an infantry weapon known as the bazooka, three clustered launching tubes were suspended under each wing and armed with 5.3-lb warhead rockets. Schilling was none too impressed with the results, the rockets going "every which way". The installations were cumbersome and a liability if enemy fighters were encountered. Apart from the new ordnance for ground attack, electrical release for the bomb rack shackles were to be installed to give a more assured release than the mechanical type in use. Another improvement was the K-14A 'gyro' gun sight. Based on a British development, this improved the chance of obtaining hits when firing a deflection burst. Gerry Johnson, at the time considered the best shot in the group, had been selected by Ajax to fly with the RAF for a few days in October 1943 in order to form an opinion of this sight and found for the affirmative.

The V-1 bombardment, unleashed by the Germans a week after the D-Day landings, brought another aerial target although rarely in the 56th operating areas. The first claimed by the Eighth Air Force fell to a P-47 of the air/sea rescue squadron at Boxted but thereafter little opportunity was presented for 56th pilots to down these missiles. Only the odd example over-flying the London target area ended its journey near Colchester. That is, until 31 August, when for some reason a flush of 'buzz bombs' came Boxted way. James Chew, 62nd Squadron mechanic:

> "Colonel Schilling was giving us a lecture near No. 2 hangar concerning how good a fighter plane the P-47 was. He was standing on a flat bed truck and the GIs were standing around listening to him give the spiel. All of a sudden the Colchester air raid alert sounded. Schilling stopped talking long enough for the sirens to finish and when they stopped he continued on with his speech. A few minutes later the unmistakable sound of a buzz bomb broke in on his speech. All the GIs ran out onto the airfield to get a better look at the buzz bomb. And just then the motor conked out and the bomb dived into the ground about a mile from us with a huge plume of smoke and dust and a loud roar. All the guys stood there shouting and talking among themselves in the excitement. As they wandered back to the truck, Schilling was seen standing spread-legged with his hands on his hips, looking intently at us as if to say, what the hell are you running out there to see that buzz bomb for. I'm more important than it is."

Six more passed near Boxted that warm sunny afternoon. The following day, during a fighter-bomber mission over the Netherlands, the group probably got a more telling experience of V weapons when wagons in a freight train attacked suddenly exploded damaging three of the P-47s involved. Dutch underground intelligence suspected that the train was carrying V-1 warheads. Within a few weeks the Luftwaffe launched V-1s at night from aircraft over the North Sea and the dreaded put-put sound, like an unsilenced motorbike engine, would be all too familiar throughout the winter of 1944-45.

By the autumn of 1944 many of the early replacement pilots that survived were finishing their tours and to the ground crews the turnover in new pilots appeared to have accelerated; as indeed it had as during the past six months total losses were more than double those incurred during the first year of combat. The old hands, with few exceptions, were those who had returned for a second tour. All but two of the Polish fliers in the 61st had returned to resume RAF service. Remaining were Witold 'Lanny' Lanowski and Michael Gladych who preferred life with the Americans. Lanowski was a regular Polish Air Force pilot who had reached France via Rumania. When France collapsed he escaped from Marseilles by ship and arrived in Britain where he flew 79 sorties with the RAF before being rested. Prior to arriving at Boxted in May, Lanny had first tried to join the Mustang-equipped 354th Fighter Group at the same base earlier in the year but they would not let him fly combat. His relationship with Gladych was not particularly close as they were two very different personalities. Gladych was, within bounds, a law unto himself. William Hartshorn:

"One afternoon in September 1944 several of the 61st pilots watched a British Spitfire enter the landing pattern at Boxted, land and taxi into our squadron area as our own Squadron Leader Mike Gladych walked out to greet the visiting pilot. Mike, an ace several times over, was somewhat older than most of us and, for this second lieutenant, appeared to be a mature and business-like leader who got my respect. Anyone who had survived five years of combat and who had Spitfires and Hurricanes and goodness knows what else in his background was someone to look up to. I had had the privilege of flying his wing on several occasions. Mike called me 'Air Boy' after a character in a newspaper cartoon, possibly in deference to my youthful appearance. I'm sure I looked at least seventeen. In any event, on this occasion, with the Spitfire now parked in front of our squadron ready room and with Mike chatting with his friend from the RAF Polish unit, I walked over and was introduced. After several minutes of looking over what was probably viewed by many as the most famous fighter plane of the war, I couldn't help but make the observation that this would have to be the dream plane for any pilot to fly. Mike gave me a look, turned to his friend and after a few words in Polish turned back to me and I found myself being helped into the cockpit with an RAF helmet on my head.

"After too briefly pointing out several key instruments and showing me where the throttle, gear, and flap handles were, Mike's friend produced what appeared to be the starting mechanism and with a sharp explosion the Merlin engine was turning over. With the beautiful sound of a V12 coming to life, the radio on, and last minute instructions to close the coolant flaps just before take-off, here I was on the taxi-way actually about to fly a Spitfire. In position at the runway and with clearance from the tower, I pulled out onto the active, advanced the throttle, and after a short run we were flying. Looking out over the long nose and out to the side at those famous elliptical wings, I was introduced to the light touch and responsiveness that were the symbol of the airplane. By contrast, the Thunderbolt took longer to get off and then as the name might imply, 'thundered' off across the countryside as you picked up speed and adjusted trim. Once up to speed, the two thousand horses in the nose delivered the power necessary to make the P-47 as fast as any fighter then flying. But certainly, the feel in the air of the Spitfire was different. It went up like an elevator. And so I climbed out away from the field relishing the moment and getting familiar with this beautiful bird. After a few turns at probably 6,000 ft, I saw a P-47 from our group off to one side, up no doubt on a local flight. Who under these circumstances could resist rolling over and slipping in behind him to await his reaction to the challenge. Would he allow this Spitfire to stay perched behind him in such a compromising position? True to the spirit of the day, the Thunderbolt immediately rolled around in a sudden turn and round and round, up and over we went. The seventy-five hundred pound Spit' I was in hung in there on his tail for a few turns and then the P-47 pulled up, rolled over and dove away at a speed I couldn't match. Little did that pilot know that he had been up against one from his own group, enjoying the exhilaration of the moment. Now after a few more manoeuvres it was time to return this aircraft to its owner; but first, what about my pals on the ground wondering how I could be so lucky. Shouldn't they be included somehow? And so down I dove positioning myself to the east of the field for a low level pass over our squadron flight room. With the engine turning up I hopped over the trees at the boundary of our airfield and at minimum altitude roared at and over the roof of the ready room. Pulling up into a steep chandelle, I headed out of the immediate area, suspecting the control tower would be wondering what was going on over our squadron area. Someone has said that the Lord sometimes chooses to watch out for the young and the foolish and so it must have been on this occasion. As it turned out the windscreen on this particular plane had lost some of its transparency through long exposure to the sun and weather so that vision forward was not the best. Add to this fact that my pass across the field was made into an afternoon sun and I just missed seeing the radio mast on the roof of the squadron building. Which side I passed it on I don't know but I can only assume 'His eye was on the sparrow' on this occasion for which I am thankful. Meanwhile, back on the ground after an uneventful landing I found that a call to our squadron had been made to find out what was going on. The upshot of this call led to a tongue in cheek reprimand from the Squadron Operations Officer, Captain Don Smith, to satisfy some HQ officer who ordered something be done about it. In addition a fine of five pounds was levied which I thought fair. The $20 it had cost me was worth the experience. And, of course, I was ever grateful to Mike Gladych for making this possible."

These Poles were not the only pilots who escaped 'resting' by the RAF. There were still a few Americans who preferred to fly with the British service. When Jack Bradshaw was retired to a non-combat post after flying Spitfire XIVs he volunteered for transfer to the USAAF, ending up flying a tour with Thunderbolts in the 56th. In November two Polish American pilots who had been flying with the RAF joined the Wolfpack.

In combined air and ground totals of enemy aircraft destroyed, the 4th Fighter Group had led the Eighth's fighter groups since 10 April. On 5 September the 56th regained the leading position when credited with 71 enemy aircraft destroyed through strafing and nine shot down, becoming the first group to pass the 700 destroyed mark. In the matter of air victories alone the 56th had been champion throughout the year with a hundred more than the 4th. On the bountiful day the 700 mark was passed the Wolfpack carried out two missions, the first a sweep of enemy airfields in the vicinity of the route a following bomber stream would take to hit oil targets in south-east Germany. Led by Major Dade, 15 claims were made for aircraft destroyed on the ground and seven through air action. The cost was two pilots and four aircraft, the latter battle-damaged having reached friendly territory in France and 'bellied in'. That afternoon Schilling led a strafing mission to the Giessen area of Germany where the Luftwaffe was caught unawares with some 60 aircraft on Gelnhausen airfield, where 47 were claimed totally wrecked and another dozen damaged. Claude Chinn:

"Pilots who flew Thunderbolts in combat all knew the awesome power of eight machine guns carried in the wings. Few, if any, I suspect, experienced that power first hand. I did! Colonel Schilling was leading the group and I was leading his element. The attack began in the usual way, the leader and his flight going across the airfield at full speed, drawing fire from the gun positions. The second flight came in close behind us and shot up the gun positions, making it safer for following flights. The Colonel, after a few passes over the field, ordered the first squadron up so the next could make their run. It was on the pull-up to the right that my experience began.

"The normal pattern, in breaking off, was to make an extra wide climbing turn so as to allow the next flights to begin their runs on the target. With my wingman close in tow, we made the turn a little too wide and flak from another airdrome caught me good. The shell, probably a 20-mm, hit the accessory section behind the engine and in an instant there was no oil in the airplane, it was all on the outside. We had heard stories about the engine running awhile without oil, now it was my turn to find out if they were true, and if so how long. General Patton's army was on a swing south-east of Paris, so I released my wingman back to the squadron and headed off in the direction of where friendly troops might be. I had left my throttle at the climb-out setting after the hit, so I was covering ground at a pretty good clip. Thirty minutes or so later, a convoy of trucks showed up on the highway I was following. German trucks did not travel during daylight hours, so I assumed these were Patton's and decided to belly in close by. The wheatfield I chose seemed okay, so I made a circle approach anticipating that my engine would freeze-up, it did. The landing was quite exciting. The ground view was not nearly as friendly as that from the air. There were no troops to be seen so I set the plane on fire and ran into a wooded area off my right wing and forward of the aircraft. American troops showed up after a few minutes, coming over a slight rise in the elevation on the other side of the field, off the left wing, also in front of the now burning plane. I raised my hands and with caution stepped out of the woods. The troops, six men in two jeeps, called for me to hurry as there were Germans in the area. I set out at a fast clip straight towards the group of men. When directly in front of the plane all eight of the machine guns, that only a few minutes earlier had been strafing a German airdrome, started shooting at me. Fortunately, I was lined up on the axis of the plane, about fifty yards out from the nose. The bullets were passing on either side of me. The plane moved a little but kept the nose and tail lined up. The firing stopped after only a few seconds and the soldiers were again calling for me to come on. However, there had been no tracer bullets. Knowing that the last few rounds in the guns were tracers, I held fast to the nose to tail line-up and started towards the plane, figuring that if the guns did not fire the tracers, I would climb over the wing. The tracers came as I was about twenty yards out front. Gingerly stepping across the gun path, I joined the Third Army."

Chinn, coming down south of Troyes, was back at Boxted five days later.

No other P-47s were lost in the attack on Gelnhausen, but coming out one P-47 was hit by flak near Antwerp. The pilot baled out and evaded capture. Flak was to make September the most costly month of operations for the group. Seven pilots were lost in as many missions during the first two weeks with another seven battle-damaged aircraft wrecked or scrapped. Two pilots had to 'belly in' on the continent twice in a week; for Lieutenant James Jure it was his third crash-landing. One of those lost was the popular Mike Quirk, the 62nd CO and last of the squadron's original combat pilots. Quirk, seen to bale out and land in a tree, survived as a POW, as did another of his squadron, Billy Edens, who was brought down by ground fire while attacking the same German airfield. Schilling moved second-tour Leslie Smith from the 61st to the 62nd to take over command.

However, the worst and most devastating losses occurred during the Allied airborne invasion of the Low Countries, operation Market Garden. On the opening day of this venture, 17 September, the 56th was not directly involved, and was sent to attack the rail marshalling yard at Amersfoort. Ground fire encountered there was intense and one Thunderbolt was shot down and seven damaged. Michael Jackson:

"Dave Schilling was leading the group that day and I was flying his wing. We did some dive bombing, then went up to the Zuider Zee, reformed and headed south to the Nijmegen area to make strafing runs. I heard somebody screaming over the radio, 'I'm hit, I'm hit.' I looked around: it turned out to be Schilling. His P-47 was flying through the air with a streamer of fire some thirty feet long coming back from his left wing. I went over to him and under him and I could see the fire was coming from his left wheelwell. Suggested he drop his gear which he did and the flame just blew out. I told him the fire was out and his tyre had burned off. His response was, 'Fairbanks here. Going Home.' So I climbed to look around to see who I could join up with but couldn't find anybody. Then I got a hit on the right side of the bubble canopy. A 20 mm came in one side and went out and exploded the other. As result I picked up some shrapnel in my left knee and left hand. Superficial. Powder marks on my left hand and knee. When I got back to base the crew chief stuck a ruler in the canopy and said, 'My God, you were just 12 inches short of having your head blown off.'"

Schilling got back to Boxted for a crash-landing. Lieutenant Carl Westman also got his P-47 back to England despite battle damage only to have it burst into flames before he could land. Westman's clothes caught fire and his face was burned on opening the cockpit canopy to bale out. The Thunderbolt narrowly missed some cottages near Wattisham when it crashed. Lieutenant Darrell McMahan's P-47 was hit by two 40-mm shells. One penetrated just forward of the windshield and exploded in the cockpit near the rudder pedals; splinters hit McMahan in the forehead, left leg, right knee and arm, but he was able to apply a tourniquet to his right leg. Russell Fredrickson:

"McMahan returned to base with considerable battle damage to his aircraft and extensive personal injury. His right knee was, for all practical purposes, missing. Everyone was absolutely amazed that he not only flew the airplane back to Boxted, he landed it safely. With the engine shut down and the canopy open, the Flight Surgeon of the 62nd Squadron, James Biggins, jumped up on to the wing to assess the situation. Not liking what he saw, he reached across the cockpit and lifted Darrell out of the airplane single-handed. An extraordinary feat of strength."

If the 17th had been an unusually bruising day what happened on the morrow was a slaughter. The situation facing the airborne landing forces, particularly those at Arnhem, was critical. Supplies and reinforcements had to parachuted to them and the 56th was one of the units detailed to fly ahead of re-supply aircraft to shoot up enemy anti-aircraft sites to help minimise losses to bombers hauling the parachute-delivered supplies. 'Flak busting', a dangerous mission in any situation, was made even more hazardous on this occasion in that because of the danger of shooting up Allied forces the pilots were briefed not to attack until fired upon. Leadership of this mission fell on Bunny Comstock, the 63rd CO:

"I was scheduled to lead and got up at 3 o'clock to check the ops order and the weather. The weather was terrible. We were scheduled to go ahead of the bombers, who were re-supplying the ground troops, to take out any flak. These were all B-24s. and as usual they got the nasty job. The field order read that we could not shoot at anything until it had shot at us. Between that ridiculous instruction and the weather I went back to the Wheelhouse and awakened Dave Schilling and told him that I considered it impossible. Dave put on his clothes and came down and read the field order and agreed with me. He picked up the phone and went through to wing and argued against the mission. He asked the senior officer to whom he was talking to repeat a statement he had just made, holding the receiver out so I could hear the officer say 'You will go at all costs.' Dave slammed the telephone down and turned to me and said, 'You heard him.' I briefed the mission as instructed. When we got to the coastal area I spread the other two squadrons to diffuse the number of airplanes and tried to contact the bombers. When I got on the bomber channel it was obvious they were already in the area. The weather was down to about 500 feet. I did not wish to let down through the weather and went in underneath. One of the first people shot down was my wingman, Charlie Rotzler, who bellied in straight across a ditch at a high rate of speed. From that point on it was pandemonium with people saying I'm hit, I'm baling out, and I'm going in. This probably went on for four or five minutes when I called an abort and to climb up through the overcast. There was only one aircraft in my vicinity and it turned out to be from the 61st. He joined up and we headed out. When we got near the cost the weather lifted and I could see B-24s returning home. The only comment I got from Dave on the mission was that I should have aborted sooner. Hindsight is great! Lost six pilots from my squadron including Gordon Stevens, one of the bomber pilots who having finished a tour wanted to fly fighters. He was killed as was Lt Raymond who managed to get his shot-up P-47 back to England, only to crash. Tom Gurerro, an outstanding football coach, crash-landed. The Germans found him and put a steel plate in his head; his injuries were such he was repatriated. Kling and Rotzler got picked up by our troops and eventually made it back. Kelley became a POW. They later gave the group its second Presidential Citation for this mission; supposedly for achievement, really for sacrifice I think."

Of the 39 P-47s that took off from Boxted early that afternoon, 16 did not return and of those that did 15 had battle damage. For the de-briefing officers it was difficult to gain a clear picture of what had occurred other than that the group's pilots had encountered devastating ground fire over Holland. Faced with an overcast as low as 500 feet in some places and visibility restricted by varying degrees of haze it proved exceedingly difficult to locate enemy gun emplacements, but it was claimed at least 14 had been shot up. Some of the missing were believed to have survived and over the next few days it was established that 12 had come down in Allied territory or evaded capture, of which one was known killed. The other four remained Missing In Action. One originally believed to be in enemy hands was William Hartshorn:

"On the way we passed the troop carriers and gliders. Saw some gliders that had been cut loose down in the water. We went all the way at tree top level. Caught a lot of flak. At one place there was a line of fire in a field. When we went up over a bank there was a P-47 sitting in the water. Just happened so probably one of ours. Somebody was shooting at us so we started to make a turn to go back and get him when there was an explosion in my right wing root. A big hole and fire and the indictor showed my wheels came down. Terrible weather, low ceiling. The engine still running, I pulled up just under the overcast and flew back for a couple of minutes. Couldn't crash-land with the wheels down so called, 'Somebody tell me if my wheels are down' but I was all alone. The thing was burning and I was sitting on gas. Looked down and saw a column of trucks with white stars on the hoods and decided to bale out. You were supposed to go out on the right side because the propeller made a flow of air along the fuselage which took you away. But because of the fire I went out on the left side, got about halfway out then the slipstream just took me, bounced along the fuselage and hit the tail and broke my leg. After the chute opened I saw a cottage and woman watching me; I was concerned I was going to hit the fence on either side of the road but I landed hard on the road. The guys in the truck convoy must have seen me as one of the weapons carriers came over and picked me up. Took me to a local town where I had a splint put on my leg. Ended up in a field hospital with wounded Germans and GIs. While there somebody stole my good luck pink shorts. After a couple of days I was removed to Paris, then flown back to the UK and ended up in a US hospital near Cardiff. Had been there a few days when down the corridor comes Don Smith. He and another guy had taken a small liaison plane and flown over to see me. That's the sort of guy Don was."

Morale at Boxted had been taxed during the first weeks of September, and understandably it fell away even further on the evening of the 18th. Even the most stoic pilots were troubled about their future. When they received notice from wing headquarters to prepare for another flak-busting mission the following day, a disturbed Schilling contacted General Auton and argued against committing the 56th to this duty again in view of the losses sustained. It is said that Auton threatened to relieve Schilling of his command: even so, the altercation was soon resolved, as a field order was then issued for an escort of B-17s to Hamm. Schilling led the 32 P-47s that the group was able to muster. No enemy aircraft were encountered and there was no strafing.

The disquiet was partly lifted on the 21st when the group was given the task of providing area support for RAF Stirlings carrying out supply drops at Arnhem. Flying south under the cloud towards Lochem at around 3,500 feet the group chanced upon a low flying formation of FW190s flying east. With the advantages of height and surprise the Wolfpack claimed 15 shot down for the loss of two in the ensuing battle. Three of the claims were made by Dave Schilling, group leader that day. This raised his personal score to 17 and one shared air victories. Any displeasure at higher headquarters that might have arisen over his objection to commit the group to another flak-busting mission during the Netherlands airborne landings was short-lived. On 1 October Schilling was promoted full Colonel.

22 Young Men's Fancies

"The people like the ground officers, the men in the various support outfits and the ground crews had a better appreciation of what was going on than the pilots did. The pilots were like spoiled children and we the proud parents. And we let 'em get away with it because we knew that when a guy went out on a mission he was putting his ass on the line." This comment from a flight chief is true to the ethos of the group well into the second year of operations. Only a few of the original combat officers and early replacements remained to carry the torch, and while new pilots were well indoctrinated that they were part of an elite outfit their commitment would only be for the duration of their tours. The group ground personnel, with few exceptions, were the ongoing entity, there from the beginning and likely to stay until the end. The prowess of the 56th Fighter Group may have been generated by the pilots but the ground men now embraced this fame and proudly carried it forward. The *Stars and Stripes* service newspaper frequently carried items on the group's standing in the competitive totals of enemy aircraft claimed destroyed, and became as much a major source on information as the base squadron bulletin boards. Boxted men had an unshakeable belief that the Wolfpack was the best fighter outfit in the Eighth if not the whole USAAF (albeit that competitors held similar beliefs for their groups).

Relationships between pilots and ground crews had the officer – enlisted men barrier to contend with and at the flight line varied from an easy joking friendship to a detached coolness. Some pilots never got to know their assigned crew chiefs very well. Some ground crews did not want to know their assigned pilots for the simple reason of less personal hurt if the man was lost. Having strapped a pilot into the cockpit the period of awaiting engine start time was difficult for the sensitive crew chief. This delay was for many pilots the most stressful part of a mission and it showed particularly with the nervous. Crew chiefs made a point of talking to their pilot about anything they thought would take his mind off the oncoming flight.

The range of intellect and experience among the ground personnel was immense: from an intellectual college tutor to a hobo; from considerable civilian wealth to the other extreme. And these extremes were not necessarily distinguished by rank. A citizen's airforce could find a use for all. Angelo DeCarlo, 1126th QM Company:

"We had an older fellow in our quartermaster unit, an ex-coal miner from

Logan, West Virginia, named Emory Ellis. Probably one of the old group
drafted by the army. A friendly individual but he could not read or write.
And he was taught just to sign his name so he could sign the sheet once
a month just to get paid: the payroll sheet. He never had a job in any
particular section. They just used him as a utility to do the jobs that
needed a little physical effort but none that required any great
responsibility. At Boxted he was put in charge of our area. All he did was
clean up the area every day and eventually put up little picket fences,
painted them white and kept the place spotless. In the evening before we
returned to our barracks he'd make sure the fires were started in each hut.
He would do anything asked of him; very congenial. For some reason he
took a liking to me and as he couldn't read or write he would ask me to
write letters to his girlfriend. He'd sit down with me and tell me what to
say. I'd paraphrase it and read it back to him; that's how he wrote his
letters. Likewise, when he got a letter he'd come to me to read it to him."

At the other extreme was the 62nd Squadron's statistical officer, 1st
Lieutenant Samuel Cabot, who had a remarkable ability for mental
arithmetic. He was able to add six figure numbers as fast as they could be
written down, a feat that earned him several winning bets. Not that Cabot
was a gambling man; the wagering was usually conducted by Dave
Schilling on any unsuspecting newcomer to the Officers' Club bar.

Off-duty entertainment for both officers and men was the
responsibility of the so-called Special Services Officer, Captain Alfred
Mellor, who excelled at his task. On-base dances, variety shows and
concerts were organised at regular intervals for both officers and men. He
was apparently something of a wheeler-dealer, his activities extending
beyond the base. Angelo DeCarlo:

"Mellor was quite an operator. He was in charge of our Boxted band,
Schilling's Serenaders. He would get us off duty for three or four days,
take us to London to play in the Strand Hotel and the Stage Door
Canteen. My First Sergeant would say to me that he didn't understand
how I had so much pull to get an order to be pulled out of my normal
duties in my quartermaster unit and authorised to go play in London. One
man in the band was out of the intelligence section, another a medic for
the pilots, and we also had a parachute rigger and an ordnance man. We
all wondered how Mellor was able to work these orders."

This band was an expansion of the original Jivin' Yanks and two of
the musicians were officers: Leo Butiste (a 62nd pilot who later changed
his name to Battista), on saxophone and Merle Woods, the 63rd Flight
Surgeon, on trumpet.

Sports were encouraged and during the summer months softball was
by far the most popular. Matches were arranged with other units. As a
gesture towards Anglo-American goodwill a soccer match was arranged
with an RAF team. Claude Chinn, 63rd pilot: "One man in our team of

scrubs had played soccer in college but the rest of us were raw meat. The RAF men were good, at least in our inexperienced eyes, and they really gave us a beating. The game soon became a shambles and nearly ended in a fight. My feet were sore for several days from blisters caused by the too-small shoes given me to wear."

By the autumn of 1944 several ground men were well entrenched in various off-duty activities in the local community. Cycling forays had resulted in genuine friendships with local families and the exchange of goods and services. Many an enterprising GI had some scheme to better his life, a few quite illegal. Urban Sweeny: "Down near the railroad station at Colchester there was a pub on the corner of Mile End Road and the man there had a taxi. Just up from the pub was a big hedge and around once a month when we went by with the truck we'd drop five gallons of petrol there. Any time we needed a taxi he was always ready for us." Unauthorised appropriation of motor fuel was a serious offence, yet for those handling vehicles there was apparently little risk of being apprehended. Personal motorised transport of any kind was not permitted US servicemen although this did not deter Sergeant James Putzlocker from purchasing an aged English motorcycle and using it around No. 2 hangar area until it met an untimely end. The fuel was high octane gasoline dregs drained from used drop tanks, effective if far too volatile for this machine as Rolland 'Red' Wagner discovered:

"First time on a motorcycle and I'm gunning the engine in front of the armament tent. Bob Helwig said, 'Red, watch when you put it in gear; its going to take off.' I told him I have all the airbase to drive around in. I put it in gear and held on. Didn't even have enough sense to release the gas and I'm heading straight at a gun emplacement pit. I thought if I go left the bike will come on top of me, if I go right I'll run in the men's outhouse and I wasn't about to go in that direction, so I took it straight into the gun pit. The bike went down and I went right over landing on the sand bags the other side. Everyone had a big laugh out of that and I went to base hospital to be patched up."

Unfortunately, further English motorcycle adventures by 62nd mechanics resulted in more serious injuries which came to the notice of the group Ground Executive. The driver, Staff Sergeant Tom Bradshaw, only sustained a few cuts and bruises, whereas his pillion passenger, Staff Sergeant Oswald Cottrell, suffered concussion and a fracture, ending up in a base hospital bed for a few days. Bradshaw was tried by summary court martial, found guilty and had to forfeit $25 of one month's pay.

A major attraction to associations with the local inhabitants was fresh food, particularly eggs. While the men were well and amply fed, powdered egg was the fare for all but pilots. Eggs were on the British ration list and the produce of back-garden hens was supposedly only for the householder and not to be sold or traded. This was almost impossible to police, however, and clandestine selling and trading of eggs was commonplace in country districts. Certain commodities then rarely available to the British, such as tinned fruit and juices, were available on American bases and popular in illegal trading for eggs or poultry. 'Home cooking'American style and variety were sorely missed by many, even if they understood the economies of army cookhouse catering in a foreign land. The desire of some individuals for variety could be pursued too enthusiastically. Private First Class Belmont Nicheson discovered what he identified as a sweet chestnut tree in a hedge on the 41st Service Squadron domestic site. When they ripened he collected about a bushel and immediately began to roast them on the top of his Nissen hut stove. Others were not invited to share as they had not contributed to the harvesting. Having indulged all evening his stomach began to feel uneasy. About three in the morning his hutmates had to call an ambulance as Nicheson was in great pain.

Missed more than anything else in the matter of sustenance, however, were chilled food and drink. Common in the United States where a continental climate regularly called for a cooling intake during summer, in the early decades of the twentieth century it was still a luxury and to some extent unnecessary in the temperate UK climate. Ice cream was sorely missed, for while it was a feature of a pre-war British summer it was, like most confectionery, no longer available. There were attempts to fly an ice-cream mix to freezing altitude in a drop tank which only produced a cold slush. At Halesworth, in a more successful effort to meet this need, Lieutenant John Truluck devised and built an ingenious ice-cream machine, but it eventually broke down and was abandoned.

While David Schilling was on leave in the States he took practical, if unofficially approved, steps to obtain an ice-cream maker for the 56th. One day in late summer, Sergeant Bill Billings, who in the past had been involved in carrying out dubious commissions for Schilling and plainly had his trust, received an unusual order:

"Sgt Warren Schaffer, Group HQ, had a set of written orders from Colonel Schilling. He sent me to the west coast of Scotland to locate a US Navy ship, an LST, at a small port near Gourock. The order said pick up electrical machinery and transport it to our base electrical shop. It was late in the evening when I located the ship, reporting to the Chief Petty Officer. He said he was expecting me and asked if I had chow as the late mess was on now and also if I had a bunk for the night, as they could not load the machinery until morning. I was worrying about the truck but the CPO said the watch would look after it. Next morning, after removing the canvas from the body of the truck, the ship's boom lowered the machinery on to the truck along with two wooden boxes of parts. The machine was wrapped with canvas which the CPO said was to protect it from the weather. I think it was so no one could see what it was. I had the sailors secure it with a rope as it was top heavy. While they were replacing the canvas top on the truck, the ship's boom lowered another draft, three cases of American beer. The CPO called down and said it was for me but not to try and drink it all at once. Returning to Boxted I drove the truck in thru' the back gate near Mile End Road as my living site, No. 10, was near the back gate. I deposited the beer at my hut. Back at the motor pool the truck was turned over to the night driver and he drove it to the base electrical shop. I never saw what was under the canvas, but all of a sudden the base had an ice-cream machine. Later the scuttlebutt was that Schilling's cousin was the captain of that LST."

Even though this act of subterfuge, if discovered, could have marred his military career, it was the kind of enterprise in which Schilling delighted. When the electrics of the machine were adapted to the British supply and ice cream became available at both officers' and enlisted men's parties, Schilling's distinctive chuckle was as much personal satisfaction at beating the rules as for the praise he received.

Candies were available, if rationed, in the base PX store, and that of chocolate bars was always fully taken up. And in summer these were preferred chilled by some, particularly by Fred Christensen. He had Tommy Myres, his armament man, put Milky Way bars in the gun compartment before a high altitude test flight so that on return to terra firma Fred had his frozen delights.

The American palate's expectation of chilled beer was particularly disappointed in Britain where its availability was only to be had in expensive hotels equipped with refrigeration. Warm beer was an ongoing joke, even if most GI drinkers eventually took to this booze which was deemed tepid and bland at first. It was soon established that it did not lack in alcoholic kick and two or three pints reduced the novice to a state of inebriation. Each beer drinker sought out his favourite pub and often remained loyal for the duration of his stay at Boxted. Many of these favourites were several miles from the base. Close by were The Crown, and Lion and Lamb on the main Ipswich – Colchester road, and The Fox, and Shepherd and Dog on the north-west side in the hamlet of Langham Moor. Beer was rationed to the public houses with a weekly delivery which, unfortunately for the local drinkers, often became known to the GIs who were there in force on the day to 'drink the place dry', requiring under-the-counter action by the innkeeper to remain in favour with the villagers.

An example of these drinking forays was on an August evening when a farmer and his son were inspecting some late mown hay near the northern end of the main runway adjacent to the little group of houses that included The Fox. A rather rotund and heavily beer-breathed sergeant suddenly appeared through a gap in the substantial boundary hedge near the pub and enquired of the farmer, "Hey, pop, can you give me a ride round to the main gate if you're goin' that way?" The farmer answered in the affirmative, whereon the sergeant called back to persons hitherto unseen, "Okay, fellas, we got us a ride back to camp." Whereupon at least another nine GIs clambered through the gap. The farmer protested that while he was happy to offer transport, his aged Talbot car normally only seated three and the driver; this to no avail as those of the merry band that could not squeeze in hung on the sides and back. While the heavily overloaded car proceeded slowly round the airfield perimeter track to the main gate, a distance of a mile and a half, the sergeant, who had taken the front passenger seat with the farmer's son perched on his lap, proceeded to jab a yellow rose under the nose of the farmer and anyone else in reach with the beaming question: "This was given me by the English lady at The Fox: a real English rose. Don't that smell nice?" Unfortunately, the overwhelming odour in the car was beery breath. On depositing the travellers at the main gate the farmer was asked how much he was owed. When he refused to take payment the happy sergeant told his men to empty their pockets of spare change which against protest was thrown in the open car windows.

Sadly, in some individuals alcohol unleashed belligerent action. A sergeant who liked to drink and tended to return to his 63rd hut in irritable mood, discovered that one of the two fire extinguishers in the building was empty. It irritated him that the British works party, who were responsible for such maintenance on the base had failed to refill or replace the extinguisher. The sergeant would vent his annoyance by turning the empty extinguisher upside down and striking the plunger on the floor. One night he failed to notice that the extinguisher he had so regularly abused had been changed. When the plunger let loose he and a good part of that end of the hut were covered with foam.

The availability of beer on the base was more strictly controlled and usually only available at parties for enlisted men and there was no authorised liquor. Robert Carnachan:

"One thing the officers had which was not available at the enlisted men's dances was liquor, other than beer. The flight surgeons had access to pure grain alcohol which they would bring to the dance where it was mixed with canned grapefruit juice, making a smooth concoction called the Velvet Hammer. It went down easily, but too much and the next morning you suffered. Pilots usually had the good sense not to overdo with the possibility of an early morning flight next day. If hangovers did occur however, the usual cure was to go out to their planes and breathe oxygen from the masks for awhile. After each mission every pilot was entitled to a shot of whiskey for medical purposes. I don't know of any who took advantage of this, but they saved up their allotments until they were able to get a full bottle. Bourbon whiskey, not Scotch. As most were very young and not regular drinkers, they would frequently make a present of the bottle to their crew chief, or save it up for an officers' dance."

As meeting the opposite sex was a desire of most young men, the organised on-base dances proved a good starting point with truck loads of interested young women brought in from local towns, mainly Colchester. The serious associations that developed were predominantly among the enlisted men who were around for many months. Over fifty eventually married British women, mostly met in the area. The proportion of married men when the group came overseas was much higher among the enlisted men who were also, on average, older. There is no doubt that British girls found Americans attractive with their smart uniforms and Hollywood-style accents. The GI was generally less reserved than British servicemen and quite willing to strike up a conversation with ease. With lower ranks being paid three times as much as the equivalent British serviceman, the GI was a favourite target for prostitutes, as was discussed earlier and many women were drawn from London to operate in East Anglian towns. Americans were no more sexual adventurers than any other Allied servicemen in a foreign country, but, as everywhere, there were ardent womanisers and others drawn into temptation. One young prostitute made regular taxi trips out to Boxted during the summer, paying the taxi driver to wait for her at Runkins Corner, while she went across a field to a remote aircraft parking area of the 62nd Squadron, there to provide service for two older mechanics on the stub of a farmer's straw stack.

Officers had less opportunity to get to know local girls and two or three-day passes were usually taken in London. Faced with the difficulty of obtaining hotel rooms all three squadrons found flats to rent on a regular basis. Robert Carnachan:

"I was not married before going overseas, but did make a whirlwind engagement to a college sophomore after one week's acquaintance just before shipping out. However, after six months in England, I broke the engagement. Never got the engagement ring back, though. Often got down to London on a 48-hour pass and usually stayed at the Jiles Club run by the Red Cross for American officers. One time when I spent a whole week in London I stayed at the Cumberland Hotel by Hyde Park. Then, during my last few months with the 63rd, the squadron officers had rented a five bedroom flat for £75 a month near Berkeley Square. We all pitched in a couple of pounds a month for the rent. It was a great place to stay for London trips. Well stocked with canned American fruit cocktail and condoms. It was there that I lost my virginity two months before my 25th birthday to a 19-year old from Northern Ireland. She was sort of semi-pro, I never paid her any money but she did get many gifts from me."

23 From Dearth to Plenty

On 26 September Major Gordon Baker assumed the duties of the group Flying Executive Officer as Pete Dade returned to the United States on compassionate leave. Baker got the post because of his seniority although he had only joined the group in the summer. Schilling made Captain Donovan Smith the new 61st Squadron CO and had him promoted to major. For a long time Smith had answered to the nickname Dieppe, earned for an early escape from the flak put up over that French Channel port, but this was now rarely heard with so few of the 'originals' still around. A well-liked individual and considerate of others, he had not long turned 20 when the group came overseas, its youngest pilot – and he looked it.

Following the Allies' airborne assault on the Netherlands the group received several new pilots as replacements for the dozen lost in the support missions flown. A change of policy was afoot in that the Atcham operational training base was being wound down and each fighter group would have to have its own training section, something the 56th had started the previous year. While recent replacement pilots had generally undergone longer and more varied training in the US before coming overseas, those received at Boxted were needing additional instruction. Probably without exception, newcomers willingly acknowledged the benefit of this extra tuition. Typical are the comments of Russell Fredrickson who arrived in July:

> "I was one of five replacement pilots. We all considered ourselves to be adequately trained to start flying ops immediately. Boy were we wrong! First of all our squadron instructors proved that we didn't know how to fly at best, and we were unable to fly the P-47 to its maximum capability. Additionally we attended much needed ground training classes to ensure our readiness to fly combat over the continent. Aircraft and landmark recognition exercises were administered daily until we could pass with a perfect score. We didn't fly combat until our instructors, with their infinite patience, said we were ready. The training programme established by the 56th was invaluable. It not only assured better qualified replacement pilots, but it was a confidence builder for the individuals who were subjected to the training."

The attention to training begun when the 56th arrived in England was still being pursued.

Once more Ramrods became the main operational duty with only the occasional fighter-bomber mission. By now the Luftwaffe was rarely encountered in the air and even the longer ranging Mustang groups had few substantial air battles during October. The decline in enemy fighter opposition to the Eighth Air Force bombers had become more apparent as the months passed, and the decline in the quality of the pilots more so. Although Allied intelligence agencies believed the Luftwaffe was suffering a dearth of fighters, production was actually rising. However because of battle damage, often acute spare parts shortage, and a growing concern over securing sufficient fuel, despite its priority, it was considerably disadvantaged. Such had been the attrition suffered by the Jagdverband pilots that few of the Experten remained to lead the ill-trained replacements; many had but a few hours on fighters before being committed to combat, and they were up against far more proficient Allied pilots.

By October 1944 the majority of the P-47s operated by the 56th were the 'bubble' canopy D models with the extra 65 US gallons of internal fuel, which gave greater endurance after drop tank release. This allowed the range of the Thunderbolts to be extended still further over Germany and missions could be pushed to five hours' duration. Such was the case on 2 October when Bunny Comstock led the group to give bomber escort in the Kassel area. FW190s, seen in the distance, were gone before they could be intercepted. The high power-settings of the chase reduced fuel reserves and Comstock decided to land and refuel at the recently established RAF airfield at Antwerp. Comstock's wingman Bob Daniel applied too much brake as he taxied in, and the aircraft went tail up, damaging the propeller. Bunny Comstock:

"I wanted Daniel back so I gave my parachute to one of the others to bring home, put Daniel in the seat of my plane and sat on his lap and flew back to Boxted. The statistical people at fighter wing could not understand how you could send out 16 aeroplanes and only get 15 back with 16 pilots. When they learned how I got my ass chewed out. What I didn't know was that my plane had taken a hit in the belly; the fuel I thought I had was not really there. The tank had swelled up and given a false reading. My crew chief found a hole in the bottom. When they checked the fuel they found there was hardly any left. I could have lost both Daniel and myself. It was a damn fool thing to do."

For the old hands such as Comstock the losses that really hurt were of those who like himself had chanced a second tour. Captain John Eaves began his second tour with the 62nd Squadron in October and while leading a local flight his P-47 suffered engine failure. With little altitude Eaves had no option but to 'belly in'. The aircraft slid across a field and a country road at Debden, and hit a bank with two trees. Although the cockpit was only slightly crushed Eaves suffered a fatal head injury. He was the last of the 62nd combat originals in the squadron.

Bunny Comstock, the mission leader on 1 November 1944, took some confirming photographs of the group's first successful action with an Me 262 jet while on a Ramrod.

"We were on our way out and had finished with the bombers. Complete undercast. A P-51 group off to the right. One of our people off to the right called out a P-51 had been hit. Another said, 'Its a 262.' I looked out ahead and saw the jet in a shallow dive going for the clouds and heading west. I thought he would be coming back since the clouds were on the ground at the coast. Then he was spotted going east far below us and both groups went into a dive. There were P-47s and P-51s all over him. He was between both groups and was quickly hit in the left engine. He ejected and immediately deployed his ribbon chute. He should have free fallen first. I came by him and he was okay but it was reported he was fired on."

The Me 262 had first bounced a P-51 squadron and shot one aircraft down but during his descent towards the bombers two P-51 groups plus the 56th's P-47s had gone after it. Lieutenant Walter Groce called to his flight to spread out and catch the jet in a turn, a good move as the enemy aircraft did just that in an effort to evade north. Groce's fire scored several hits and the jet went down. Although Groce was awarded a destroyed claim, when higher command came to review gun camera film they found that a P-51 pilot of the 352th Fighter Group had also scored hits of the jet and its destruction was subsequently awarded as a shared victory. The German pilot, Oberfeldwebel Willi Banzaff, survived, only to be killed a few days later.

The Me 262 jet, first encountered during summer air operations, had posed a threat to Allied air supremacy. Some hundred miles an hour faster than any USAAF or RAF fighters, other than the RAF Meteor jet which was just entering service, the enemy fighter had a substantial armament of four 30-mm calibre cannon. Its firepower was a bigger threat than its speed, a single short burst being sufficient to bring down a four-engine bomber, albeit that speed of closure could make accurate sighting difficult. Like the British jet, however, the engines of the Me 262, which were still underdeveloped, were not wholly reliable. It also lacked the manoeuvrability of its antagonists. Nevertheless, its ability to overtake or accelerate away from Allied fighters was a considerable tactical advantage and understandably caused the Allied air force leadership some concern.

By November 1944 only two P-47-equipped groups remained in the Eighth Air Force and by the end of the year only the 56th would still have Thunderbolts. The manufacturers looked to support the Wolfpack in retaining the type and the company's technical representative at Boxted intimated that a powerful new model was on its way and later another with greater internal fuel capacity. Eighth Air Force command however, considered the eventual conversion of the 56th to Mustangs, for it seemed better to have all fifteen groups operating the same type to effect support economies. The 56th was still ahead of other groups in the matter of enemy aircraft destroyed totals but this lead was being eroded. The P-51s, through their superior duration, were usually being given the prime positions for bomber support where enemy aircraft were most likely to be encountered. Such was the case on 2 November when the Luftwaffe came up in strength to intercept bombers making for oil targets. Mustang groups claimed over a 100 shot down in numerous fights for the loss of 10 in combat, whereas all the Thunderbolts experienced was a hit and run attack by three Me 262s causing slight damage to two 61st aircraft. The 'blow jobs' (common slang for the jets long before the same term became an obscene metaphor) were gone with no hope of intercepting them.

Nine missions later the group did see an air fight when sent to attack an oil storage depot at Langenselbold. The 61st Squadron, led by Jim Carter, had just reformed after strafing when it was bounced by FW190s. The squadron lost two aircraft and fought off the enemy with allowed claims of seven. Nearly all the 61st pilots had little or no combat experience and acquitted themselves well. Even Carter had difficulty extracting himself from this battle in which the squadron was caught at a disadvantage. He described this situation in his combat report:

".... Just south of the target at 8,000 feet I started a right turn to the north to cross over when I saw – and heard it reported – 16 or more FW190s coming in on us from out of the south east at about 5 o'clock to me. They were flying a formation very similar to ours and had evidently come down from not more than 2,000 feet above us – at first sight I had thought them to be Platform [62nd Squadron]. We broke into them and the fight started. Three or four took turns firing at me from 90 degrees on down and finally one hung on to me. At different times I'd take stray shots at other 190s as they crossed in front of me. 47s and 190s were all over, but this one joker stuck tight to me, firing for the most part out of range. I could out turn him until he'd stall, but on recovery he could accelerate faster and again he'd be on me. About the fifth such turn I felt my plane on the verge of snapping and he only had about 70 degrees deflection which seemed too little to me, so I rolled it over and hit for the deck with water injection. As long as I'd fly straight I would gain slightly and increase my lead to about 1,000 yards. I hung to the ground with full power praying he'd run out of ammo or get tired – just when I thought he'd do neither he pulled up. That old 47 sure put out for 20 or 30 minutes. I climbed to 15,000 feet and except for an occasional burst of flak made it home without further mishap."

Elsewhere the 62nd and 63rd Squadrons brought down another five. Superior training and tactics won out again. Captain Mike Jackson, who claimed an FW190, described his means of out-turning the enemy: "... dropping flaps 20 to 25 degrees then siphoning them back to the up position to get some speed and not stay in the turn too long to stall out."

Other pilots believed the P-47 could turn with the Messerschmitt without the use of flaps; one example was Lieutenant Russell Fredrickson on November 27th:

> "We were sighted by a flight of four Me109s as we dove down from above. One element broke right while the leader and his wingman turned left. My wingman and I went after the lead element while my No.3 went after the other two Me109s. We ended up in a classic Lufbery and went round five times with me shooting at the number 2 German and number 1 shooting at my wingman. We were fairly low to the ground when I hit the number 2 man from 400 yards and he went in. I was then able to get after number 1. He too went in after another 360 turn. I'm not sure the Germans ever did learn that the P-47 could turn inside the Me109."

But the FW190 remained the greater threat in a turning fight, although if initiating the interception there was a successful tactic. Edmund Ellis: "A FW190 in a dead flat turn could turn inside a P-47. We learned to make what we called a scalp turn. You dive in, pull the nose up high and kick inside rudder and you could make a skidding turn."

On 2 December there was another successful air fight. Vectored by the MEW (Microwave Early Warning) control, which had moved to the continent to provide extended search and was operating under the call sign Nuthouse, the Wolfpack led by Paul Conger sprang a surprise, claiming 11 shot down. None of the three group losses was due to enemy action. Tragically Captain Eugene Barnum flying top cover with the 61st took it down to intercept some Me109s when a recent replacement pilot on his first mission, 2nd Lieutenant Wyman Baker of the 63rd, cut across and struck Barnum's aircraft. Both men were killed. Barnum was another combat original recently starting out on a second tour. The third pilot lost is believed to have suffered vertigo in the undercast when descending to refuel.

Two days later the group went out on bomber support and then successfully strafed an airfield at Neuberg. Although briefed to expect moderate high altitude winds over the continent, the reality was that these were much stronger, forcing several pilots to land in liberated areas to refuel. Additionally, an extensive undercast hugged the ground in many places and when only half the force arrived back at Boxted there was concern about the fate of the remainder. It was known that several had landed on the continent to refuel, but when all aircraft were accounted for, the sorry story was that of the 21 missing nine were wrecks through crash-landings or bale-outs. Fortunately, all pilots were safe although Major Robert Hall, a recent recruit to the 62nd, was injured in a parachute landing in Brittany.

The last few months of 1944 were considered wetter than the previous year. For those replacement pilots, particularly from the Mid-West and more arid areas of the States, the impression of England was a place of persistent cold damp chill. S.D.Ulch, who joined the 62nd, found several layers of newspaper over his cot helped sleep. There was not much convenient woodland to plunder for the stoves at Boxted and the coke ration for barrack huts was far too meagre. However, there was a useful fuel alternative. Claude Chinn:

"We were given all the bomb rings we wanted to use as fuel. A bomb ring was a laminated piece of pressed cardboard that had surrounded the bombs when they were shipped. There were two rings to a bomb and they made the job of storing and handling easier. They were about three inches wide and about two inches thick, coated with a heavy waterproofing wax. The rings burned fiercely and put out a lot of heat. Getting them started was another story. We had in our Nissen hut a cast iron stove for which we developed a cannon-like technique of starting a fire. We usually had no kindling or other material to use, but for some reason we could get all the cigarette lighter fuel we wanted. The lighter fuel became our starting agent. First the stove was packed solid with bomb rings which had been cut in quarters. Then a can of lighter fuel was poured into the stove and the iron lid replaced. It was too dangerous to stand by the fire when it was being lit, so we would take another can of lighter fuel and make a trail across the floor to the door and out. A match to our fluid trail started the fuse and when the fire reached the stove we had instant heat. We also had several dents in the ceiling where the stove lid had made contact."

Waste oil drained from engines was another excellent starting medium for the stoves in some huts even though this use was officially banned. Someone discovered that there was a vast amount of felled timber at Great Dunmow airfield, which had formerly been a deer park. Most weeks a truck with 40-feet long trailer was sent to collect this wood, which was then sawn for burning. The buildings on the communal and administrative site did not normally want for coal or coke even if the heating stoves were inefficient. As winter's grip descended other measures were taken. Major Mike Jackson:

"Our squadron room was a large Nissen type hut and as we often didn't have a lot to do when we weren't flying in November we thought we'd do a little decorating. Pop Nolan, a younger pilot than me, said why don't we get some warmth into this place? I said okay and assigned Pop to be the foreman of this operation. The first thing we did is make a hole in the wall and then we built a fireplace. We bought the bricks from a local firm and the people on the base who were our liaison with the British said we could use their tub to mix our cement in. They said we want it back. So we got a truck and went to the yard where this stuff was stored and took it back to make our cement. I admonished the boys and said when we've finished with the tub it has to be washed out and dumped back in the compound where they kept this stuff. Two days later we're in the room when our CO comes in with the RAF liaison officer who wants to know who left the cement in the tub to harden over two days. I got fined £15 –

which came out of my pocket to save the boys embarrassment. The guys
of the 63rd next door thought what a wonderful thing the 62nd had done.
So we advised them how to build a fireplace just like ours. When it was
completed and dry enough for them to have a fire we heard about it. So
I got one of my guys to get a piece of plywood and climb up and put it
on top of their chimney. Of course as soon as the 63rd boys lit the fire the
smoke all came back into the ready room and they were getting out of the
place fast."

The horseplay was on-going and even stretched to the senior officers who
also cherished warmth. Bunny Comstock:

"Don Smith and I took my jeep from the Wheelhouse and drove over to
the communal site to see a movie. When we came out the jeep had gone
and we suspected Les Smith of taking it. So we walked back home and
sure enough when we got back there was the jeep sitting outside. All
three squadron commanders and the top group fliers lived in the
Wheelhouse. When we went in the door looking for Les he wasn't to be
found, but we could hear the bath water running and guessed he was
about to have a dip. The old farmhouse heater was coal-fired and
produced just enough water for one bath and that was it. So we decided
to get back at Les and as we could hear him in his room we let all the hot
water out of the bath and ran cold. To make it more uncomfortable Don
said close the door and I'll sit on the pot. I was outside the door watching
out for Les when here comes Dave Schilling in longjohns. So I beat on
the door for Don to come out as we've made a mistake. Dave looked at
me and said, 'What are you two little bastards up to?' I knew we were in
deep trouble. Dave wasn't at all pleased. He looked in the bathroom,
which now had an unpleasant odour, and then he really read the riot act.
Didn't see it as a joke; was really irritated. Didn't get his bath that night
because there was no more hot water and no more coal to fire up the little
furnace. Of course Les Smith laughed his head off when he heard how
our prank had misfired."

Capers were far from being the prerogative of fun-seeking pilots. Enlisted
men were more inhibited on the station through the censure of rank. Off
base there was less restraint. Herbert Newhall:

"One day I was in the Red Cross Club in Colchester when I was surprised
to meet a fellow called Bill Stewart who was from near my home town.
He was a top turret gunner in a B-17 outfit at a nearby base and I met him
on a number of occasions. When he completed his tour of 35 missions his
crew or some of the people at his base arranged a party at The Rose and
Crown to which I was invited. We all got a little happy and my friend was
anxious to get me back to Boxted early in case there was a mission next
day – I was a 62nd crew chief. I told him there was plenty of time but he
wouldn't listen, called a cab and said he'd ride back with me – he had had

more than a few drinks. When the cab arrived he hustled me in and got in himself, only to immediately lay back and close his eyes. As I didn't want to leave the party yet I simply slid out the other door and sent the taxi off. When they got to Boxted the gate guard looked in the back to check who was in the cab. Stewart woke up and said he was just taking his buddy back to the base. Then he saw there was no buddy. He wasn't very happy with me when he came back to the party."

As in the previous winter the dark evenings and inclement winter weather found a majority of both officers and men seeking entertainment in the warmer communal buildings of the station. The cinema had two showings each night, and recreational games rooms were very popular. In the Officers' Club there was nearly always a card game for money. Ed Ellis:

"We would start to play Red Dog on pay day. The game went on and on and sometimes the pot got built up quite big. We had to leave to go and get some sleep because there might be a mission next day. So instead of ending the game the warrant officer in charge of the Officers' Club would pick up the table cloth, tie it in a knot and put the money in the safe. Next night we'd set it down, open it up and the game would go on. This could go on for a week. Sometimes one of the guys in the game would be lost, so we had a rule that when somebody went missing their money didn't come out of the pot; the pot stayed as it was."

Colonel Schilling had lost none of his zest for the social life under the pressures of command. Apart from amorous liaisons he frequently flew to other British and US-manned airfields of interest and introduced himself, establishing a wide circle of friends and acquaintances. In the autumn, discovering that the Royal Navy had target gliders, Schilling managed to acquire some, persuading high command to let the group have an AT-23 for use in towing these targets. A heavy cable winch was installed and having overcome initial problems the gliders proved much better targets for gunnery practice than the usual canvas sleeves. The AT-23 was the designation of a training version of the twin-engine Martin B-26 Marauder bomber and proved exceptionally useful for 'communications' work. A frequent use in the hands of the Colonel was for pleasure trips, notably to France. Mike Jackson: "Officially to get coal. Only the coal came back in bottles."

While he might play hard, Schilling was ever mindful to further the standing of his 56th Fighter Group. Eighth Air Force bombers had attacked the major source of synthetic oil production in the Merseburg area several times but the plants still functioned and their flak defences inflicted heavy losses. The idea was floated of using a small force of specially trained fighter-bombers against the vital elements of these targets. As the heavy calibre anti-aircraft artillery and gun-laying radars were placed to counter high altitude attack it was thought that with surprise the low level fighter-bombers might succeed unscathed. A job for Thunderbolts, and the choice of unit to carry out the task was obvious: the 56th Fighter Group's CO was summoned. Schilling embraced the plan whereby the 56th would send three flights, each with a specific target at the important Leuna complex. Apart from the distance involved, it seemed like a suicide mission to those pilots selected to participate, a flight from each squadron led by its CO. As one of the latter dryly commentated: "Our Colonel was always dreaming up ways to get us killed." Schilling would lead the first flight, Comstock the second and Don Smith the third. Each flight leader picked his men, telling them they were to train for a very dangerous and exacting mission but only if they wished go. Nobody refused. Schilling picked Lieutenants Stovall, Fleming and Winters from the 62nd, and Comstock, Fahringer, Groce and Andermatt, who were all 63rd men. The last flight only consisted of two, Don Smith and Joe Perry. The target area had thirteen tall chimneys, some only about 300 feet apart, which would have to be negotiated. Practice flights were undertaken using a factory complex in the Manchester area as the mock target and a model of the real target was made for pilots to study. Training for a similar mission against the Zeitz oil plant was also ordered, this to be led by Les Smith and would be only one flight from his 62nd Squadron, Lieutenants Nolan, Hale and Buchmiller. In low level training over the sea Lowell Buchmiller was killed when a wing tip hit the waves during a turn. His place was taken by Lieutenant Ball. Expectation of an order to brief remained for several days but after the RAF seriously damaged both plants with its larger bombs the project was abandoned. There was some relief amongst those involved: "We weren't looking to be heroes. The more we studied and trained the more it looked suicidal."

To allow for carrying bombs on the wing racks yet still with sufficient drop tank fuel capacity for such a long mission, Schilling encouraged the Bovingdon experimental station to design a larger tank that could be carried on the belly shackles. Due to the ground clearance limitation this could only be achieved by lateral expansion and the resulting tank, rated at 208 US gallons, had an even broader head-on profile than the 150-gallon type. A bigger capacity belly tank also gave advantage in that the wing rack pylons reduced performance and could be removed. The new tank, put into limited production in Britain, came into use a few months later.

There were those who thought Schilling mentally reckless, carried away by his wild ideas; a bravado played out to the full to hide his hidden fears. The 62nd Squadron's first Flight Surgeon, Clifford Tichenor, had recognised a tendency for Schilling to seek pleasure to compensate for stress, although most pilots did this to some degree. Alcohol was one route and at times Schilling did imbibe too much although it never became a serious problem for him. The showman and genial demeanour were facets of a character that also displayed a sense of purpose. Schilling always faced up to the demands of command. And on 23 December 1944 he was to reach the zenith of his time with the group.

In mid-December an unusual period of calm weather descended on western Europe with cloud cloaking the land largely as fog. It was then that the Wehrmacht chose to launch a counter-offensive through the Ardennes with some initial success. Such was the fog and vertical cloud extension that from the 19th visibility at ground level in much of England was so restricted that Eighth Air Force offensive operations ceased for three days. By the 23rd freezing conditions had taken over, enabling some bombers and fighters to be despatched to attack communications targets in the Saarbrücken area. The 56th Group was ordered to provide area support under MEW control, assembling 56 P-47s for take-off at 1000 hours with the expectation that the Luftwaffe would be up to aid the land campaign. Schilling led, for the first time since the end of November due to leave and indisposition. Hostile airspace was entered an hour later whilst climbing through 17,000 feet, whereupon Schilling ordered the squadrons to spread out; in his view this gave a better chance of encountering the enemy, although it caused problems for the MEW controller. As the group reached 26,000 feet in the Bonn area at 1140 hours, by which time six 61st and two 63rd P-47s had aborted with problems, Nuthouse vectored it east to intercept a large number of bandits. Two minutes later a suspected enemy formation was seen to the north, only to disappear into clouds before the Wolfpack could intercept. As the original vector was resumed, another gaggle of enemy aircraft was lost in the same way. Feeling frustrated Schilling called Nuthouse, questioning its judgement for still vectoring the group on the same bearing when they had just missed the opportunity to intercept two enemy formations. He was told "Don't worry. Stay on original vector for bigger game at 22,000 to 23,000 feet."

Shortly thereafter Bunny Comstock, leading the 63rd, called in a huge formation of FW190s right below. Schilling was about to order action when another large formation of enemy fighters was seen several miles ahead at about a thousand feet lower than the Thunderbolts. Schilling told Comstock to take the 63rd and 61st down to bounce the bigger formation while he took the 62nd after the formation ahead. With the advantage of surprise and some 4,000 feet of altitude Comstock led the attack on what was quickly identified as a formation of FW190s. In the ensuing combat he despatched two and damaged two others, despite sensing something was wrong with his firepower and before his ammunition was exhausted. On return to Boxted he was informed the armourer had mistakenly forgotten to cock the guns in the right wing. In total the 63rd claimed 11 during a ten-minute air battle, where the enemy turned to fight shooting down one P-47 and damaging three others with 20-mm fire. Comstock's wingman, Flight Officer Melvin Hughes, was pursued down to ground level by Focke-Wulfs, and evaded by flying up a valley, damaging a wing on a treetop. One of his pursuers was seen to misjudge a turn and crash into the hillside. Another 63rd pilot, Lieutenant Bob Daniel, had to bale out of his damaged P-47 over friendly territory and returned to Boxted next day. Meanwhile the 61st Squadron, providing top cover, had become involved, claiming five FW190s without loss.

Colonel Schilling's quarry was Me109s, and as he took the 62nd in on the rear of this formation in a gentle turn surprise was achieved. Possibly, if this approach was seen, the enemy pilots thought the aircraft were Focke-Wulfs. The bounce provided Schilling with the opportunity to destroy three Me109s of the nine despatched in that attack. Reforming, Schilling headed east encountering two gaggles of FW190s. Again with the advantage of height and surprise Schilling led the 62nd to claim 10 of the enemy of which he was responsible for two. The fight was not one-sided for two P-47s were lost. The only damaged aircraft of the squadron on return to Boxted was Lieutenant William Stovall's which hit a tree while he was escaping pursuers. In total the group claimed 37 enemy shot down, one probably destroyed and 14 damaged, which was approximately half the destroyed claims for the Eighth's fighters that day. It was the most successful mission the 56th had ever undertaken. Back at Boxted Schilling dismissed his own success to the public relations people with, "My major trouble was to get my fighters back into formation to come home when we were running low on gas. They just wouldn't quit fighting." Perhaps some credit should have gone to his wingman 2nd Lieutenant Frank Aheron who watched over his leader while he despatched five Luftwaffe fighters. Wingmen had a vital part to play in combat with few opportunities to do any shooting: their aircraft were mostly those shot at. Later that day Schilling played Father Christmas at a Colchester Officers' Club party for children whose fathers were prisoners of war.

On the morrow the group was given a similar mission under MEW control, and Schilling again took the lead. The vectors received all turned out to be Mustangs. The group was more fortunate on Christmas Day when another Nuthouse-controlled mission brought them a bounce on a low flying Messerschmitt formation of which they shot down eight 109s without loss. Incongruous as the situation was, the victors could happily indulge in Christmas celebrations without thought of the enemy pilots they had probably killed. This was the nature of the business; air combat was in terms of aircraft not the men within them. It did not do to dwell on your enemy as being anything other than a Messerschmitt or a Focke-Wulf. Or if you did he had to be a Nazi, someone you could hate. In quiet moments the individual might be troubled by the human element, but it did not do to entertain such matters. Most combatants accepted it was a case of 'he or me'.

By its second Christmas overseas the group's mess staff were able to produce dinner fare that would have been the envy of their severely rationed British neighbours. Not only were a greater variety of foodstuffs forthcoming from the USA by this time, but knowing where to go shopping in England added considerably to the menu. Tomato juice, turkey rice soup, roast turkey, sage dressing, cranberry sauce, snowflake potatoes, candied sweet potatoes, giblet gravy, hearts of celery, buttered asparagus tips, French baked peas, marble cake, vanilla ice cream, sliced pineapple, hard candy, oranges, apples, hot rolls, butter, bread and coffee.

Much was from cans but oranges and ice cream were not found on British Christmas tables that winter.

With the serious situation on the continent brought by the Wehrmacht ground offensive, missions were flown every day but one for the next two weeks even though weather conditions were very poor. Boxted was sometimes 'socked in' by freezing fog and returning aircraft had to put down elsewhere. Everything was festooned with ice, pretty on the eye but miserable for the ground men who had work to do. On the last two days of the year there occurred incidents that were particularly dampening to morale. Harold Comstock led the mission on the 30th, his 130th and last of his second tour. It was considered uneventful and on return 2nd Lieutenant Sam Batson was asked to air test his assigned aircraft which had just undergone an engine rebuild. This was the first P-47D with a bubble canopy received by the 56th and had been the personal aircraft of Zemke and later Comstock. Batson, 'a bright, personable young man', took off and apparently immediately encountered engine trouble. He did a circuit of the airfield and came into land on the east-west runway. When about a half mile away on his approach the engine failed. As had been proved many times in such circumstances the hefty structure of the P-47 gave a pilot a good chance of walking away from a crash-landing if the landing gear was still retracted. It was a different matter if the wheels were lowered, however, as in this case. The aircraft crashed in a field at Wick Farm, went over on its back and burst into flames. There had been several fatal accidents involving 56th pilots, most far removed from the base. This close-by pyre was clearly visible in the winter sky and the horrific details related by those who went and attempted rescue soon circulated among other personnel.

Next day the bombers headed for strategic targets in Germany, the first time in two weeks, when the Wolfpack was sent to support B-17s. Soon after meeting the bombers MEW control notified Fairbanks of bogies near Quackenbruck and the 62nd led by Captain Felix 'Willie' Williamson, was sent to investigate. Williamson, who joined the squadron as one of the first replacements in May 1943 and had just returned for a second tour of duty, was vectored to a small low-flying mixed formation which appeared to be two Me109s and seven FW190s. Although having the initial advantage the interception developed into a confused dogfight. Second Lieutenant Donald Armstrong was on his eighth mission:

"There were three of us shooting at an Me109. One P-47 from the right coming in, one coming in from the left, and I was directly behind the Me109. Stovall's plane came up from below me and flew between us just as I started to shoot. Thinking I might have hit him I broke off pursuit of the enemy aircraft and watched Stovall pull up, roll over, and go straight down into the ground and explode next to a farmhouse. Stovall did not say anything on the radio and that led me to think he might have been dead before he hit the ground. I saw a large hole in the left wing root when he flew up in front of me. It was a very long flight back to base for me because I thought I had shot down a friend. After landing I found a strand of wire cable wrapped around the outside gun sight. I was so nervous I told the mechanic he could have it. I told Doc Biggins, the Flight Surgeon, what I thought had happened and he went to the CO. My gun camera film was developed and plotted on a graph. I was told next day that I did not hit Lt Stovall."

The tragedy was compounded; as Bunny Comstock related:

"When I came into the Wheelhouse to get a drink of water or whatever here sat Colonel Stovall, young Stovall's father. The Colonel had been a First World War fighter ace and was now on General Spaatz'staff. Prior to that he had been at Ajax and we had got to know him. He had flown over from Paris to see in the New Year with his son. I knew the son had gone down as there was a lot of chatter about it. His first question was, 'How did the mission go, Bunny?' I said we lost a few Colonel. I sort of got panicky. How was I gonna tell this man that his son was one of them. I jumped in the jeep and went back and got hold of Dave Schilling, and his remark was, 'Oh shit'. He rounded up other squadron commanders and we all went back to the Wheelhouse and finally Dave broke the news to him that it was his son. It seems that another pilot was firing and young Stovall had let down right into the stream of bullets. The lieutenant who did the shooting stopped as soon as he saw this airplane come into view but it was already too late. The father sat there and tears rolled down his cheek. I guess he had manipulated the system to get his son assigned to the 56th because we were the tops in air fighting. He asked if he could talk to the young lieutenant who did the shooting and Dave sent for him. He came up and Stovall asked him just how it happened. The Colonel told the pilot he understood how things like that happened and that he did not hold him responsible. We eventually left the Colonel and Dave alone. He stayed there that night and next day we flew him back to Paris in the C-78."

The atmosphere in the Officers' Club that evening was not as congenial as might be expected on New Year's Eve.

24 Winter Blues with the P-47M

For some weeks the group had been planning to celebrate its second year in England and the weekend selected was 6-7 January. Meanwhile the war went on and a new idea had been proposed for the Wolfpack. MEW control was supposed to be precise in its navigational ability, so how would it fare in conducting a tight fighter formation to bomb a target from high altitude? The formation had to be tight and practice flights were made, packing three dozen Thunderbolts into a diamond-shaped assembly some 450 feet long by 250 feet wide, and stacked in a wedge 300 feet deep. Flying at the pre-determined airspeed, the ideal was not easy to hold for long at 20,000 feet, the altitude planned for an operation trial against a precision tool factory at Siegen east of the Ruhr on 5 January. Schilling led, and the bombing formation was not taken up until under MEW control. On target approach Nuthouse called and told Fairbanks to break off and come back for another run. Schilling was incensed and voiced his displeasure, saying he could not hold the formation for long and they were receiving attention from the flak gunners. On the second run Nuthouse gave the order to drop and each aircraft released two 250-lb bombs into the overcast.

Returned to Boxted pilots were not happy about having to fly straight and level in a flak barrage. A similar mission led by Les Smith was run next day, and this time each aircraft carried a single 500-lb bomb to obtain better stability. Again the target was obscured by an overcast. Russell Fredrickson:

> "I had the honour to lead the 63rd Squadron with 12 planes in tight formation. We were above an overcast flying under MEW control maintaining heading and altitude. The heavy flak was really scary. I heard at least five rounds explode in close proximity to our formation. The battle damage to my airplane was minor but it did bring the total number of patches up to 72 on my third bird. The ground crews had some neat tools for patching holes in the fuselage, tail and wings. Mostly circles of varying sizes that looked like they belonged there. No rough edges."

Don Armstrong:

> "This time we sent two P-47s down to check the results. They reported that we had missed the target by 5 miles. There was some flak on this

mission and I was so tensed up and my back – with which I'd been having problems – hurt so badly I could hardly get out of the plane after landing. The crew chief had to hand me the parachute because I could not lean over to pick it up. Doc Biggins diagnosed lumbago and I got two days in hospital."

Like previous attempts at high level bombing this technique was a failure and never attempted again, not least because accurate flak bursts in such a tight formation could cause catastrophic losses. There were no losses so the group personnel could better indulge their anniversary parties.

Apart from the second anniversary, the group also included the celebration of the 800 victories mark which occurred on Christmas Day. Three dances and vaudeville shows went on at the same time at Boxted on the evening of 6 January, one in the Officers' Club and for the enlisted men in the Little Wheels' Club and Red Cross Aero Club. Some officers served ice cream and cake in the enlisted men's parties and those with musical talents filled in the string section of the orchestra playing at the Little Wheel dance. No doubt impressed by the sympathy the group officers conveyed on the loss of his son, Colonel Stovall flew in from Paris when asked to respond to the group toast. At the Officers' Club dinner Schilling rose from his position at the head of the table and raised his glass. "To the 56th – and especially to those men of the 56th who have gone and who cannot be with us for this anniversary dinner tonight." Stovall responded: "To the fighter group with a fighting spirit unexcelled in the forces of the United States or any other nation. If every other branch of the service had this same sort of fighting quality, the war would be over!" Following dinner dancing commenced to the music of the 'Flying Eagles' service band. The inevitable high jinks among junior pilots ran to cutting off ties as souvenirs of the occasion. Schilling had invited several outsiders including women with whom he was rumoured to be particularly friendly. Dave asked his squadron commanders to be attentive and dance with these women even though two had come with husbands, a senior British Navy commander and a Scottish mill owner. The third woman was a married WAC Captain of a more adventous nature. Earlier that day Schilling asked Comstock to take the two-seat Thunderbolt and collect her: "Returning to Boxted I drove her to the Wheelhouse and when I asked where she wanted her baggage she told me Dave's room. Her comment was, 'Why Bunny, you're blushing.' I guess I was still somewhat naïve."

During his visit Colonel Stovall learned that Don Smith and Bunny Comstock had just finished second tours and invited both to fly to Paris where he would introduce them to General Spaatz. The invitation was accepted, both young men considering it an honour to be invited to meet their country's top air force commander in Europe. Arriving at Spaatz's headquarters they met the General for dinner, who pronounced that there was a real treat in store for them, fresh oysters, which his personal pilot had flown in from St Malo earlier that day. Neither Smith nor Comstock had ever eaten raw oysters or wanted to but went through the motions of enjoyment for the sake of not appearing ungrateful. After listening to tales of air fighting in the First World War, the two Wolfpack veterans retired to their assigned room. Bunny Comstock:

> "This room was usually that of a WAC, a Captain, on Spaatz's staff. Hers was the only one with two single beds and she was away I guess. The room reeked of perfume, typical girl's stuff. We got ready for bed. I pulled the covers back and there was a set of pyjamas placed between the sheets. So I undressed and having nothing else climbed into these pyjamas. During the night, no doubt due to this atmosphere and being a young man who had not seen his wife for a long time, the inevitable occurred. Next morning when I saw what had happened to the pyjamas, I was too embarrassed to leave them there, so stuffed them into my B4 bag and went off to enjoy Paris. We trudged around in the snow and had a great time."

Back at Boxted interest was focused on the promised new model Thunderbolts, the first of which was being readied for Colonel Schilling as his personal mount, though he was never to use it operationally. Externally the P-47M appeared identical to the latest D models and was basically a D with a lightweight and more powerful re-design of the reliable Pratt & Whitney R-2800 originally developed for use in US Navy aircraft. The new engine, giving the P-47M a top speed of 460 mph at high altitude, made it the Allies' fastest propeller-driven fighter in operational service. The 56th was informed that this was a limited production especially for them and would be followed by a much-changed model with larger fuel capacity. Indeed, all but two of the 108 P-47Ms produced would see service with the 56th. Following the discontinuation of camouflage finishes on the production of most US warplanes, Eighth Air Force fighter groups were advised to paint the upper surfaces of 'silver' aircraft with camouflage paints in preparation for moving to the continent after the cross-channel invasion, where their bases might be more liable to enemy air attack. Movement to liberated France or Belgium was still a distinct possibility and with the P-47Ms it was decided that each squadron would have distinctive camouflage schemes: the 61st all matt black upper surfaces; the 62nd a disruptive pattern of green and grey; and the 63rd a disruptive pattern of two shades of blue. Once again the 56th was projecting its individuality with concealment compromised by each squadron emblazoning the camouflage with bright insignia. It was an indication that these were not aircraft of just any fighter group, but those of the elite Wolfpack.

So far the weather of winter 1944-45 was considered worse than the previous two experienced in England. With the New Year conditions became severe and on the night of 9/10 January there was a heavy fall of snow. Lt Colonel Lucian 'Pete' Dade, who had returned from the USA two weeks earlier, took out a mission to conduct a sweep in support of bomber operations. The icy weather brought mechanical and equipment concerns for pilots and no less than 18 turned back for various reasons, including Pete Dade. One abortive never made Boxted, but belly-landed near the coast at Clacton. The mission was something of a fiasco owing to navigation difficulties; one of the squadrons blundered over Cologne at low altitude, quickly having to evade the bombs being dropped on the marshalling yards by B-17s high above. From the amount of flak encountered it appeared the German gun-laying radar had picked up the Thunderbolts instead of the bombers. The cold spell continued with extra discomfort and difficulties for the ground crew, yet some professed to prefer the hard snow to the damp drizzle so often prevalent.

At least the skies were clear on 14 January when the Luftwaffe again challenged the Eighth Air Force, but the enemy's losses showed the deteriorating standard of their pilots. A total of 155 enemy aircraft shot down were claimed by the 15 groups, of which the 56th's share was 19. The Wolfpack had despatched its strongest force for some time, 39 in an A group and 24 in a B group to sweep the Stendal-Magdeburg area, the 'Happy Hunting Ground' of the previous spring. Paul Conger led A group using a P-47M, as squadron commanders had each been issued with the new model. In shooting down an Me109 he was impressed with its climb performance. Mike Jackson led B group, in which Willie Williamson headed the 62nd Squadron flights. In a mêlée with a large number of enemy fighters Willie claimed five and was so credited, a success tempered by the loss of his wingman during the action. The only other pilot lost that day had to bale out to perish in the icy North Sea before the rescue teams could reach him.

When Majors Donovan Smith and Harold Comstock completed their tours, command of the 61st and 63rd squadrons passed to Majors James Carter and Paul Conger respectively, another two 'originals' on 'second chances'. Paul Conger had proved to be an able fighter pilot with the necessary aggressive attitude to combat. Thick set, of average height, he looked older than his 26 years. In the early months of service he had a drink problem, tending to become belligerent when having taken too much but the problem had been conquered. Paul was dedicated although his directness was such that he was not popular with everybody. Robert Carnachan:

"Paul was essentially a bully. He came into my office one evening after the last mission was in and we were assessing what had to be done to which planes. He said that he wanted his P-47M to be ready the next morning. I turned to my line chief and asked about its status and was informed it would not be ready to fly. So, I turned to Paul and said: 'Major, that plane will not be ready for service tomorrow.' Conger said something to the effect that it better be ready, and my response was that I was the Engineering Officer and responsible for the status of the aircraft and that the plane would not be available. A few weeks later he had me transferred to the 41st Service Squadron."

Significant transfers affected the group hierarchy during January. Colonel David Schilling, near the end of a second tour, was showing signs of the strain of leadership. Auton and Kepner decided it was high time the then top scoring fighter ace of the Eighth with a combined total of 33 victories – 22 and a shared in the air, and 10 and a shared by strafing – should be given a staff appointment at 65th Fighter Wing. Command of the group was passed to Lt Colonel Dade, for long the deputy. There were some misgivings about this among group staff and pilots as Dade was not generally popular. Another combat original, he was still on his first tour, as there had been a long period when as Group Operations Officer he flew few missions. Because of this, and unfairly, he was considered to have picked easy missions. It was also noted that Dade had experienced several turn-backs, but this could be more indicative of a particularly careful pilot than any reluctance to face combat, as on some occasions he had obtained another aircraft and caught up with the group formation. Not only was Dade a competent pilot but he was proven in battle having shot down three enemy aircraft and shot up several on the ground. He was also methodical and reliable in his assigned duties during his time with the group. Dade's unpopularity had more to do with personality clashes; a stickler for military conduct, he did not get involved in boisterous activities; genial, yet hard on juniors who stepped out of line, which some offenders regarded as pettiness. Zemke and Schilling, the icons, were hard for any follower: Dade gave of his best. The position of group Flying Executive went to the senior squadron CO, Major Leslie Smith who still had several hours of combat time left to complete his second tour. His place at the head of the 62nd Squadron was taken by Captain Felix Williamson. Although Schilling flew his last mission on 5 January his official transfer and relinquishing of the group command did not take place until three weeks later.

Winter's grip held fast for most of January 1945 with more snowfalls followed by thaws, the resultant fogs causing diversions. The mists and clouds were so bad over Boxted on the 16th after a bomber support mission that aircraft diverted to other airfields while pilots who could not find a haven baled out. The bad weather brought an increase in accidents for most units of the Eighth Air Force, and 21 January was a particularly black day for the 56th. During the launch of an escort mission two aircraft collided during the take-off run. A 63rd Squadron wingman, 2nd Lieutenant Robert Hall, had an engine problem but failed to issue a radio warning and did not pull off the runway. The leader of the following element, 1st Lieutenant Willard Scherz, whose view was hidden by the nose of the Thunderbolt until too late, hit Hall's aircraft, the propeller slashing into the fuselage. Hall was killed and a badly shaken Scherz escaped from the fire that engulfed the two aircraft. Remaining take-offs were switched to another runway, and the mission continued with pilots too busy to conjecture on the fate of those in the runway crash. That would wait until later when they also learned that two of the group's OTU Thunderbolts collided and crashed during a training flight over south-east

Essex; one pilot, a recent replacement, was killed. There was another crash incident this day, although the damage sustained was repairable.

The 61st Squadron was placed on non-operational status to make a complete conversion to the P-47M model. It had been found that the more powerful engine with different power settings and responses to the P-47D made for difficulties in uniform control when flying the two different models in the same formation. A decision was made to convert one squadron at a time, withdrawing the Ds and bringing in the Ms. At around mid-day on the 21st, 2nd Lieutenant Edward Lightfoot was slow timing a P-47M and had climbed to over 30,000 feet when the engine cut out. Being over his home airfield Lightfoot elected to make a belly landing and called the tower: "I'm making an emergency landing on runway number five." The runway was kept clear. When the Duty Flying Control Officer saw the aircraft approaching he hastily radioed, "You have no wheels!" Lightfoot answered, "I have no engine either!" The actual touchdown was alongside the runway on the snowy mush and apart from the propeller and cowling damage the airframe suffered little. The cause was found to be a breakdown in the ignition harness between magnetos and distributors. Similar cutting out at high altitude had been experienced on another P-47M under test but the engine had restarted at lower altitude. In consequence P-47Ms were grounded until an inspection of all ignition harness was undertaken revealing four other aircraft with broken leads.

Weather continued to reduce operations with only three more missions during the remainder of January and on the last of these there was nearly another runway tragedy. An element leader experienced engine trouble on the take-off run and while trying to deal with it drifted in front of his wingman. Fortunately there were no injuries although both aircraft had severe damage. Despite the ignition lead problems with the P-47M the group was able to muster enough aircraft for what was to be its longest mission of the war, a sweep ahead of the bombers making for Berlin, entailing over a 500-mile penetration. Pilots were issued with Russian 'blood chits' in case they came down in Soviet-held areas, the front line being reckoned as 50 miles east of the enemy capital. Each aircraft carried 200 US gallons of fuel in drop tanks providing for the flight out to the German capital. Anticipation of encountering the Luftwaffe was fulfilled, as south-east of Berlin some 15 FW190s were seen climbing, believed to have recently taken off from an airfield. Paul Conger, who was leading the group, went down with the 63rd and 62nd Squadrons to intercept but the enemy aircraft turned to meet the attack. In the ensuing combats nine fighters were claimed for the loss of Lieutenant David Magel, whose brother Robert had been shot down the previous August, originally reported killed but later found to be a prisoner. David, seen to bale out of his burning P-47, was reported to have landed safely. However he was killed; the reason was not ascertained but some speculated it was through lynching by civilians. From engine start to shut down the mission had taken five and three-quarter hours and many pilots complained of feeling somewhat stiff that evening.

The enemy would only claim one more life of a 56th Fighter Group pilot; accidents would claim ten. A few of these fatalities were due to on-going problems with the P-47M. The 62nd Squadron began full conversion on 3 February but unlike the 61st retained a number of its D models. Two weeks later the 63rd followed suit and also kept most of its P-47Ds for a while as troubles with the M had multiplied. On 9 February George Bradley, a former B-24 pilot who had joined the 61st in November, suffered an engine failure at altitude and tried to belly in on a large field at Dedham. Two young oaks on the boundary fence were in his way and passing between them most of both wings were shed. Bradley climbed from the wreck with no more than a banged up head. On inspection the engine failure was found to be another case of cracked ignition harness and a programme of replacing all with new neoprene-cased high tension leads was undertaken. Annoyingly, similar problems had been experienced with ignition leads two years previously and yet the manufacturer had failed to get to grips with the problem. The fault in the new engine of not reaching the required operating temperature, was remedied by a baffle on the pre-heater ring and lagging push rod housings. Failure to develop full power at high altitude led to re-adjustment of the throttle to turbo-supercharger correlation.

The technical problems and modifications prevented the 61st from flying any missions with the M during January and it was not until Valentine's Day that the first mission with this model took place. The other squadrons were also limited in operational activity during this period, using retained P-47Ds. The load on the ground crews of the 62nd and 63rd was particularly heavy, most crews had two aircraft to maintain, a D and an M model. The service squadron personnel were also hard-worked with lines of P-47Ms in each of the two hangars awaiting required modifications. Pilots spent time on slow timing engine flights and during the latter part of February another problem with loss of power was identified as being due to carburettor poppet valve diaphragms splitting which led to grounding Ms on the 26th. Fortunately, Bendix carburettor representatives were able to obtain suitable material from the British to make replacement gaskets and all 67 Ms at Boxted were modified within 24 hours. At the same time a local modification to the poppet valve was made to prevent a recurrence, allowing the grounding to be lifted. All this severely reduced the group's operational commitment and though 14 missions were flown they were mostly at no more than two-squadron strength, borrowing P-47Ds from one another. Total sorties for February only amounted to some 400, half the number that, for example, had been flown in the previous November. Understandably it was a frustrating time for pilots, particularly those who had been around for some months and embraced the ethos of the group. People at Boxted felt let down by Republic. The new model Thunderbolt that the manufacturers had claimed would give the group a performance advantage proved a poorly tested stopgap. The destruction of enemy aircraft in the air or on the ground that had come to be the yardstick of unit achievement, and for which the 56th had led the way throughout the past year, was now left to the Mustang groups. After the success of the 3 February mission the 56th's only other claims for a month were four enemy aircraft by strafing, albeit that the Mustangs did not have a great deal of contact with the Luftwaffe during this period. Even so, a few of the P-51 equipped groups were gradually overhauling the 56th's lead.

Colonel Schilling, who had got himself seconded to the RAF intelligence organisation, had not lost interest in his old group and using his well known persuasive charm got the RAF to release a captured Luftwaffe fighter leader into his care for a few days. Jim Carter:

"One day Dave Schilling arrived at Boxted and introduced us to a German fighter CO at a group briefing. They stayed a few days. The German officer wore his uniform sans insignia to make him less conspicuous in his travels to the dining hall, etc. This because some of our ground personnel objected to seeing a Luftwaffe pilot on the base who may have shot down some of our own men. Schilling thought there might be some value in discussing tactics with an adversary."

Word soon got round of the German's presence and a few men of Jewish faith did register their objection to his presence. It was typical Schilling opportunism, from which he would have also derived amusement at the surprise engendered at Boxted when an enemy pilot was suddenly produced. The Luftwaffe officer was a Gruppe commander, shot down while leading his unit during the mass Luftwaffe raid on Allied continental airfields on New Year's Day 1945. Schilling kept in touch with his old command until April when he returned to the USA.

By the end of February it was believed the problems with the P-47M had been surmounted and the remaining D models were withdrawn. Unfortunately, the M was still beset with engine failures. On 4 March the 62nd Squadron took out an all-P-47M formation for the first time, only to have six of the fourteen despatched return early with technical troubles, mostly through loss of engine power. One line of thought was that the trouble was connected with the high-grade fuel being used. Tests were conducted with plain 130 and the enhanced 150 octane, known as PEP, but the results were inconclusive. The use of water injection was also suspected, but again tests gave no positive answer. Missions continued to be dogged by abortives. Then on 11 March 2nd Lieutenant Frank Aheron, on a training flight, had a piston failure causing the oil tank of his P-47M to rupture; oil covered the windshield and cockpit canopy making it difficult to see out. Aheron attempted an emergency landing at RAF Cranfield, only to crash, and lose his life. This was not the first case associated with oil loss at high altitude and warranted closer investigation. The following day 2nd Lieutenant Alfred Bolender's engine lost oil during a mission. His wheels-down emergency landing on a deserted airstrip in Belgium resulted in a complete nose-over in mud. Two girls came to his rescue and literally dug Bolender out of his inverted and partly submerged cockpit. During an escort mission on 14 March, when the group found and shot down three enemy aircraft – two being the new Arado 234 jet-powered bombers – another 62nd Squadron P-47M developed an oil leak. The pilot, 2nd Lieutenant Earl Townsend, turned for home with an escort, only to have the engine fail completely while still over the North Sea. Townsend baled but in doing so is believed to have hit the tail as he was killed; his parachute did not open until just as he hit the water. Next day during the launch of another escort, the M flown by 1st Lieutenant Willard Scherz, was climbing out after take-off from the main runway when the engine failed. With the flight attitude and the aircraft's full fuel load, air speed diminished abruptly precipitating a flat spin. Scherz, who had escaped from the runway collision a few weeks earlier, was killed in the resultant crash on allotments near Colchester railway station. Eighth Air Force Technical Section, plus Republic and Pratt & Whitney, might be doing their utmost to resolve the situation with the P-47M, but it had gone on far too long for Eighth Air Force HQ which had a war to fight. On 16 March all P-47Ms were grounded and a dozen war-weary P-51 Mustangs were withdrawn from other units and sent to Boxted together with a few mechanics to advise on maintenance of liquid-cooled engines.

Despite misgivings about the P-47M few at Boxted wanted to see the group convert to what were derisively known as Spam Cans, not least the ground crews. Their allegiance to the Thunderbolt was strong, as many had been with the P-47 since the very first B models came off the production line at Farmingdale. A renewed effort to solve the M's problems was made. Sergeant Wiley Noah, the crew chief on the P-47M originally assigned to Major Michael Jackson – who finished his missions in late February – noticed that pulling the propeller through to clear the cylinders had become increasingly easier. With this obvious lack of compression he had tests run and it was found dangerously low on several cylinders. A programme of compression testing was undertaken and several engines were found to be lacking on some cylinders. Meanwhile an engine that had been stripped down revealed that poor compression was due to the iron oil-wiper piston rings having rusted. It further revealed that in cylinders with poor compression air was being pumped up the oil breather lines and the pressure was such that it caused the lines or oil tank to fail. Evidently the engine components were not given the proper protective treatment in the USA before overseas shipment. In transit salt-water atmosphere got into the engines, causing corrosion. After the engine had been run a few hours the oil-wiper rings failed or corrosion scaled off and caused engine damage. Eventually, a decision was made to change all engines with less than 50 hours running time which amounted to around three-quarters of the complement. An intensive effort by the service squadron and squadron mechanics during a nine-day stand-down in mid-March led higher authority to be convinced that the problem had at last been solved, albeit that another pilot was killed following an engine failure and flat spin during this period. Pilots made introductory flights with the training Mustangs until the end of March when these aircraft were withdrawn, much to the relief of the ground crews.

25 Final Weeks of Combat

In the winter of 1944-45 the US Army devised a plan whereby wounded and weary infantrymen on the continent would be replaced by a number of non-specialist personnel from the Army Air Forces in Britain. Most if not all Eighth Air Force stations made a contribution, even if few men were happy to exchange a relatively safe life for the risk and discomforts of the front line. Boxted gave and received from the support units. Angelo DeCarlo:

"I was in the commissary one day when five or six guys reported in. Here I was a Pfc and all these guys were staff sergeants or above who had been transferred in from the battle fronts with wounds. They were to work under me as I had to instruct them what to do, how to break down and sort out the stores. I was careful what I said to them as they all outranked me; but we got along fine. These replaced some of the men who were taken out of our unit to go to the infantry."

While accepting the Army's decision, having to train men for ground duties was an additional burden to an organisation already stretched in the maintenance and repair area, apart from the regular pilot tuition. There was an opinion amongst the senior staff that several of the replacement pilots received during the winter were not up to the job; the general standard of selection had slipped. Training commands in the USA were turning out large numbers but many were found not of the right temperament for a fighter cockpit. The group, as always, put new pilots through its own training programme, which intensified this opinion as some of the newcomers had not even flown a P-47. The ground crews also voiced their views that some new pilots were lacking. Frank Gyidik:

"One day a replacement pilot came out to get familiar with the P-47 and fly it for two hours. I tied him in as usual and then got off the wing. So he goes to start up, energises the engine, engages the starter, it hardly turns over. I motioned to him to cut it, went up there and looked around, and found he had turned on the radio and about every switch that uses electric power. It's a big engine and takes a lot of power out of the battery and he'd all the electrical power on. So I shut everything off, told him to turn on the master switch, be ready with his ignition and mag' switches, energise it and then hit the starter and she'll fire. Next day he comes out again and I hear the engine dying away as he tried to start it. So I climbed

up and again he'd got all the switches on. I tried to start it but the plane
was dead by then. So he got out of the plane and left. The battery on a P-
47 is between the firewall and the engine and it seemed to weigh a ton
when you had to stretch over to take it out. So I changed the battery. Next
day he comes out again and does exactly the same thing but I managed
to get it started. I says, 'Lieutenant, how many times have I told you how
to start this thing?' Later the operations officer comes out and says the
lieutenant who been flying your plane complains you have been kind
of reading the riot act to him. So I explained what he was doing. Next
morning I'm sitting in the cockpit having pre-flighted the machine, and I
looks across towards the control tower and I see a pilot with his parachute
on walking all the way across the field and it turns out to be this
lieutenant. I said what's happening – and I see he has a tech' book. He
says, well I'm supposed to get in the cockpit and read the tech' book on
how to start an airplane and sit here for an hour until I've mastered it.
Come noon time, he walks way back across the airfield. I never saw him
again and heard he had been transferred out."

Operations resumed on 24 March, the day the Allies launched their
offensive across the Rhine. Two uneventful missons were flown. The
following day an escort for Liberators encountered a few 'blow jobs', but
the P-47s gave chase to no avail as Me262s could easily pull away. Major
George Bostwick, who had returned from leave in the USA and replaced
Paul Conger as the 63rd CO earlier in the month, took his squadron to
Parchim airfield where several jets were seen. The squadron was orbiting
at around 12,000 feet when 2nd Lieutenant Edwin Crosthwait spotted an
Me262 in flight and called it in to Bostwick. As neither Bostwick nor
anyone else could pick it out below, Crosthwait was told to intercept and
with the element of surprise caught the jet in a turn and shot it down.
Meanwhile Bostwick had seen another Me262 flying low over the
airfield. He dived to attack transferring his attention to another 262 which
had just taken off. The pilot of this jet saw Bostwick's approach and made
a violent turn to the left. In so doing the left wing struck the ground
causing the aircraft to cartwheel and crash. Incidents this day confirmed
the superiority of the jets' speed, and that the best opportunities to destroy
them in flight were in turning actions or during their take-offs or landing
approaches. Me262s were encountered on four of the following eight
missions, which was indicative of the Luftwaffe's attempt to use this type
to counter the daylight air offensive. At this stage of hostilities, with vast
numbers of Allied fighters over German territory in daylight, there can
have been little hope of their having a major effect. Even so, for some
months, Allied air force commands had been concerned about this
formidable aircraft. The RAF, moving its first operational squadron of
Meteor jets to the continent in April, hoped to counter the Luftwaffe jets,
but their poor endurance, restricting radius of action, thwarted this
purpose.
   The 56th claimed its fourth Me262 on 5 April when Captain John

Fahringer, the 63rd Operations Officer, caught one in a turn, when its pilot seemed to have his attention on attacking B-17s. Two days later the Luftwaffe chose to make one of its last major efforts attacking Eighth Air Force bombers with some deliberate ramming reported. After chasing an Me262, George Bostwick found some Me109s near Celle and promptly despatched two himself while 63rd pilot, Lieutenant Charles McBath, was credited with another. Elsewhere Captain Robert Winters of the 62nd chased a lone Me109 and shot it down.

These were the first piston-engine fighters encountered in more than three weeks, but the dearth would now hopefully be reduced by employing a new piece of equipment. Back in the previous August Staff Sergeants Thurman Schreel and Charles Taylor, of the 41st Service Squadron, proposed to their engineering officers that when one of the older Thunderbolts was retired from combat use they be allowed to convert it to carry a passenger behind the cockpit. Their idea was passed to Colonel Schilling who gave enthusiastic permission. A P-47D retired from the 62nd Squadron was made available and conversion work started, although it was not to take precedence over other tasks. In fact, Schreel and Taylor did much of the work in their spare time or at night. In three weeks they had removed equipment aft of the cockpit, cut away the decking, added strengthening members and lining, fitted a seat and provided a new oxygen system that could be used by both occupants. Their most difficult task was fashioning a cockpit canopy allowing the egress of both pilot and passenger in an emergency. Completed in under a month, each man had devoted over 220 hours to the project; a test flight was carried out on 10 September. Thereafter the so-called Doublebolt had frequent use for fast communications and light transport, including the occasional surreptitious ferrying of lady friends. The British had developed an airborne radar interception device called Prospectus which within a range of 50 miles could pick up enemy fighter VHF radio talk and give a bearing on the transmissions. Through the Bovingdon-based Technical Section a set was acquired and installed in the Doublebolt, with the intention of flying the aircraft in the van of a formation in the hope the radar operator would be able to lead the group to enemy aircraft. By this time the Doublebolt's airframe had amassed well over 300 hours flying time and was supposedly classified 'war weary' and restricted. Nonetheless, with Lt Colonel Dade as pilot a first operational trial was made on 9 April with a long-range sweep towards Regensburg. No enemy aircraft were detected, however, and although three further missions were carried out with Prospectus during April, they were all disappointing as no contacts were made.

Group pride took a blow on 4 April when the 4th Fighter Group, long its main rival, had boosted its combined total of enemy aircraft destroyed to fifteen more than the 56th's total, although figures were frequently amended as headquarters reviewed gun camera film and reconnaissance photographs. The goal of 1,000 victories had been the desired milestone for some time, but now it appeared the war would be over before that figure was reached unless there was some sort of last ditch stand by the

Luftwaffe. The Eighth Air Force despatched bombers and fighters against airfields in the Reich from which the Luftwaffe was still believed to be operating on 10 April. Sweeping ahead of the bombers the 56th, with 60 P-47Ms, had an eventful day strafing airfields and water landing sites, returning with initial claims of 47 aircraft destroyed. Ground fire was intense at some locations and 15 Thunderbolts suffered hits. Fortunate was Lieutenant Ed Ellis:

"We were firing at planes stacked under trees, travelling at around 300 mph and down below tree level. I was just starting to pull up when a flak burst went off on my right side and took off about four feet out of my wing. The concussion blew me back down into the trees. I flinched. There was a sound like someone dropping a pile of wood on a buzz saw. Opening my eyes I couldn't see out. Thought I'm dead. That was ridiculous because then I could see the instrument panel. So I cranked my canopy open and looked out. My wings were in terrible shape through hitting the trees and flying through them. Didn't realise at that moment I'd also been hit in the head by a small piece of flak, as I was too busy keeping the airplane in the air. Called my CO and told him I was going back home. To keep the plane flying had to come in to land at near 200 mph with the gear retracted."

Three P-47s did not return to Boxted but it was learned one had landed and another crash-landed at RAF-held airfields. The third, piloted by 2nd Lieutenant Paul Stitt of the 62nd, crashed on approach to another Belgian landing ground; Stitt died of wounds and injuries next day. When 62nd flights were returning two Me262s were engaged. Captain William Wilkerson and 1st Lieutenant Bill Sharbo being credited with the destruction of one each, although Wilkerson's was later reassessed as a probable. The day's score raised the 56th's total past the 900 mark, re-establishing the lead over the 4th Group. The main source of this rivalry was the *Stars and Stripes* newspaper. There was still some concern in high command that while this competition encouraged aggressiveness there was also the risk of over-eager fighter pilots unnecessarily endangering their lives.

The following day a strafing ban was imposed because of a fear that Allied land forces might be attacked during the fluid situation existing on the battlefronts. There were no operations on 12 April and respects were paid at Boxted to President Roosevelt whose death had been announced. More immediate concern was the death of Ed Lightfoot, the pilot who was involved in the first crash-landing incident with a P-47M back in January. Lightfoot took on a P-51 from a neighbouring group in a mock dogfight which resulted in a collision over a wood at Raydon; both pilots were killed. This was the fifth collision since mid-January, resulting in all in the deaths of six 56th pilots. While collisions were a familiar hazard in formations, this spate gave the group headquarters worrying concerns about air discipline. The standard of airmanship among new pilots was already questionable but some of the fatalities had involved experienced men.

Allied command reconsidered the strafing ban, and relaxed it for certain defined areas on 13 April. The 56th received a field order to provide freelance support for bombers going to targets in northern Germany. The 1,000 destroyed goal was in the minds of senior group officers and a hurried study was made of known airfields in the assigned area, particularly those that hitherto had received little attention. And there was still the expectation of one last great stand by the Luftwaffe. Eggebek, an airfield south of the Danish-German border, was singled out for investigation and placed first on the list. Led by Lt Colonel Dade, 48 Thunderbolts plus spares took off from Boxted in the early afternoon and reached their objective approximately an hour and three quarters later. Eggebek was crowded with an estimated nearly 200 of various types of aircraft. Appearing to be just the target the Wolfpack was seeking, two squadrons were placed as top cover while Pete Dade, with the 63rd, tested the airfield defences. These did not appear to be heavy and the initial strafing concentrated on silencing as many as possible. During these runs Lieutenant William Hoffman's Thunderbolt took a hit, causing him to bale out. At only some 200 feet altitude he apparently did not have time to open his parachute and was killed. The 63rd then went in to shoot up enemy aircraft, claiming more than 30, with Lieutenant Randel Murphy alone destroying ten. When the 63rd had used up its ammunition the other two squadrons were called down in turn. The action lasted some 80 minutes, leaving a vast pall of smoke rising over Eggebek. Back at Boxted an initial assessment of claims brought a total of 95 enemy aircraft destroyed and another 95 damaged. To achieve this 339 individual passes had been made and 78,073 rounds of ammunition expended. The Wolfpack had reached their 1,000 destroyed goal on the second anniversary of the group's first mission. However, not all pilots were happy about this day's action. Alfred Bolender:

"Everyone knew the war was over ... I didn't agree with the mission when it was announced, because I believed it was a duck shoot to pick up a lot of aircraft in order to beat the 4th Group which was close to us in total kills. The result was that we destroyed some 90 aircraft, lost one pilot and my plane received considerable damage – 18 holes through the wing, fuselage and canopy. My radio was knocked out and I left the strafing pattern to return home. I had several good friends who lost their lives during my time with the 56th but none have left the bad feelings I still have about that needless fatality."

During the next two days Eighth Air Force attention shifted to enemy strongpoints still holding out on the French Atlantic coast, then on 16 April the bombers went after mainly rail targets in Germany. Their escort engaged in extensive strafing with the extraordinary tally of over 700 enemy aircraft destroyed for losses of near 40. The 4th Group, eager to overhaul the 56th's total, shot up airfields in southern Germany and Czechoslovakia with claims of 105 to take them past the 1,000 mark. The cost was dear: eight Mustangs missing and several damaged. Elsewhere the Wolfpack could only claim four aircraft in ground attacks, having met heavy defensive fire. B group P-47s took several hits and the leader, Willie Williamson, only just managed to make St Trond for an emergency landing before fuel escaping from a severed line brought flames. Captain Edward Appel was not so fortunate:

"We let down to strafe Muldorf airdrome about 50 miles east of Munich. Came in on the deck and was shooting into Me109s sitting on the field. Picked up a lot of flak. Saw holes appear in the wings then the engine started running rough and losing power. I started to pull up which I shouldn't have done right over an enemy airfield, then they really started to get in the hits. Anyway, was soon out of range. Was at full throttle but no power, airspeed kept falling off. Tried to get over one last hill before bellying in, too low to bale out. But as I started to clear the hill the right wing stalled and went under, and the plane cartwheeled across the country. I thought school was out again. Broke the wings and tail off but by some miracle came down right side up. Cut my knee and elbow a little bouncing around in the cockpit. Thought I was all bloody but it was just hot engine oil from the ruptured oil tank. Left the Mae West and parachute in the seat and crawled out and took off running. Some farmers were watching but they didn't bother.

"Ran into some trees but after the trees there was a little village strung along a road. Had to get past this village as the German soldiers were coming from the airfield. As I came up to the village two soldiers came out and drew their guns and hollered 'Halt!' With all the shooting going on behind me I thought I'd pretend I was a German running away from the Americans. I yelled back, 'Nicht halt, American kommen.' They turned and looked back where I'd come from with wide eyes and I kept on going. Then they swung back towards me again pointing their guns and yelling 'Halt'. I stopped and waved an arm back towards the woods and yelled 'Nein, Nein, nicht halt, American kommen.' They again turned round and watched the woods for the Americans they thought were there and I made tracks. I ran into some woods and actually sat down and laughed thinking about how they would catch hell when other German soldiers came and they had let me go. Couldn't find any place to hide in the woods as the underbrush was all cleaned out, so I climbed to the top of a big tree and sat there. There were lots of trees. The Germans soon came, line abreast again, hunting round under the trees with rifles, but they kept right on going. Stayed in the tree until dark and then crawled down and took off northwest towards the front lines. Walked at night and hid in the daytime again. Had a couple of escape kits along that had compasses, maps, hacksaw blades and concentrated rations in them. Also had my 45, which was a big consolation even if I didn't fire it. Came to the Danube river at night. Used the hacksaw blade to saw a chain in two that moored a boat. The boat was on a cable across the river. I jumped in and used the tiller and went right across because of the terrific current coming down from the Alps. Came to the Isar river and did the same thing. Stole a boat with the hacksaw blade and went across. Came to what I thought was another river and done the same thing again, sawed another boat loose and used the oars in the boat to paddle. Only thing is, this time when I was out quite a way I could see in the moonlight I was in the middle of a lake. I could have walked around it. Felt like a sitting duck out there. Got to some place in the mountains that looked like a big hotel or hospital. Didn't see anybody around. One end was a barn with a horse in it. The rest of it was the inn or hotel or eating part. Anyway, between the two was this driveway. I walked into the driveway and opened a door into the barn part. I took the blanket from the horse and filled my pocket with some potatoes and started back out. Just then some German soldiers came out and walked right past the door where I was hiding. After they left I ran as fast as I could for the woods. Thought I'd get shot but I didn't.

"Another time I was just sitting in the woods in daylight waiting for night when I heard a noise behind me. Turning round I saw two civilians with axes raised coming towards me. Pulled my 45 and pulled down on them and hollered halt but they would not stop. Hollered halt some more, one finally did stop and the other one kept coming. He was only a few feet away and would not stop. I was already aiming between the eyes and starting to squeeze the trigger before he swiped me. The other one said something to him and he stopped. Then one of them left and the other stayed there to watch me. I suppose they were going to get more help. Anyway I didn't want to kill anybody if I didn't have to or I would be in trouble if they caught me. So I took off a running with this guy behind me hollering halt. But I out-ran him and kept on going. Would go up to a house right after dark and knock on the door. Usually the dad would come to the door. I told him straight out that I was an American flyer and hungry; needed food. Many times they would have me come in and sit at the table and give me bread, meat and coffee. I wouldn't let anyone leave the house while I was there. Kept my gun on the table and everybody at a distance, then would leave and make many miles that night so they wouldn't catch me. Some families would give me extra food to take along. Got near the front lines where there was a lot of shooting. Hid under some small thick evergreens in a hollowed out spot. Looked like an old World War I foxhole. Anyway, one night the German army moved over me and then for two days I was between the two lines that were shooting at each other, mostly artillery. The shells that hit the trees would really blast things around there. One night the shooting went to the east so next morning I crept out to the edge of the woods and watched the roads. Down the roads were going our weapons carriers and tanks. I watched a few go by before waving any down. Wanted to make sure they were ours. Then came out with my hands up. Didn't want to get shot by our own army. Went back through an artillery outfit that was the same outfit that I came through the first time I evaded, the same officers, the same colonel. The colonel was a little suspicious of me; thought maybe I was spying for the other side. Anyway, I was out again and by the time I got to Paris the war was over."

Ed Appel had flown 30 missions as a B-24 pilot before being shot down behind enemy lines in September 1944 when he had managed to avoid capture. Like several other time-expired bomber pilots he volunteered to fly fighters and contacted Dave Schilling who said, "Sure. Come on down. We'll check you out." Appel had flown 16 missions with 62nd Squadron before being brought down again and making his remarkable second escape. Although there had been some concern about bomber pilots' ability to adapt to fighters following what had befallen the original six whom Zemke had taken in during the previous spring, others had been accepted. Fred McIntosh was another and was reported missing. 'SD' Ulch, another 62nd pilot: "It was believed Fred wasn't coming back. In the scramble about personal possessions over what stayed and what went to headquarters, I wound up with Fred's prized German flying boots; a cherished possession. Days later, Fred returned and was glad we had saved some of his prizes and thanked me profusely for saving his boots!" Appropriating desirable items from the lockers of missing pilots was common among the less squeamish comrades who knew that such would not be returned to next of kin. McIntosh's case was far from the first where a pilot thought missing had gone down in Allied-held territory on the continent and turned up sometime later to find his possessions had been disposed of.

In four subsequent missions, the last of which (the group's 463rd) was on 21 April, there were no aerial encounters and no strafing targets, as on the 18th this latter activity was again banned as a potential danger to the Allied advance. The news that Adolf Hitler was dead and that the Russians were in Berlin suggested it was only a matter of days before hostilities ceased. Yet there was still the possibility of that last show of strength by the Luftwaffe. The Eighth's bombers and fighters were not called on for four days and only a medium-sized force of B-17s and B-24s were sent to attack targets in southern Germany and Czechoslovakia. Then it was announced that the strategic campaign was concluded and that the Allied air forces on the continent who were giving tactical support to the ground forces, would be left to deal with any final Luftwaffe air activity. There was still a chance that the Eighth's fighters might be called upon and the Thunderbolts at Boxted were armed ready for the call. Those imbued with the ethos of the Wolfpack were still eager to go out to battle, to further endorse the group's standing. It stood at the top of the table for enemy aircraft destroyed, 1008, even if this was only five more than its rival the 4th Fighter Group. In the matter of air victories alone the 56th was a hundred ahead of the nearest competitor, and its hope had been for an opportunity to raise the 686 total to 700. To present mortal combat in competitive terms may have troubled many observers, yet this was how the majority of those involved viewed it at the time. And, as previously shown, commanding generals saw competition as a vital key to esprit de corps.

As the days passed so the likelihood of further action receded and there was a growing sense of relaxation at Boxted, particularly amongst the pilots who could now be fairly confident they were going to survive the defences of the Third Reich. There was one notable incident that brought two pilots considerable admiration from the inhabitants of Colchester. On the evening of Saturday 28 April, 1st Lieutenant Alfred Bolender and 2nd Lieutenant Tobin Armstrong* of the 63rd Squadron were walking a couple of girls home after a visit to the Red Lion in Colchester. They had just crossed the river bridge in North Station Road when they heard and saw a British army lorry coming down the very steep hill from the centre of the town and obviously out of control. It crossed the road at the bridge and went through the railings, landing upside down in the river. Bolender and Armstrong ran back and realising there were men trapped in the cab they jumped into the river and managed to get the four occupants out and back to the bank. It was so cold Bolender could hardly speak when he returned to the bridge. They were taken back to one of the girls' homes and dried out until picked up and taken back to Boxted. For their brave action both were later awarded the Soldier's Medal by the US authorities.

Flying practice and training continued, and a reminder of the inherent dangers came on 1 May when 1st Lieutenant Albin Zychowski was killed. Four Thunderbolts on a cross-country flight engaged in some low passes over the USAAF Rest Home at Knightshayes Court, near Tiverton, Devon. Zychowski, who was third in line, apparently misjudged his height and mushed through some treetops, crashing into rising ground beyond.

There were some readjustments in command at this time with Major Jim Carter, CO of the 61st, exchanging positions with Major Gordon Baker as group Operations Officer. The group Flying Executive was Lt Colonel Donald Renwick who took over when Leslie Smith finished his second tour and was reassigned at the beginning of April. 'Doc' Renwick had been one of the 61st flight leaders in the early days of combat and was transferred to the Atcham P-47 training organisation when Hub Zemke was required to supply a suitable officer for instructing. Renwick became commanding officer at Atcham and remained until that station was closed, later to return to his old group.

On 7 May the group headquarters was notified that the following day would be declared VE Day, the official end of the war in Europe. This meant that the group's last mission had been that of 21 April; its last of 686 air victories had been the Me262 shot down by Lieutenant Sharbo on 10 April; the last of 322 aircraft ground victories those on 16 April ; and

---

* In the 1970s Armstrong's wife was the US Ambassador to the Court of King James.

Captain Ed Appel's on the same date was the last of 128 group aircraft missing in action. Of the pilots of those missing aircraft 35 had been made prisoner, nine evaded capture, six were rescued from the sea and, on 13 April Lieutenant William Hoffman was the last of 78 killed. Twenty-seven pilots were wounded in action, nine more than once.

26 Waiting to go Home

Eighth Air Force HQ ordered personnel to be confined to their stations throughout the UK on VE-Day and for 12 hours prior to it to avoid any GI ebullience in local community celebrations. However, all but a few manning flying control and key communications positions were released from duties with free refreshments, including beer, provided in both officers' and enlisted men's clubs. The main topic of conversation was, understandably, their return home, a subject that also predominated during the weeks ahead. The army announced a points system of eligibility for return to the USA, the criteria based on an individual's period of overseas service and other personal factors. The average for long service ground personnel was around 80 points; the highest rating on the station being that of the 61st's Master Sergeant Carl Matson who had 145. Rumour, an ongoing feature of service life, now embraced movement: the 56th was going straight to the Pacific, it was being sent to Germany with many variations on the future disposition of personnel. However, there was to be no quick departure of the group from Boxted as priority went to other forces. The Eighth's bombers would be among the first for they could fly back to America and carry some ground personnel as passengers. Before that exodus began the bombers were used to transport ground personnel on aerial sightseeing tours of some of the damage inflicted on Germany by the strategic campaign, which was in the way of a thank you for their endeavours. They were known as Trolley Runs, and Liberators arrived at Boxted on the mornings of 10 May and three following to collect passengers for a seven-hour flight at around a 1,000 feet. The planned 900-mile route went from Southwold to Leyden in the Netherlands, then north-east to Hamburg by way of Osnabrück and Bremen, south to Brunswick, west to Hanover and down over several towns in the Ruhr, turning west again at Essen and out over The Hague. The sights of the devastation were to remain impressive memories for those conveyed.

With the expectation that some personnel, if not the group, would go on to the war with Japan, a training programme relevant to aspects of service in the Pacific areas began. It seemed all very transitory for the high-points men moving to homebound units and the reception of low-points men continually disrupted programmes. The low-points men transferred into the group ranged from 'dog trainers to motor boat drivers', most with little knowledge of aircraft support and maintenance. In this they had to be trained, hopefully 'to eventually realise the prop was not there to cool the pilot'. A significant problem was that most of the high-points men were those in vital jobs such as crew chiefs or technical specialists who could not be released until replacements were received or trained. Even so, the first men withdrawn from the Boxted complement were the ground specialists, presumably to meet a demand from the Pacific theatres of war. Master Sergeant John Brady, Communications Chief, was one. The procedure involved in return to the USA was not to his satisfaction:

"I was always in the first group to receive instructions, as personnel were routinely selected alphabetically. Such was without regard to rank, position, status or whatever. Two days following the alert, the group into which I was selected boarded a train at Colchester. I was not given any instructions as to what to do about all the communication facilities I was responsible for. It was as if I just closed the door, left the equipment running and walked away. I remember just leaning my bicycle against my barrack building and leaving it. After an overnight journey during which we did not know where we were going, we arrived at a compound near, as we later learned, Preston. The compound was exactly that. An area fenced about ten feet high. We were confined, restricted with locked gates and guards. It was quite similar to a POW camp – and that is exactly how we felt. At this point all anyone knew was that we were on our way back to the US. From then on this type of treatment continued until I was discharged from the air force. The Army then, I feel, considered rank merely a position on the pay scale with added responsibilities thrown in. Personnel were just people, as a group all uniforms were without rank. We remained in the compound for about two weeks before being entrained and moved to a port of embarkation I knew not where. We boarded a ship at night and sailed next morning. I learned then that the ship was the *Aquitania*. Since leaving Boxted I had been given no information or instructions about anything. After arrival in the States I was eventually sent to Lackland air base in Texas where rumour held that we radio men were to be processed for movement to the Pacific. The end of the war put a stop to that but at no time was I officially told a thing."

Several of the pilots who had been made prisoners of the Third Reich returned to Boxted for a few days. On 22 May the 'Head Shed' staff were delighted to welcome Hub Zemke. He was flown in from Rheims by a friend in a Beechcraft C-45, addressed an assembly of men in a hangar and stayed overnight before moving on to be interviewed by General Kepner, his old Fighter Command boss and now head of the Eighth Air Force. Apart from Pete Dade, Jim Carter, and three or four others, the pilots were all new to Hub. The ground staff were still largely unchanged, the solid foundation of the entity. A request from Eighth Air Force shortly thereafter was to supply a P-47 for the planned USAAF exposition to be sited beneath the Eiffel Tower in Paris. Dade, his HQ staff and the squadron commanders agreed this should be painted up in the markings carried on Hub Zemke's aircraft and the epithet Zemke's Wolfpack emblazoned across the fuselage together with 1,000 Destroyed. Zemke, a man with a good hold on his emotions, would later remark that he was greatly touched on visiting the exposition and seeing this tribute. As for the 1,000 destroyed, the Eighth Air Force section given the task of reviewing claims had reduced the 56th's and increased the 4th's. There was a murmured suspicion at Boxted that the controlling fighter wing's bias in favour of the 4th was behind the re-evaluation, although there was no real justification for this belief. Flying exercises continued with restriction on low flying. Its danger aside, buzzing may have provided experience for wartime operations but was not welcomed by the British public or farm livestock. As a deterrent aircraft identification letters were painted large under the left wing of the P-47s so that dangerous low flying could be reported. Post-war the 56th's pilots 'bent' a few aircraft but the only fatality during this period was a 61st pilot on detached service with the RAF. Lieutenant Franklyn Rader, who had been sent to the RAF's Central Gunnery School at Catfoss, Yorkshire where the USAAF maintained a study detachment. On 22 May Rader, flying from Tangmere on a ground-attack training exercise in a Typhoon, apparently misjudged height and crashed at Selsey, Sussex.

The group maintained its aircraft strength, even adding the few remaining P-47Ms from the air depots to its inventory. The model was by then fairly trouble-free, apart from high-octane fuel eating away the Neoprene water regulator diaphragms. To overcome the problem, as high speeds were no long necessary, the water injection boost was disconnected. An old B-17 was acquired for transport use, but was no sooner stripped and readied for service than it was withdrawn by higher authority. On 7 July the men at Boxted were surprised to see a Heinkel He111 land. This and an FW190 had been acquired by three Wolfpack pilots who had been employed in ferrying selected aircraft found on German airfields to Cherbourg. These were to be loaded on a British aircraft carrier and conveyed to the USA for experimental testing at Wright Field. Major James Carter:

"Captain McIntosh, Hauptmann Braun, and I had flown a Ju88 from Grove, Denmark, to Cherbourg; and Felix Williamson had escorted a Do335 from Oberpaffenhofen to Cherbourg where his P-47 had engine trouble which was going to take a few days to repair. We asked about the Heinkel that was sitting on the field and when told that it was not going to be shipped to the US, enquired if it would be all right if we used it to fly home to England. The officer in charge of the aircraft collection team said we could have it so we took it. We encountered only one problem on the flight to Boxted. We could not fathom the transfer of fuel from the rear tanks. We never solved this problem."

The Heinkel, which had been used as a transport by the Luftwaffe, was duly painted up in the black and red colours of the 61st Fighter Squadron and flown at low altitude over the English countryside, much to the surprise of many of the population who had last seen an He 111 in a far from peaceful situation. The acquisition was condoned by Colonel Dade, notably in more relaxed frame of mind at this time. Jim Carter:

"The only real objection to my having and using the Heinkel as my private aircraft was made by a crusty old colonel commanding the outfit at Wattisham. A Dutch air/sea rescue unit had invited 15 of our pilots for a visit to Holland. We arranged for a C-47 to come to Boxted on August 3rd and fly the pilots to Wattisham where they would be transported to the Dutch rescue craft at a nearby port for the trip across the North Sea. The C-47 never showed. Our B-26 was out of commission. I thought it a terrible shame for our pilots to miss out on such an adventure, so I loaded the 15 into the Heinkel and flew them to Wattisham. The Heinkel created quite a stir at Wattisham and, unfortunately, even the CO came out to see what was up. When he saw the 15 pilot passengers disembark, he rightly and vigorously chewed me out for 'risking their lives in that thing', that in his opinion I wasn't properly qualified to fly. He reluctantly gave permission for me and my crew chief/co-pilot, T/Sgt Barney H. Hunter, to take-off for our return to Boxted, but, first, I had to promise that I wouldn't come in the Heinkel for the 15 pilots three days later on their return from Holland."

Felix Williamson managed to find an FW190A and flew it to Boxted. He was fortunate in safe arrival for on servicing the engine it was found that metal filings had been put into the sump. Efforts were made to obtain another engine but there was never an opportunity and eventually the Focke-Wulf was broken up.

In early July the service group and squadron personnel were alerted to prepare for movement, and equipment went to Barry docks, Wales. The word was they were headed for the Pacific. In mid-April there had been a reorganisation of support units on all Eighth Air Force stations, placing all under a single headquarters. In this reorganisation the 33rd Service Group was redesignated the 450th Air Service Group and the 41st Service Squadron as the 826th Air Engineering Squadron, but in practice things went on much as usual. When the service group left, much of the detailed engineering work had to be performed by squadron mechanics, although aircraft with need of anything but simple repair were now salvaged (the term for scrapped). Near half the pilots were transferred to the holding camp at Stone in the middle of the same month prior to return to the States, leaving more aircraft than pilots at Boxted. The solution was to ground 20 P-47s in each squadron. Two pilots with a predicament were the Poles who preferred to fly with the Americans. Mike Gladych had somehow managed to be accepted as a USAAF officer. Lanny Lanowski continued to hold RAF rank and received no pay from the USAAF. On leaving Boxted he initially had to obtain support from Polish contacts.

The overall strength at the station was reduced from the wartime 1,750 average to around 1,100. At the end of August Lt Colonel Dade was transferred to the US Strategic Air Forces in Europe headquarters in France and Donald Renwick took over command of the 56th with James Carter as his deputy. Some slightly disturbing information was forthcoming from VIII Fighter Command during July. The final re-assessment of enemy aircraft destroyed claims had elevated the 4th Group's to $1052^1/_2$ and reduced the 56th's to $985^1/_2$. While the 1,000 destroyed boast was now in question, the Wolfpack still reigned supreme in the matter of air victories with some 60 more than the next group in line. What was even more to the 56th's credit was that these were obtained before the standard of their Luftwaffe opponents deteriorated. VIII Fighter Command's decision that whether shot up on the ground or shot out of the sky an enemy aircraft should rate equal in a pilot's achievement, was open to question. There was the argument that while strafing a stationary target on a heavily defended airfield could be more dangerous than air combat, many other ground targets had been equally well defended and brought no special accolade. The 56th could also point to having the best ratio of destroyed claims to own losses, eight to one. Nothing would persuade its champions other than that the group's record was by far the best of all those that fought over Europe.

Despite the wish to go home, those staying during the summer of 1945 generally had a pleasant time with a short working day and few restrictions in leisure hours. A recreation many missed was swimming, and GIs discovered that beside Crown Lane, Ardleigh, just east of the base, were some large, deep pits with clear water. In fact, these were where much of the aggregate used to build Boxted airfield had been excavated two years earlier. Despite the cold water, it became a popular place for a dip on warm days. Using old drop tanks for buoyancy a raft was constructed and floated on one of these pit ponds as a diving platform. Tragically, one June afternoon Pfc James Money, a 63rd mechanic, was apparently caught up under the raft and drowned, and thereafter the ponds were declared off limits.

The Japanese surrender in August put an end to thoughts and rumours about further service in the Pacific theatres of war. In early September the orders for departure from Boxted were received with the remaining P-47s to be ferried to the Stansted air depot. There was the matter of Jim Carter's Heinkel for which there was no official paperwork and which if deposited at some USAAF base without it, would probably provoke official reaction and repercussions for those responsible for the aircraft's acquisition. Not wishing to court trouble that might delay his passage home, Major Carter devised a simple plan. Early one morning he took off from Boxted with the Heinkel and flew to RAF North Weald some 40 miles away. On landing the Heinkel was parked near the control tower. Meanwhile the group's Norseman communication aircraft had landed on the same airfield and parked some distance away. Carter and his crew chief ambled across to the waiting Norseman and were flown back to

Boxted. After a few days the RAF wondered why the Heinkel was still present, and when their enquiries to USAAF agencies met with no success they finally assumed the aircraft had been abandoned. Twenty-six-year-old James R. Carter was the only original combat pilot still with 56th at the end of its time in England. Apart from six weeks' leave in the States between tours, he had served continuously from assignment in July 1942 and flew 137 combat missions.

The last Thunderbolts took off from Boxted at around 1100 hours on 14 September, and the three squadron formations gave a low level fly-by before heading for Stansted. Lt Colonel Wilbur Watson, for long the stalwart of the ground staff officers, departed with a fifth of the ground personnel, sailing for New York on the *Europa*, on 19 September. Doc Horning went home with a Nazi flag, an SS sword and dagger, trophies obtained from the defeated land. The remaining personnel moved to the airfield at Little Walden near the fighter wing headquarters, then to a holding camp near Southampton; boarding the *Queen Mary* and sailing for America on 11 October. Two days after arrival at New York the 56th Fighter Group and its three squadrons were officially inactivated, operative one minute to midnight 18 October 1945. There was no ceremony, merely the signing of papers by a USAAF HQ officer. For most of the men the group had ceased to be when the last of its Thunderbolts took off from Boxted and the last truck turned out of No.1 gate. As a veteran later observed: "The outfit just came to pieces at the end. There was nothing left other than memories." He was wrong. What remained was fame, distinction at the least.

27 Epilogue

The 56th Fighter Group was brought into being again under Strategic Air Command on 1 May 1946 at Selfridge Field, Michigan. Colonel David Schilling was appointed commanding officer and gathered many of the old Wolfpack pilots to serve with him. Even so this peacetime incarnation was far removed from the wartime entity. The few regulars and others who wished to continue with a military career had varied Second World War experience, and those assigned to the new 56th being a typical, sample had served in many different theatres of war. Where possible Schilling recruited others from the wartime 56th, although they remained only a small element of the new. Starting with a few Thunderbolts, the group progressed to P-51H Mustangs and then to Lockheed P-80 Shooting Star jets. With the latter, Schilling led a trans-Atlantic exercise to Europe in the summer of 1948, the first of its kind for USAF jets, during which one or two red-nosed P-80s swept low over the old haunts of Halesworth and Boxted. Although remaining at Selfridge Field, the group status was supplanted by that of a wing organisation and, in the early 1950s, further changes resulted in a gradual demise and eventual inactivation. As is the wont of the military the numerical designation was given to later formations, and the 56th took several forms in the USAF during the rest of the twentieth century.

Of those notable contributors to the Wolfpack's success, many sought to continue with an air force career. Following his capture Hubert Zemke became the Senior Allied Officer of a large prison camp at Barth, Germany, and took the surrender of the German staff before liberation by the Soviet army. Remaining in Europe he was involved in a controversial movement of Zeiss optical works personnel to the west. He later commanded air force units in Germany and the USA. Always his own man, like some other wartime commanders, he did not adjust easily to the bureaucracy of peacetime service where it was not wise to express oneself forcibly to generals. Retiring from the USAF in July 1966, still a colonel, Hub Zemke took up an interest in woodworking, settling on a little almond ranch in northern California. He died aged 80 on 30 August 1994.

Dave Schilling continued to be active in the development of Strategic Air Command fighter employment during the immediate post-war years, taking part in several record-breaking flights and undertaking some pioneering work for in-flight refuelling. Following the suicide of his first wife in 1950 and overcoming severe hepatitis, he was given a posting with a SAC division in England. Tragically, this dynamic personality was killed on 14 August 1956 when the Allard sports car he was driving collided with a bridge parapet near Mildenhall.

Francis Gabreski also continued with an air force career, commanding F-86 Sabre units during the Korean War where he was credited with shooting down six MiG jets and sharing in the destruction of another. He left the USAF in October 1967 to take a consultative appointment with Grumman Aviation and later the presidency of Long Island Railroad, retiring in 1987. 'Gabby' Gabreski died on 31 January 2002, just turned 83. For a half century he was acclaimed as America's greatest living fighter ace.

After his return to the USA in May 1944, Robert Johnson had no further operational assignments and served as an instructor. On leaving the service in 1945 he did consultative work for Republic Aviation and later Grumman, although remaining in the USAF Reserve. He died in December 1998 aged 78. The most successful career of those Wolfpack men who continued in the air force was that of Gerald W. Johnson who rose to the rank of lieutenant general. Like Schilling he served in Strategic Air Command, transferring to bombers. This astute and personable man went on to hold several commands culminating in that of the Eighth Air Force during the strategic bombing campaign against North Vietnam in 1972. He retired in September 1974 following a year as Inspector General of the USAF. He died aged 83 in July 2002 following a fall during a visit to Britain.

After his return to the USA from Britain in the summer of 1944, Walker Mahurin went on to fly combat with P-51s in the Philippines. He was credited with shooting down a Japanese bomber. Only one of the few former 56th men who went on to fly combat against the Japanese is known to have been killed, Walter Frederick, who was brought down by ground fire while flying a P-47. Like Gabreski, Bud Mahurin also flew Sabres in the Korean War, claiming three MiGs and sharing in the destruction of another before being shot down and made prisoner in May 1952. He was subject to severe treatment during his sixteen months of captivity in North Korea. Several other Wolfpack men served in Korea, and at least six lost their lives. These included three who been accorded some notability during the Second World War: Robert Sheehan, the first pilot to evade capture and return to England; Glen Schiltz, the first with triple victories and Joe Powers, the 15 victories ace who is credited with bringing down the top Luftwaffe Experte Günther Rall. A few who served in Korea went on to fly in the South-East Asia conflict of the late 1960s; notably Harold Comstock who flew two tours in Vietnam.

Of the two Poles who flew with the group for over a year, Gladych became a US citizen and ended up running a physiological clinic. Lanowski stayed in the UK, although he did finally get paid for his wartime service by the US government.

Of the Second World War ground personnel, some sought to continue in the military although the majority returned to civilian life with employment ranging all the strata of United States society, from such extremes as the judiciary to milkmen. Being part of what had been largely a citizen's air force, the great majority of men had turned their backs on the military at the first opportunity. They wanted no more than to raise families and pursue a livelihood far removed from the service experience. Their wartime bases in Britain were soon subject to change. Only Wittering, where the 63rd Squadron was briefly stationed , survived as an active RAF station into the twenty-first century. King's Cliffe reverted to farmland, as did Boxted, after a nine-month spell with the RAF. Runways and other hard surfaces were broken up as hard core for new highways. Those at Halesworth mostly survived, being used to support turkey-rearing sheds in a large-scale poultry enterprise. Horsham St Faith became the city of Norwich airport.

In a further post-war examination of fighter pilot claims, those of the 56th's produced revised figures increasing the air victory total to 664 destroyed. Ground claims were not re-assessed as the USAF had de-rated aircraft destroyed on the ground to the same status as other strafing targets. Precise figures for the total of aircraft shot down by any one unit, either Allied and enemy, were never established owing to the confused nature of air battles where many units were involved. Published figures are nonetheless indicative of the most successful and the 56th had some 70 more than the second group in line.

The Second World War was a truly global conflict of the twentieth century and in its overall human involvement and loss of life is unsurpassed in man's sorry history of belligerence to his kind. Airpower came of age in the years 1939-1945 with a proven decisive part in many campaigns, not least that in Europe. There the United States Army Air Forces' 56th Fighter Group played a starring role in the achievement of air supremacy. For the young men that were its core it was the best, albeit that those of every other group thought likewise of its own. The 56th could boast the leading fighter aces, a total of air victories higher than any other unit in that theatre of war, and of having led the way in establishing the prowess and viability of the long-range fighter. The determination of leaders, tenacity of pilots and dedication of ground personnel were the substance of the ethos that embraced achievement. As a result the Wolfpack has become something of a legend in the story of American airpower. Those men who flew and fought to earn that fame came to look back with varying sentiments. Perhaps the most pertinent reflection is from Hub Zemke, the prime motivator in those long gone days: "Wars are stupid. They are not acts of gentlemen no matter how much we try to romanticise them. You can't kill anyone chivalrously. You just kill them."

Index

People
Adrianse, Lyle 51
Aggers, William 113, 114, 115, 166
Aheron, Frank 212, 222
Allison, Richard 43, 47,
Andermatt, Eugene 210
Andersen, Milton 28, 76, 111
Anderz, Tadeusz 158
Appel, Edward 230, 232, 234
Armstrong, Donald 213, 215
Armstrong, Tobin 233
Arnold, Gen.H.H. 84, 103
Auton, Jesse 111, 176, 194, 219

Baker, Gordon 178, 202, 233
Baker, Wyman 206
Ball, Sanborn 210
Banzaff, Willi 204
Barnum, Eugene 206
Barron, Louis 69
Batdorf, Gordon 55
Batson, Sam 213
Battista, Leo 196
Beckham, Walter 143
Bennett, Joe 144
Bevins, Hiram 83
Biales, Albert 20
Biggins, James 192, 214, 216
Billings, William 39, 40, 198
Bolender, Alfred 222, 223, 229, 233
Bolles, Anthony 151
Bostwick, George 174, 176, 226, 227
Bracken, George 157
Bradley, George 221
Bradshaw, Jack 189
Bradshaw, Tom 101, 168, 197
Brady, John 47, 89, 101, 156, 157, 236
Braun, Hpt 237
Brennan, Joe 180, 186
Brennan, John 140
Brooks, Norman 111
Brower, Lawrence 46, 62
Brown, Jack 91

244